W9-CRN-122

OUT OF THE DESERT?

OUT OF THE DESERT?

ARCHAEOLOGY AND THE EXODUS/
CONQUEST NARRATIVES

WILLIAM H. STIEBING, JR.

PROMETHEUS BOOKS
BUFFALO, NEW YORK

Library of Congress Cataloging-in-Publication Data

Stiebing, William H.
    Out of the desert : archaeology and the Exodus/Conquest narratives / by William H. Stiebing, Jr.
        p.   cm.
    Bibliography: p.
    Includes index.
    ISBN 0-87975-505-9
    1. Exodus, The. 2. Jews—History—To 1200 B.C. 3. Bible, O.T. Exodus—Antiquities. 4. Bible. O.T. Joshua—Antiquities.
I. Title.
BS680.E9S84   1989
222'.12093—dc19   88-36768
                                                                            CIP

To Kim,

who since childhood has wanted to know
not only "what," but also "why."

Contents

Figures

Tables

Preface

There long has been a need for a book-length assessment of the relation-ship between archaeological evidence from Egypt and Palestine and the biblical stories of an Israelite exodus from Egypt and conquest of Canaan. Earlier works, such as those of J. W. Jack (1925) and H. H. Rowley (1950), have been outdated for many years. Many relevant new archaeological discoveries have been made throughout the Near East in the last two or three decades. In addition, studies by Donovan Courville (1971), John Bimson (1978), Ian Wilson (1985), Hans Goedicke (1987), and others have suggested historical and archaeological correlations for the Exodus and Conquest period that are very different from those that have been generally accepted in the past. Yet no work has discussed this new evidence and critically evaluated the revisionist theories against the more traditional views.

Moreover, despite the large number of works appearing on the Exodus and Conquest over the last few years, none has tried to understand these events as part of the larger social and cultural collapse that was taking place throughout the eastern Mediterranean at the end of the Bronze Age. Hittitologists, specialists in the archaeology of Greece, Egyptologists, Assyri-ologists, and biblical archaeologists have largely ignored one another as they sought to explain the changes taking place in the areas of their own interests. But turmoil, crisis, population movements, and social conflict pervaded the eastern Mediterranean world. Surely, these events were related. It is clear that the Exodus and settlement of Palestine need to be seen in historical context as part of this wider upheaval. That is why I have written this book.

The subjects discussed below obviously are of interest to a number of people besides archaeologists and biblical scholars. Many students, members of the clergy (both Jewish and Christian), historians, and members of the general public would like to know whether an historical and archaeological context can be established for the Exodus and Conquest and, if so, what that context is. I have therefore attempted to make this work comprehensible to a broad, general audience. Specialists in biblical studies or biblical archaeology undoubtedly will find much here that they will regard as elementary, especially the material in the first chapter. I have included this information to make the subject accessible to nonspecialist readers. I believe, however, that both specialists and the lay public will be able to read the book with profit.

Portions of Chapter 4, which deals with various revisions of the date or archaeological context for the Exodus, have appeared in slightly different form in my book *Ancient Astronauts, Cosmic Collisions and Other Popular Theories About Man's Past* or in a series of articles I have written for the Velikovskian journal, *Catastrophism and Ancient History.*

It is impossible to list all those who have made this work possible either through their intellectual influences on me or through more direct assistance during the preparation of the manuscript. As always, a debt of gratitude is owed to my wife, Ann, who has helped make this book possible in ways too many to number. She has been patient during the times I have been preoccupied with research or writing, and when I hit snags or the work seemed to be going slowly, she provided inspiration and encouragement. Thanks are also due to many of my students at the University of New Orleans, who have helped shape the text through their interest in the subject and questions in the classroom. The Research Council of the University of New Orleans helped me to complete the manuscript more quickly by granting me a 1988 Summer Scholar Award, which enabled me to work on this book rather than teach at the university during this past summer. And gratitude needs to be expressed to Doris Doyle, Robert Basil, and the staff at Prometheus Books, who once again have shepherded one of my manuscripts through the presses with admirable skill and speed. Finally, special thanks should be given to Professor James B. Pritchard, who encouraged me when I was a young graduate student to pursue my interest in the history and archaeology of ancient Palestine. The *Mudir* ("Director"), as Professor Pritchard is affectionately known to his workers and staff, also gave me archaeological field experience during the University Museum's excavations at Tell es-Sa'idiyeh in Jordan and Sarafand in Lebanon. Professor Pritchard's careful, dispassionate scholarship, his ability as a writer and lecturer, his sparkling sense of humor, and his equanimity and grace in every situation have provided a model his students and colleagues can only try to emulate.

New Orleans, Louisiana
Summer 1988

1

Textual and Archaeological Evidence

The story of Moses and the Exodus is one of the best-known stories from the Bible. It is recalled and celebrated every year in the Jewish observance of Passover. Christians are continually reminded of it as well, as when they celebrate the Lord's Supper, or Eucharist—especially on Maundy Thursday (or Holy Thursday, the Thursday before Easter), which commemorates the day Jesus ate his Last Supper with his apostles at Passover time. Accounts of the Israelite conquest of Canaan are not as familiar to modern audiences, though many people know at least part of the story of Joshua's conquest of Jericho.

Jewish and Christian theologians have made much use of the biblical accounts of God's deliverance of Israel from bondage in Egypt and his gift of the Promised Land to his Chosen People. But this study will not be concerned with the theological implications of these stories. This is an historical study, and historians want to know whether the Exodus and Conquest events described in the Bible really happened. Is the Bible a reliable source of information for Israel's early history? And, if the Exodus and Conquest *were* real events in the past, when did they occur? What were their historical contexts?

To answer these questions, biblical accounts must be subjected to the same kinds of analysis that historians utilize in studying other ancient documents. Before the historical reliability of the biblical narratives of the Exodus and Conquest can be judged, we need to know as much as possible about when the various accounts were written, who wrote them, why they were written, and the sources of information available to their authors. There are many ways to glean such information. One is what scholars call the "historical-critical method," in which the text itself is subjected to rigorous internal analysis. In addition, we can learn a lot about the biblical narratives by comparing them to other ancient texts. And, beyond written legacies, archaeological discoveries can give us marvelous insight into our ancient heritage.[1]

A Summary of the Exodus and Conquest Account

The Exodus story is alluded to frequently in the Bible, for God's salvation of his people from Egypt is one of the major themes of ancient Israelite religion.[2] Our basic sources of information on the Exodus, though, are the biblical Books of Exodus and Numbers, which now form part of the Torah, or Pentateuch (the first five books of the Bible). The story of the Conquest of Canaan is found in the Books of Joshua and Judges.

These books relate the following story. The Egyptians became fearful of the growing numbers of Hebrews who for many years had lived peacefully in the delta region. The Egyptian pharoah tried to decrease the Hebrew population first by forcing them to perform hard labor, then by killing their sons (Exodus 1). One of the Hebrew boys, Moses, was hidden by his family in a basket in reeds at the side of the river. He was found by the pharaoh's daughter and raised as her son. After reaching adulthood, Moses one day killed an Egyptian who was beating a Hebrew slave, and he was forced to flee into the Sinai Peninsula to escape from the pharaoh's wrath. There, Moses married and lived among seminomadic tribesmen for a number of years. Then, he saw a burning bush on a mountainside and heard the voice of God calling him. God commanded Moses to return to Egypt and lead the Israelites out of the delta to Canaan, a prosperous land that God would give to them (Exodus 2-6).

By this time, a new pharaoh was on the throne of Egypt, and he refused to allow the Hebrews to leave. So God sent a series of plagues upon the Egyptians—the Nile water turned to blood, frogs overran the land, swarms of gnats and then flies made life miserable for man and beast, disease struck down the livestock in the fields, boils broke out on the skin

---

1. For a discussion of the historian's approach to the Bible, see Miller 1976 and Ramsey 1981: 3-23.

2. Sarna 1986: 1-5.

of the Egyptians and their animals, a fierce rain of hail destroyed crops and living creatures caught out in the open, hordes of locusts descended on the land and ate whatever vegetation was left, and then complete darkness covered Egypt for three days (Exodus 7-10). Finally, when the pharaoh still would not relent and allow the Israelites to leave, God caused the first-born child of every Egyptian to die (Exodus 11-12:30).

Pharaoh now decided that Moses and his people could leave. But soon after they set out, he changed his mind once again and pursued the Israelites with a force of chariotry, catching up with them near a body of water called the *Yam Suph* (usually translated "The Red Sea" or "The Sea of Reeds"). God caused the water to move aside, allowing the Israelites to cross on dry land. When the Egyptians tried to follow, however, the water flooded back, and the pharoah's whole army was drowned (Exodus 12:31-15:21).

The Israelites followed Moses through Sinai to the holy "Mountain of God," where they formed a covenant with Yahweh, their God, and received His commandments (Exodus 16-31, 33-35). From the Holy Mountain they proceeded to Kadesh-Barnea on the southern fringe of Canaan. But, when they heard reports of strong cities and gigantic warriors in Canaan, the Israelites rebelled against Moses, which angered God. As a punishment, God decreed that, except for Caleb and Joshua, none of those who left Egypt with Moses would enter the Promised Land (Numbers 10:11-14:45). So, for almost forty years the Israelites had to camp in the desert around Kadesh-Barnea.

Finally, Moses led his people through Transjordan to Mount Nebo near the Jordan River, where Moses died (Numbers 21-24, 32-33; Deuteronomy 34). It was Joshua who led the Israelite tribes across the Jordan into Canaan. In two systematic campaigns in southern Palestine and one in the north, the kings of the major Canaanite cities were defeated and killed; much of the land was then occupied by the Israelites (Joshua 1-24).

After Joshua's death the leadership of the Israelite tribes fell upon charismatic figures called *shophetim*. The usual translation for this term is "judges," but these leaders were generally military commanders, not legal authorities. Related terms in other ancient Semitic languages show that the basic meaning of the root *sh-p-t* was "to govern" or "to be in authority."[3]

---

3. An Assyrian *shapitu* was a governor, Phoenician *shuphetim* were "regents" or "rulers" of city-states, and according to various ancient authors, the Phoenician colony of Carthage had two chief administrative officials, called *Sufetes* (a Latinized form of *shuphetim*). See Kraft 1962: 1014 and Boling 1975: 5.

The Israelite *shophetim* or "judges" were temporary rulers who helped Israel defeat enemies and consolidate her hold on Canaan (Judges 1-21).

This, in brief, is the biblical account. Who wrote it? When was it written? And how historically reliable is it?

Literary and Historical Criticism of the Pentateuch

Traditionally, the Pentateuch—the Books of Genesis, Exodus, Leviticus, Numbers, and Deuteronomy—have been credited to Moses. This attribution would make the Exodus narrative an eyewitness account by the person in the best position to know all of the facts. But careful study of the Pentateuch has gradually made scholars aware of many inconsistencies, duplications, contradictions, and differences in style and vocabulary. This evidence, in turn, has raised the question of whether all of this material could have been written by the same person.

In Exodus 6:2-3, for example, God tells Moses that Abraham, Isaac, and Jacob had known Him as El Shaddai ("God Almighty"), not Yahweh, His true name. Yet the patriarchs refer to God as Yahweh a number of times in Genesis, and God Himself is depicted as revealing His name Yahweh to Abraham (Genesis 15:7) and to Jacob (Genesis 28:13).

Other discrepancies abound even in the account of the Exodus, the portion of Israel's early history that Moses should have known intimately. According to Exodus 3:1 and 18:1, Moses' father-in-law was named Jethro, but in Numbers 10:29 (as well as in Judges 4:11) he is called Hobab. Numbers 21 describes a route that the Israelites followed from Mount Hor into Canaan that differs from the one described in Numbers 33. Moses' brother Aaron died and was buried at Mount Hor, according to Numbers 20:22-29, 33:38, and Deuteronomy 32:50. But Deuteronomy 10:6 claims that Aaron died and was buried at Moserah (also known as Moseroth), a place that Numbers 33:30-37 places six stages before Mount Hor in the Israelites' itinerary.

There are also differences among the various accounts of the laws that God is supposed to have given Moses. According to Exodus 20:24, sacrifices are to be offered on altars built in every place God chooses to have His name remembered. Yet Deuteronomy 12:1-14 states that there shall be only *one* sanctuary of God and only there should sacrifices be performed. Exodus 21:2-7 specifies that male Hebrew slaves are to be freed after six years of service, but that female Hebrew slaves are not entitled to such release. On the other hand, Deuteronomy 15:12 states that both male and female

Hebrew slaves are to be released after six years.

Indeed, many passages in the Pentateuch clearly were written long after the time of Moses. As early as the second century A.D. doubts arose over the Pentateuch's reference to Moses' death.[4] The medieval rabbi Isaac ibn Yashush (died 1056) recognized that Moses could not have described Edomite kings as reigning "before any king reigned over the Israelites" (Genesis 36:31), since in Moses' time there was no way of knowing that Israel would one day have a king. And Abraham ibn Ezra (1089-1164) noticed that Genesis 12:6 ("and the Canaanites were then in the land") must have been written when the Canaanites no longer represented a major portion of Palestine's population. Ibn Ezra also saw a problem with Deuteronomy 1:1, which refers to the territory east of the Jordan as "the other side of the Jordan." Obviously, this passage was written from the perspective of someone on the *western* side of the Jordan (Canaan)—yet Moses died *east* of the Jordan, having never reached Canaan.[5]

In the eighteenth and nineteenth centuries many other anachronisms and discrepancies were recognized; and, since the latter part of the nineteenth century, virtually all biblical scholars have agreed that Moses did not write the first five books of the Bible. A consensus developed in support of the theory that the Pentateuch was formed by weaving together four distinct documents, or sources, that were written down in stages from the time of the monarchy through that of the Babylonian Exile. These sources were called J (for "The Yahwist" or "Jahwist"), E (for "The Elohist"), D (for "The Deuteronomist"), and P (for "The Priestly Author").[6]

The Exodus story generally has been regarded as a composite account formed by blending together all of these sources. Two books of the Pentateuch, Leviticus and Deuteronomy, are essentially unitary works. Leviticus, a series of instructions about cultic matters, seems to be primarily the work of the Priestly Author, who compiled his material during the Babylonian Exile (the sixth century B.C.).[7] And except for Chapters 1-4 and 30-34, which seem to have been added by later editors, Deuteronomy was the product of the Deuteronomist, who composed it probably no more than

---

4. *Talmud*, Baba Bathra 15a.

5. Bermant and Weitzman 1979: 46.

6. For a description of the methods and results of "source criticism" of the Pentateuch, see Pfeiffer 1948: 134-141; Rowley 1950b: 15-46; Speiser 1964: xx-xxxvii; Bermant and Weitzman 1979: 44-58.

7. Milgrom 1976: 541. Martin Noth (1965: 10-15) credited the narrative portions of the book to P, but argued that the "Holiness Code" (Leviticus 17-26) and other blocks of material were combined with the P narrative by a later editor.

a generation or two before King Josiah discovered it in the Temple in 621 B.C.[8] On the other hand, the Books of Exodus and Numbers seem to have had a more complex literary history, for they contain elements normally credited to J, E, and P.[9] Scholars usually assert that the earliest material about the Exodus is contained in the J tradition, generally thought to have been written down in the tenth century B.C., during the reign of Solomon or soon after his death.

The view of Julius Wellhausen,[10] that these sources were literary creations reflecting primarily the time in which they were written, predominated until after World War I. Around this time, however, a number of scholars began adopting new approaches to the biblical text, approaches called "form criticism" and "tradition criticism" (or "tradition history"). These methods sought to isolate the individual units of tradition that had been utilized by the biblical authors in constructing their works. These traditional materials were then studied to determine their genre and function, and to trace their origins, development, purposes, and method of preservation.[11] After it was convincingly demonstrated that there was a prehistory to the materials in the biblical texts it became evident that the date and accuracy of a given story could not be judged simply by noting the source in which it occurred.

Today, support for the documentary hypothesis is not nearly as strong as it was a generation or two ago. The cohesiveness, date, and even the existence of some of these sources as independent documents have been questioned.[12] For the historian dealing with the era of the Israelite Exodus and settlement, the most important challenges to the documentary hypothesis are those that concern J, since this work was regarded as the oldest of the sources and the core around which the Pentateuch developed. The older view (still widely held), that J represents a tenth-century-B.C. written version of an old epic tradition from the era of the "judges,"[13] gave many scholars confidence that the Exodus and Conquest stories were essentially historical. After all, the poetic epic upon which J was supposedly based would have

---

8. Lohfink 1976: 230; Mayes 1983: 22-39.

9. The Yahwistic and Elohistic strands in the Exodus story are difficult to disentangle, and they are often thought to have been combined with one another before the P material was added. Thus, scholars often divide the traditions in Exodus and Numbers into J-E on the one hand and P on the other, with a few passages being added by still-later editors.

10. Wellhausen 1885.

11. For a description of "form criticism," see Tucker 1971 and 1976. "Tradition criticism" or "tradition history" is described in Coats 1976.

12. See, e.g., Van Seters 1975: 125-131; Fretheim 1976: 259-260; Blenkinsopp 1985; Kikawada and Quinn 1985; Rendsburg 1986; Damrosch 1987: 144-181.

13. See, e.g., Cross 1973: viii-ix; B. Anderson 1986: 152-158, 245-246.

been created when legitimate traditions about the events of the Exodus and Conquest were still widespread and well-known. But in recent years a number of scholars have argued persuasively that the Yahwistic material in the Pentateuch was composed or collected during or after the Babylonian Exile rather than in the tenth century B.C.[14] If these scholars are correct, historians could not assume the historical accuracy of *any* of the Pentateuchal traditions.

Moreover, modern study also has indicated that while there may have been historical events behind the traditions recorded in the Pentateuch, the accounts have been modified and developed into their present shape in order to make *theological* affirmations. Biblical authors were interested in history not for its own sake, but as the stage upon which God acted and made known His glory and power. Furthermore, in some instances Pentateuchal "historical" accounts seem to have been written primarily to provide hope and guidance to people of the period in which the stories were written down or edited rather than to accurately preserve valid memories of the past.[15] Of course, discovery of theological motifs in a biblical "historical" narrative does not prove that the event being described never happened. Recognition of the theological intent of biblical accounts of the past *does,* however, make the historicity of these narratives at least open to question. And as a result, they must be examined in the same way that a good historian examines all of his other sources for validity and accuracy.[16] The days when scholars could automatically assume the accuracy of the "historical" statements in the Pentateuch (or elsewhere in the Bible) are long past.

Debate over the date and nature of the sources in the Pentateuch will certainly continue, but it is unlikely that scholars will ever again believe that Moses authored this material. It is clear that the written biblical accounts of the early history of Israel belong to the period of the monarchy or later, centuries after the events they describe. Yes, the traditions that lie *behind* these written accounts may have originated much closer in time

---

14. Winnett 1965; Van Seters 1975: 263-278, 309-312; 1983: 355-362; Schmid 1976; Rendtorff 1977a, 1977b, and 1977c; Damrosch 1987: 157-181.

15. For example, the account of how Abraham and his family left "Ur of the Chaldeans" and then were directed by God to settle in Canaan (Genesis 11:31-12:6) seems directed to the Judeans, who were returning from exile and followed the same route. The promises supposedly made to Abraham (Genesis 12:2-3, 7) actually are being directed to the exilic community. See Van Seters 1975: 263-264.

16. See the excellent treatment of the relationship between modern historical scholarship and faith in Ramsey 1981: 115-124.

to the events themselves, but the dates and accuracy of these traditions are difficult to determine. All of these problems make the Exodus story's value as *history* much more questionable than it is generally thought to be by devout Jews and Christians.

The Deuteronomistic History

Just as Moses was long believed to be the author of the Pentateuch, so also tradition credited the account of Canaan's conquest in the Book of Joshua to an eyewitness—Joshua himself. But with the advent of source criticism, many scholars saw the story of the Conquest as the fitting conclusion to the sources they found in the Pentateuch, particularly J and E. Thus, biblical scholars often talked of a *Hexateuch,* arguing that the Book of Joshua originally had been connected to the preceding five books. A few contemporary scholars still hold this view. Various parts of Joshua and even of Judges have been assigned to the Pentateuchal authors, but no broad agreement has been reached about which Conquest stories were once part of these sources.

Study of Joshua and Judges was put on a new footing in 1943 by the great German biblical scholar Martin Noth. Noth denied that the Pentateuchal sources continued into Joshua. He argued that the Book of Joshua formed instead the first part of a long historical work that included Judges, I and II Samuel, and I and II Kings. This history of Israel from the Conquest to the Babylonian Exile was compiled by an author who had been strongly influenced by the covenantal theology of the Book of Deuteronomy, which the historian attached to the beginning of his work by adding an appropriate narrative framework to the beginning and the end of the older work. Noth saw Deuteronomy-Kings as a theological interpretation of Israel's nationhood that explained the fall of the northern kingdom of Israel in 722 B.C. and of Judah in 587 B.C. as God's punishment for his people's failure to adhere to the requirements of the Mosaic covenant as detailed in Deuteronomy.[17] Because the ideas and language of the compiler of this history were so steeped in the Book of Deuteronomy, he is called "the Deuteronomistic historian" and his work is known as "the Deuteronomistic History."

Noth's thesis has become widely accepted by biblical scholars, though today many students of the Deuteronomistic History argue that at least

17. Noth 1943.

two authors were involved, rather than one.[18] Supporters of the two-stage hypothesis usually date the creation of the Deuteronomistic History to the time of King Josiah (c. 640-609 B.C.), arguing that it was intended to justify and support Josiah's reforms (which were inspired by the finding of the Book of Deuteronomy in the Temple). During or soon after the Babylonian Exile, this historical work was revised and extended by a redactor (or editor) to bring its account down to the time of the Exile and to explain why Jerusalem and Judah had been destroyed despite Josiah's reforms.[19]

The account of the Conquest and settlement of Canaan in the Books of Joshua and Judges thus belongs to a time some five to eight centuries later than the events it describes. But it is often claimed that most of the Conquest stories and lists used by the Deuteronomistic historian(s) were derived from pre-Deuteronomic collections. Some of these materials may have been created at least as early as the time of Solomon, and some may even go back to the premonarchic period.[20] But the accounts have become so overlaid with Deuteronomistic theological concepts—such as the holy-war theme and the idea of a total conquest of Canaan by a unified Israel led by Joshua—that their historical validity is now very difficult to ascertain.[21] And some scholars, following the lead of John Van Seters, deny that the Lists of Tribal Territories in Joshua 13-24, the Story of David's Rise in I Samuel, the Succession Story (or Court History) in II Samuel 9-20 and I Kings 1-2, and other supposedly early sources used by the Deuteronomistic historian ever existed as separate documents.[22] If this analysis is correct, it would be even more difficult—if not impossible— to discern the historical reality behind the biblical narratives of the Conquest and settlement.

Other Biblical Exodus/Conquest Traditions

The theme of the Israelites' exodus from Egypt and God's gift of the Promised Land to them is one of the most prominent in the Bible. Statements about

---

18. Freedman 1976; Mayes 1983 (especially pp. 133-137).

19. See, e.g., Cross 1973: 276-289; Freedman 1976; Boling and Wright 1982: 48-51; Mayes 1983: 19.

20. See, e.g., Soggin 1972: 7-14; Boling and Wright 1982: 62-71.

21. Soggin 1984: 28-31; Miller and Hayes 1986: 61-63.

22. Van Seters 1983: 249-353. David Damrosch argues, however, that literary analysis shows that both the Yahwist and the Deuteronomistic historian used sources that were first composed during the early monarchic period, probably during the reign of Solomon (1987, especially pp. 178-181).

these events are made in many biblical books in addition to the detailed treatment this theme receives in the books from Exodus through Judges. But in our search for the historical reality behind these biblical passages, we need focus only on those that are earlier than Deuteronomy and the Deuteronomistic History. Since the Exodus and Conquest traditions in later works, like Chronicles or Ezra, could very well have been based on the Deuteronomistic writings, they cannot help us evaluate the antiquity and validity of the materials used by the Deuteronomistic historian(s). Neither are exilic and postexilic writings useful to us in determining whether the Genesis-Numbers accounts are *earlier* than Deuteronomy, as most biblical scholars have believed, or *later* than the Deuteronomistic History, as a number of studies now assert.[23]

Themes of the Exodus and the Conquest occur in a number of psalms, but, unfortunately, these compositions are very difficult to date. Materials in the Book of Psalms range in date from the early part of the Israelite monarchy to the postexilic era some five hundred years later.[24] Psalms 78, 105, 106, and 136 (which has much of its material repeated in Psalm 135, which probably was written later) provide the most detailed treatments of the Exodus and Conquest events outside of the Pentateuch and Joshua-Judges. The number and order of the Egyptian plagues in Psalms 78:44-51 and 105:28-36 differ from the accounts in Exodus 7:8-12:30 (generally divided between J and P) and from each other,[25] but otherwise these hymns (along with Psalms 106 and 136) reflect the story embodied in the Pentateuch and the Deuteronomistic History.

Psalm 105 is probably not (and Psalm 106 is definitely not) earlier than Deuteronomy,[26] so they do not provide us with a more ancient form of the tradition. But Psalm 78 might be pre-Deuteronomic, belonging to the ninth or eighth century B.C. This poem claims that the Northern Kingdom

---

23. Obviously, similarities in style and vocabulary between J and exilic or postexilic works might mean that J was written during the Exile as John Van Seters has persuasively argued (1975, 1983). The possibility remains, though, that the writers of the Exile were drawing upon the *older* traditions of the Pentateuch and utilizing some of its themes and vocabulary, as has been asserted traditionally.

24. See, e.g., Hempel 1962: 943-944; Weiser 1962: 91-93; Dahood 1966: xxix-xxx; 1970: xxxiv-xxxvii.

25. For comparisons of the various plague accounts, see Mihelic and Wright 1962; B. Anderson 1986: 69-71; Sarna 1986: 73-78.

26. G. E. Wright placed Psalms 105 and 106 early in the postexilic period (Boling and Wright 1982: 14). Psalm 106 looks forward to the ending of the Exile (verses 46-47) and thus seems to be exilic or early postexilic in date, but Psalm 105 could possibly be a bit earlier. However, if Psalms 104-106 were originally composed as a trilogy, as Wright believes, the date for Psalm 106 would have to apply to 104 and 105 as well.

of Israel ("the sons of Ephraim") sinned against God and forgot His mighty deeds of the Exodus and Conquest era:

> Before their fathers he performed wonders,
>> in the land of Egypt, in the plain of Zo'an.
> He cleft the sea and brought them through,
>> and he made the waters stand like a mound.
> He led them with a cloud by day,
>> and all night with a fire's light.
> He split rocks in the wilderness,
>> and gave them the water of the Great Deep to drink. . . .
> He drove out the nations before them,
>> and parceled out their inheritance by lot;
> He settled the tribes of Israel in their tents. . . .
> Yet they angered Him with their high places,
>> and with their idols aroused His jealousy. . . .
> So He rejected the tent of Joseph,
>> and chose not the tribe of Ephraim.
> But He chose the tribe of Judah,
>> Mount Zion which He loved.
>> (Psalms 78:12-15, 55, 67-68)

Some have argued that this psalm's attack on the Northern Kingdom indicates that it was written after the division of the Hebrew kingdoms in 922 B.C., but before the destruction of the Northern Kingdom (Israel) in 722/721 B.C.[27] On the other hand, Psalm 78's polemic against the Northern Kingdom may have been intended as justification for its destruction by the Assyrians in 722/721 B.C., while the statements about God's favor to Judah, the Temple in Jerusalem, and the line of David point to a time of origin earlier than the Babylonian conquest of Judah and destruction of Jerusalem in 587 B.C.[28] The prophetic and Deuteronomic interpretation of Israel's history as rebellion against God's covenant and the attack on local shrines ("high places") in Psalm 78 probably indicate that it belongs to the seventh century B.C., when the Book of Deuteronomy was found in the Temple.

Psalms 135 and 136 also praise Yahweh for His mighty acts during the Exodus and Conquest, but they contain no historical allusions that might pinpoint the time when they were written. Psalm 135's statements

---

27. Dahood 1968: 238; Boling and Wright 1982: 15-16.
28. Damrosch 1987: 47-48.

that "Yahweh defends his people" (verse 14) and "dwells in Jerusalem" (verse 21) possibly indicate that it was written before Judah's devastation at the hands of the Babylonians. On the other hand, Psalm 136:23-24 praises God "who remembered us in our abjection" and "freed us from our foes." These verses might be referring to the time of the Babylonian Exile. Since Psalm 135:8-12 seems to be based on Psalm 136:10-22, if Psalm 136 was written after the Exile, Psalm 135 should be even later. Whatever their exact dates, it is unlikely that either of these psalms belongs to the early period of Israel's history.

Psalms 44:1-3 (verses 2-4 in Hebrew), 66:6, 77:16-20 (Hebrew: 17-21), 80:8-9 (Hebrew: 9-10), 83:10, 99:6, and 103:7 also contain Exodus and Conquest allusions, but like the psalms we have just discussed, their exact dates cannot be determined. However, one Exodus/Conquest psalm that almost certainly dates from the era of the monarchy prior to the seventh century B.C. Deuteronomic reform is the "Song of the Sea," which was incorporated into the Exodus account (Exodus 15:1-18). This hymn celebrates God's victories over his enemies:

> Yahweh is a warrior,
>> Yahweh is His name!
> Pharaoh's chariots and army He cast into the sea,
>> his elite officers were submerged in the *Yam Suph*. . . .
> The nations heard and they trembled;
>> pain gripped the inhabitants of Philistia.
> Then the chieftains of Edom were dismayed;
>> trembling seized the leaders of Moab.
> All the inhabitants of Canaan melted away;
>> terror and dread fell upon them.
>
>> (Exodus 15:3-4, 14-15)

The "song" contains none of the Deuteronomistic emphasis on the Israelites' rebellion and backsliding, which is found in Psalm 78 and in the Pentateuchal narratives into which the "Song of the Sea" was incorporated.

The "Song of the Sea" is often considered one of the earliest poems in the Bible, rivaled in antiquity only by the "Song of Deborah" (Judges 5:2-31). William Foxwell Albright dated this hymn to the thirteenth century B.C., the period to which he also assigned the Exodus and Conquest.[29] And Frank Moore Cross has placed its creation in the period of the "judges."[30]

---

29. Albright 1968: 11-13.
30. Cross 1973: 121-144.

However, the end of the poem (Exodus 15:17), addressed directly to God, declares:

> You brought them in and planted them
> on the mountain of your inheritance,
> The place of your abode,
> which you made, O Yahweh,
> The sanctuary, O Yahweh,
> which your hands have created.

Supporters of a pre-Solomonic date for the poem argue that these lines use terminology derived from Canaanite mythology and refer to the hill country of Palestine as the abode of Yahweh.[31] But, while Canaanite myths might have influenced the wording of this passage, it is difficult not to see it as an allusion to Mount Zion and to the Temple in Jerusalem.[32] The reference to the Philistines as one of God's enemies who are terrified by his power (Exodus 15:14) also suggests a date no earlier than the latter part of the period of the "judges," and more probably during the United Monarchy. It is likely that this poem was composed during the reign of Solomon or soon afterward. While it may not belong to the time of the Exodus and Conquest, as Albright claimed, it almost certainly was written much earlier than the Book of Deuteronomy.

Other Exodus/Conquest references that can be assigned to the pre-Deuteronomic period with a relatively high degree of probability are those that occur in the oracles of Amos, Hosea, Isaiah, and Micah, prophets who lived in the ninth and eighth centuries B.C. The sayings of these prophets were edited (and, on occasion, expanded) during and after the exile, so a pre-Deuteronomic date for any references to the Exodus or Conquest contained within them is not guaranteed. For example,

> It was I who brought you up from the land of Egypt,
> and who led you through the wilderness for forty years,
> to take possession of the land of the Amorites.
> (Amos 2:10)

has been regarded as a Deuteronomistic addition to a genuine oracle of Amos.[33] However, with the exception of minor editorial additions (such

---

31. Noth 1962: 125-126; Cross 1973: 125; Boling and Wright 1982: 19.

32. Soggin 1985: 125; Sarna 1986: 100.

33. Weiser 1929: 93-95; Schmidt 1965. James L. Mays argues that this passage is an authentic part of the oracle of Amos (1969: 44-45).

as "forty years" as the length of the wilderness wandering in Amos 5:25[34]), the authenticity of most of the following passages is probable.

The ninth- and eighth-century-B.C. prophets do not treat the Exodus and Conquest events in detail, but they do mention Moses (Micah 6:4 and probably Hosea 12:14, where it is stated that a prophet led Israel out of Egypt), Aaron and Miriam (Micah 6:4), and Balak of Moab and Balaam (Micah 6:5). They also refer to slavery in Egypt (Micah 6:4), pestilence in Egypt (Amos 4:10?), God's leading his people out of Egypt (Hosea 11:1; 13:4; Isaiah 10:26), and His guiding them in the wilderness (Amos 5:25) during which the Israelites lived in tents (Hosea 12:10), were fed by God (Hosea 13:5), and were faithful to His commands (Hosea 2:16-17). The only references to the Conquest in the sayings of these early prophets are the statement in Amos 2:9 that God destroyed the Amorites who had occupied the land before Israel and the allusion in Micah 6:5 to Balak's attempt to have Israel cursed.

It should be noted that, in contrast to the Pentateuchal depiction of the desert wanderings as a time of almost constant complaining and rebelling by the Israelites, Amos and Hosea present this period as an ideal era of simple, faithful worship (Amos 5:25 and Hosea 2:16-17, 12:10). The prophetic tradition that Israel's worship in the wilderness did not include sacrifice (Amos 5:21-25, Hosea 6:6, Micah 6:6-8) is at odds with the Pentateuchal accounts as well. It is also interesting that while Moses, Aaron, and Miriam are mentioned by name by Micah, Joshua is *not* referred to by the pre-Deuteronomic prophets, nor is he mentioned in the Exodus/Conquest Psalms. Also, the only specific remarks about Conquest events in the Psalms and the pre-Deuteronomic prophets are the references to Balak (Micah 6:5), the destruction of Sihon and Og (Psalms 135:11, 136:19), and the defeat of Sisera and Jabin (Psalm 83:9). There is *no* reference to Jericho or Ai, the two Conquest traditions that are given the most detailed treatment in the Book of Joshua and that have made the greatest impression on readers down through the ages.

The way that the ninth- and eighth-century-B.C. prophets referred to events from the Exodus and Conquest period indicates that the Exodus and Conquest traditions were well known by their audiences. Whether the prophets assumed knowledge of a written J-E account or of oral confessional traditions, like the ones embodied in the "Song of the Sea" and various psalms, or of both, cannot now be determined. We also cannot determine exactly how early this tradition arose or how many of the details now

---

34. Mays 1969: 111.

present in the books of Exodus through Judges it contained. (Prophetic statements, though, make it unlikely that the details about the wilderness wanderings embodied in the Pentateuch were widely accepted in the ninth and eighth centuries B.C.). Despite our uncertainty about details, it is clear that by the end of the tenth or early in the ninth century B.C. the ancient Israelites believed that their god, Yahweh, had saved them from Egyptian slavery, led them out of Egypt, triumphed over the Egyptians at a "sea," provided for His people's needs in the desert, and given them a land that had not been theirs before. This seems to be the irreducible "kernel" around which the later narratives developed.

Archaeology and Historical Reconstruction

The Bible is not our only source of information for the history of ancient Palestine. Inscriptions found in Egypt, Mesopotamia, and other Near Eastern areas sometimes contain information about Palestine. And a few inscriptions have been discovered in Palestine itself. These sources must be compared and correlated with the biblical accounts. However, most of this nonbiblical textual evidence that is directly relevant to events mentioned in the Bible belongs to the period of the Hebrew monarchies rather than to the earlier era of Israelite origins.

The earliest known reference to Israel outside of the Bible occurs in a stele of the Egyptian pharaoh Merneptah, which celebrates a military campaign that took place near the end of the thirteenth century B.C. Israel is listed among Merneptah's vanquished enemies in Palestine. But the absence of detailed information about the "Israel" mentioned in the inscription allows for a variety of interpretations concerning its correlation with the biblical narratives. Moreover, there are no known nonbiblical references to Abraham, Isaac, Jacob, Joseph, Moses, or Joshua—or, for that matter, to David, Solomon, and a host of other biblical characters. Nonbiblical inscriptions thus provide only indirect evidence for understanding the history of early Israel.

There is, however, another source of information upon which historians can draw when reconstructing the past—*archaeology,* the scholarly discipline that attempts to understand mankind's past through study of its material remains. When many people think of archaeology or archaeologists, they get mental pictures of romantic figures like the fictional Indiana Jones making dramatic discoveries in strange, mysterious places. In the nineteenth century, this popular conception of archaeology would have had more than a little truth to it. But over the past century archaeology has developed into a careful, methodical discipline far removed from the romantic images of the past. Today, professional archaeology utilizes the scientific method and is more often tedious than glamorous. Its primary goal is not to uncover fabulous treasures or beautiful art objects (though most archaeologists would happily welcome such discoveries if they come their way), but rather to produce *knowledge* about the human past.[35]

There has been extensive archaeological excavation in Israel, Jordan, Egypt, and other lands of the Bible since the 1930s. These "digs," especially those undertaken in the past two or three decades, have employed careful stratigraphical methods of excavation. That is, they sought to distinguish the various layers, or strata, of material customarily encountered at occupation sites in the Near East. For various reasons, a place might have been occupied by one or more groups of people over a span of many centuries. In such cases, normal repairs to buildings and the careless disposal of trash and other occupational debris produced by occasional destructions of the settlement have caused the gradual development of a large multilayered mound (known as a *tell* in Arabic, *tel* in Hebrew). During excavation of such a *tell*, modern archaeologists carefully observe where one layer ends and another begins. They keep separate the objects found in each layer, studying them to determine their functions and noting any changes in the styles and/or frequencies of the artifacts from the various layers. By comparing the finds of one site to those of another, layer by layer, it can be determined which strata were contemporaneous, and one can build up a relative chronology for the area. From such study generalized charts of archaeological periods or ages have been developed (see Table 1 for the Palestinian archaeological sequence).[36] The various archaeological periods are provided with absolute dates and related to history known from texts, including the Bible, through archaeological correlations with civilizations in Egypt or Mesopotamia that had writing at a very early date or by use of scientific dating methods such as radiocarbon dating.

For bygone eras that had no written sources (or none that can be understood), the archaeological record is our primary source of information. But, archaeology is also helpful in collecting valuable information about

---

35. Good descriptions of modern archaeology and its methods can be found in Joukowsky 1980 and Sharer and Ashmore 1987.

36. For a summary of the artifacts and cultural elements characteristic of each period, see Aharoni 1978.

TABLE 1

Chronology of the Archaeological Periods in Palestine

Date	Archaeological Period	Historical Synchronisms	Date
3300	CHALCOLITHIC PERIOD		3300
3200			3200
3100	EARLY BRONZE AGE I	EB I objects found in many	3100
3000		Egyptian tombs of Dynasty I	3000
2900			2900
2800	EARLY BRONZE AGE II		2800
2700			2700
2600		THE EGYPTIAN OLD KINGDOM	2600
2500	EARLY BRONZE AGE III	(Dynasties III-VI, c. 2700-2200 B.C.)	2500
2400		EB III objects found in some	2400
2300		Fourth through Sixth Dynasty Egyptian tombs	2300
2200	EARLY BRONZE AGE IV		2200
2100	OR		2100
2000	MIDDLE BRONZE AGE I		2000
1900			1900
1800	MIDDLE BRONZE II A		1800
1700			1700
1600	MIDDLE BRONZE II B	THE EGYPTIAN NEW KINGDOM	1600
1500	MIDDLE BRONZE II C	(c.1560-1070 B.C.)	1500
1400	LATE BRONZE AGE I	THE EXODUS? (early date) THE CONQUEST? (early date)	1400
1300	LATE BRONZE AGE II A		1300
1200	LATE BRONZE AGE II B	THE EXODUS? (late date) THE CONQUEST OR	1200
1100	IRON AGE I	SETTLEMENT? (late date)	1100
1000		UNITED MONARCHY: Saul	1000
900		David Solomon	900
800	IRON AGE II	THE DIVIDED MONARCHY (Israel in north; Judah in south)	800
700		Samaria falls to Assyria (722) Assyrians beseige Jerusalem (701)	700
587		Jerusalem falls to Babylonians	587

periods from which voluminous written documents do survive. Archaeological evidence supplements written sources, helping us to understand how ordinary people lived—what their tools and houses were like, how they buried their dead, where they worshipped, what they ate, and many other details that are seldom fully described in written materials. Indeed, because written accounts, especially those deliberately recording "history," are often biased or propagandistic, archaeological evidence can sometimes be used to raise questions concerning the historical reliability of written accounts.

Correlating archaeological evidence—even from recent, "scientific" expeditions—with written accounts is not easy. Very few sites are completely excavated down to virgin soil over their entire areas—it is simply too expensive and time consuming to do so. So there is always the possibility that crucial evidence, perhaps even an entire occupation phase, has been missed. The more extensive an excavation is, and the wider the area of its coverage, the more likely it becomes that its results accurately represent the true occupational history of the site.

Correlating archaeological sites with places known from ancient texts is also not always a sure thing. Cities like Jerusalem, Athens, and Rome have remained occupied since antiquity, so their locations are not in question. But the sites of many other places must be determined from clues found in ancient written material, and sometimes there are two or three possible archaeological sites for a given town or city. Archaeological excavation occasionally solves such disputes by uncovering on a site written evidence of its ancient identity. But the locations of many ancient cities known from texts remain debatable.

Finally, there is the problem that the "objective" evidence uncovered by archaeologists must be *interpreted*. The meaning of a burned level in an ancient city or of a change in the burial practices and material culture of a past society is not automatically evident. Archaeologists sometimes disagree over how a given body of evidence should be interpreted. But there is a small, irreducible level of subjectivity in human scholarship in every field of study and no interpretation can ever really be "final." This fact should not negate the value of the archaeological record as a supplement to written sources or as the primary evidence for prehistoric periods. It should, however, make us somewhat cautious in claiming that the evidence "proves" one thing or another. In history and archaeology absolute proof is unattainable; the interpretations and reconstructions we create are only more or less probable.

In the early stages of archaeological discovery in the Near East, many individuals sought archaeological evidence to "prove" that the Bible was correct scientifically and historically. Presumably, they believed that such "proof" of the Bible's accuracy would also validate its theological claims. But, as the great biblical archaeologist Roland de Vaux has observed, "Archaeology does not confirm the text, which is what it is; it can only confirm the interpretation which we give it."[37] By the same token, archaeology cannot *disprove* the biblical text; it can only suggest that a particular *interpretation* of the text is probably incorrect. The experience of Joseph Callaway, the excavator of et-Tell (almost universally thought to be the site of biblical Ai) is a good example of this principle. Callaway accepted the historicity of the biblical account of Ai's role in the Israelite conquest of Canaan, and he hoped his excavations would show that the Bible was correct in this instance. When the evidence he turned up could not be reconciled with the biblical narrative, Callaway was forced to change his interpretation of this portion of the Bible. However, it did not cause him to reject the Bible as a whole or to abandon his religious faith.[38]

This study is not attempting to determine the ultimate reliability or theological validity of the Bible. Our goal is much more limited. We are seeking historical information about the emergence of the ancient nation of Israel in Palestine. The biblical narratives in the Pentateuch and in Joshua and Judges tell us that twelve tribes of Israelites left Egypt under the leadership of Moses, crossed the Sinai Peninsula, entered Canaan and conquered it, destroying many cities and annihilating their populations. Most Jews and Christians interpret this account as an historically reliable narrative, though some have admitted that a few legendary elements may have been included with the factual material. It is this interpretation—that the biblical accounts of the Exodus and Conquest are entirely or at least essentially historical— that can be tested with archaeological evidence.

In the following chapters the biblical narratives will be critically compared with the evidence of archaeological excavations in Egypt and Palestine, with the uncertainties and problems of the archaeological evidence being noted. If the archaeological finds seem to fit quite well with the biblical accounts, it might be claimed that the traditional view of the Exodus and Conquest accounts as *history* is probably legitimate. On the other hand, if the archaeological evidence does not correlate well with the biblical narratives, it is probable that these narratives are not historically accurate, and believing Jews and Christians should seek some other way to view

---

37. de Vaux 1970: 78.
38. Callaway 1985.

them in the context of their faith. Whatever the result of our investigation, we hope to produce an historical reconstruction that will do justice to the physical remains of archaeology and at the same time explain the existence of the various biblical traditions about the Exodus and Conquest.

2

Dating the Exodus and Settlement

In order to place the Israelite exodus and occupation of Canaan in its proper archaeological and historical contexts, we must know when they occurred. On the basis of king lists and various inscriptions, Egyptologists have put together a chronological list of the pharaohs of ancient Egypt and the dynasties to which they belonged (see Table 2). Absolute dates for their reigns have been determined primarily from references to astronomical data and synchronisms with other Near Eastern rulers and historical events.[1] Which one of the historical pharaohs forced the Israelites to build store-cities for him, and which one tried to keep Moses from leading the Israelites out of Egypt? When did the Israelite tribes under the leadership of Joshua invade Canaan and destroy Jericho, Ai, and other cities?

The Bible doesn't provide clear-cut, unambiguous answers to these questions. The pharaohs of Egypt who figure in biblical stories about Abraham, Joseph, the oppression, and the Exodus are unfortunately not named. Thus, those stories cannot easily be connected to known Egyptian history. And rulers who *are* named in the biblical Exodus and Conquest accounts—

---

1. Egyptian chronology during the New Kingdom and into the period of the Hebrew monarchies is accurate within a range of about ten to twenty-six years. The dates used here for Egyptian New Kingdom rulers and events are derived primarily from Wente and Van Siclen 1976. For recent astronomical support of their date of 1504 B.C. for the beginning of the reign of Thutmose III, see Casperson 1986; for further support of their late dates for Dynasties XIX-XX, see Bierbrier 1975: 109-113 and Casperson 1988. Some other Egyptologists favor a chronology that begins the reign of Ahmose c. 1540 B.C. (e.g., Bietak 1988).

TABLE 2

Ancient Egyptian Chronology

ARCHAIC PERIOD	3100-2700
DYNASTIES ONE–TWO	
OLD KINGDOM	2700-2200
DYNASTIES THREE–SIX	
FIRST INTERMEDIATE PERIOD	2200-2060
MIDDLE KINGDOM	2060-1800
DYNASTIES SEVEN–TWELVE	
SECOND INTERMEDIATE PERIOD	1800-1560
DYNASTIES THIRTEEN–SEVENTEEN	
Hyksos Rule in Egypt	1665-1560
NEW KINGDOM	1560-1070
EIGHTEENTH DYNASTY	1570-1293
Ahmose	1570-1546
Amenhotep I	1551-1524
Thutmose I	1524-1518
Thutmose II	1518-1504
Thutmose III	1504-1450
Hatshepsut	1503-1483
Amenhotep II	1453-1419
Thutmose IV	1419-1387
Amenhotep III	1387-1350
Akhenaton	1350-1334
Smenkhkare	1336-1334
Tutankhamun	1334-1325
Ay	1324-1321
Horemhab	1321-1293
NINETEENTH DYNASTY	1293-1185
Ramesses I	1293-1291
Seti I	1291-1279
Ramesses II	1279-1212
Merneptah	1212-1202
TWENTIETH DYNASTY	1184-1070
Ramesses III	1182-1151
LATE PERIOD	1070-525
TWENTY-FIRST DYNASTY	1070-946
TWENTY-SECOND DYNASTY	946-745
Sheshonk I (Shishak)	945-924
TWENTY-THIRD DYNASTY	745-718
TWENTY-FOURTH DYNASTY	718-712
TWENTY-FIFTH DYNASTY	712-656
Taharqa (Tirhaka)	689-664
TWENTY-SIXTH DYNASTY (Saite)	664-525
PERSIAN CONQUEST	525

the Amorite king Sihon, Eglon of Moab, or Jabin of Hazor, for example—
are not mentioned in king lists, inscriptions, annals, or other ancient Near
Eastern historical sources. Furthermore, no Egyptian texts or other nonbiblical sources directly refer to the Israelite exodus or entrance into Canaan.
However, the Bible *does* provide an internal, relative chronology for the
events it discusses. This biblical chronology, with the historical details mentioned in the accounts themselves, provides the basic information scholars
must use to determine the historical context for the Exodus.

The Biblical Chronology for the Exodus and Conquest

The most direct indication of the date of the Exodus occurs in I Kings
6:1. There it is stated that Solomon began building the Temple of Yahweh
in Jerusalem in the fourth year of his reign, 480 years following the Israelite
departure from Egypt. And, fortunately, we know, in terms of the modern
calendar, the approximate date of the fourth year of Solomon's reign. The
books of I and II Kings list the kings of Israel and Judah, usually give
the length of each reign, provide synchronisms among the various rulers
of Israel and Judah, and refer to rulers of other Near Eastern countries
and to historical events. The information provided in these books is not
always consistent, though, and the use of different calendars in antiquity
also produces problems for modern interpreters. Nevertheless, from the
data provided in these biblical books, scholars have worked out an Israelite
and Judaean chronology that shouldn't be far off the mark.[2]

The date for the beginning of Solomon's reign cannot be determined
exactly. The date scholars assign to the end of his reign varies, due to
the differing solutions they accept for problems in the biblical data, and
the forty regnal years assigned to Solomon in I Kings 11:42 might just
be an approximation (David is also given a forty-year reign in II Samuel
5:5).[3] While we cannot date his reign precisely, evidence indicates that Solomon must have come to the throne sometime during the decade between
970 and 960 B.C.[4] For our purposes, this approximation will do. If the

2. See De Vries 1962 and 1976, Finegan 1964, Thiele 1965 and 1977, and Gray 1970: 55-
75 for a discussion of the problems of Old Testament chronology and for full bibliographies.
3. For example, see Noth 1960: 225; Gray 1970: 55; Bright 1981: 195; Tadmor 1984: 383.
4. The earliest date that scholars assign to the end of Solomon's reign is 932/31 B.C. (Andersen
1969) or 931/30 B.C. (De Vries 1962; Thiele 1965 and 1977). The latest date for the end of Solomon's
reign is 922 B.C. (Albright 1945, followed by Bright 1981 and others). Most German scholars
prefer a date of 926 B.C. (following Begrich 1929). The date for the beginning of the reign varies
accordingly, depending as well on whether one accepts forty years as its correct length.

Exodus occurred 480 years before the Temple began to be built in Solomon's fourth year, then it must have taken place in the mid-fifteenth century B.C. (c. 1450-1437 B.C.).

Another indication of a fifteenth-century-B.C. date for the Exodus is the statement in Judges 11:26 that, at the time of the "judge" Jephthah, the Israelites had already controlled Heshbon and the area east of the Jordan around the Arnon River for three hundred years. The Bible states that the Israelites conquered this territory at the beginning of their entrance into Canaan (Numbers 21:21-35), and Jephthah's activity is usually dated about 1100 B.C. If by 1100 B.C. Israel had already been in Canaan 300 years, the Exodus must have occurred before 1400 B.C.

The chronology for the period of the "judges" given in the Book of Judges also is in keeping with a fifteenth-century-B.C. date for the Exodus. The lengths of various "judgeships" and periods of oppression by enemies are listed throughout the book. When these periods of time are added together and combined with the time for the wilderness wanderings, the Conquest, and the reigns of Saul and David, one obtains a figure of more than 500 years.[5] However one chooses to reconcile this figure with the 480 years that I Kings 6:1 records as the length of time between the Exodus and the fourth year of Solomon, it is clear that the author of Judges believed that the Exodus occurred no later than the fifteenth century B.C.

Extrabiblical Evidence for a Fifteenth-Century Exodus

Does a mid-fifteenth-century date for the Exodus fit what is known of the history of Egypt and the Holy Land at that time? Some scholars argue that it does. The powerful Eighteenth Dynasty had been ruling all of Egypt since c. 1560 B.C., when its founder, Ahmose, had destroyed the power of the hated Hyksos. The Hyksos were Semites from Syria-Palestine who had settled in the delta area at the end of the Egyptian Middle Kingdom, built up their power, then made themselves the rulers of Lower Egypt. Their capital was at Avaris in the delta. Ahmose destroyed Avaris and reestablished Egyptian control over the entire Nile Valley.

But Amenhotep I (c. 1551-1524), the second king of this dynasty, had no male offspring.[6] He chose as his successor Thutmose I, a general who

---

5. Rowley 1950a: 87-88; Bimson 1981: 79-81; Soggin 1981: 8-12.

6. Siegfried Horn's statement that "for three generations the royal families of the 18th dynasty kings of Egypt, from Ahmose to Thutmose II, had no male offspring" (1977: 23) is incorrect. Amenhotep I was the son of Ahmose and his Great Wife, Ahmose Nefertiri. And Thutmose

later legitimized his claim to the throne by marrying one of Amenhotep's daughters, Ahmose. Then Thutmose I (c. 1524-1518) failed to have a son by his Great Wife (the pharaoh's principal wife or Queen). She produced only a daughter, Hatshepsut. However, Thutmose I did have a son, Thutmose II, by a secondary wife. Thutmose II (c. 1518-1504) married his half-sister Hatshepsut and made her his Great Wife to strengthen his claim to the throne.

Unfortunately, once again the pharaoh's Great Wife did not have a son. One of Hatshepsut's daughters was given in marriage to Thutmose III, the son of Thutmose II and a concubine, to guarantee his right to the throne. Thutmose III was still a child when his father died, so Hatshepsut became regent for him. A little more than a year later, she had herself named pharaoh and coruler with Thutmose III. She was clearly the dominant partner in this arrangement, and she continued to rule Egypt until her death, c. 1483 B.C.

Then Thutmose III, finally able to exercise the power he had theoretically held since c. 1504 B.C., undertook a series of military campaigns in the areas to the northeast and to the south of Egypt. By the time he died (c. 1450 B.C.) Thutmose III had created an Egyptian empire that stretched from the Euphrates in Syria to Napata in Nubia, and he had established himself as Egypt's greatest warrior pharaoh (see Figure 1). (He also launched a campaign of hatred against Hatshepsut, having her name chiseled off of monuments, destroying her statues and inscriptions, and generally trying to wipe out all traces of her reign.)

Thutmose III was succeeded by his son, Amenhotep II (c. 1453-1419), who like his father was an excellent warrior and a prodigious builder.[7] He strengthened Egyptian control over Syria-Palestine and Nubia and bequeathed a fairly stable empire to his successor, Thutmose IV, whose reign closed out the fifteenth century.

It has been argued that a Hebrew infant boy might well have become the beloved foster child of an Egyptian princess during this era when many of the pharaohs' wives did not have sons. Perhaps Hatshepsut was the princess who adopted Moses, favoring him over Thutmose III, the son of her husband and a concubine. That might explain Thutmose III's great hatred for his stepmother/aunt/mother-in-law.[8]

II was the son of Thutmose I, though by Mutnefret (a secondary wife) rather than by his Great Wife, Ahmose (a daughter of Amenhotep I). See Gardiner 1961: 174, 180; Wente 1980: 127-132.

7. Gardiner 1961: 168-204.

8. Jack 1925: 251-255; Horn 1977: 23-24; Wood 1986: 93-95.

Thutmose III and Amenhotep II, whose reigns cover the time indicated for the Exodus by the biblical chronology, both undertook major building operations, including some construction in the Nile Delta.[9] Furthermore, inscriptions and tomb paintings from the time of Thutmose I and Thutmose III indicate that Semites were among the slaves employed in the construction gangs at this time. Perhaps among these slaves were those oppressed Hebrews described in the Bible.[10]

The Amarna Letters could also be used to supplement the biblical account of the Israelite conquest of Canaan if the Exodus occurred during the fifteenth century B.C. This important diplomatic archive was found near the modern village of el-Amarna in the ruins of Akhetaton, the Egyptian capital during the reign of Akhenaton. Its contents consisted of letters primarily from Syro-Palestinian rulers to pharaohs Amenhotep III (c. 1387-1350 B.C.) and Akhenaton (c. 1350-1334 B.C.). They provide evidence of almost constant quarrels and infighting among the various vassal kings ruling under Egyptian authority in Syria and Palestine, and they frequently mention unrest caused by a group called the Ḫabiru.[11] These same people appear in some Eighteenth and Nineteenth Dynasty Egyptian texts under the spelling 'pr.w ('Apiru).[12] The similarity of these terms to "Hebrew" ('ibri in Hebrew) is obvious and has been emphasized by many scholars.

If the Israelites had departed from Egypt c. 1450-1440 B.C., they would have been entering Canaan and conquering its cities in the years between 1400 and 1330 B.C., the time of the Amarna correspondence. It has been noted that the lack of letters from Jericho, Gibeon, Bethel, and Hebron might be due to their having been conquered by the Hebrews while cities such as Jerusalem, Megiddo, Ashkelon, Gezer, and Acco (all of which had letters to pharaoh represented in the Amarna archive) were still in Canaanite hands.[13] According to Theophile Meek, "This contemporaneous account of the settlement of the Ḫabiru in Palestine so exactly parallels the Old Testament account of the Israelite conquest of Jericho and the invasion of the highlands of Ephraim under Joshua that the two manifestly

---

9. Gardiner 1961: 188-189, 199; Bimson 1981: 230-231.

10. Horn 1977: 24.

11. Knudtzon 1915. In most of the Amarna Letters the term for the troublesome rebels was written ideographically (^{lu}SA.GAZ^{mes}) which does not, unfortunately, indicate how the word was pronounced. But the letters from the ruler of Jerusalem spell the word out syllabically as Ḫa-bi-ru (or Ḫa-pi-ru). The equation SA.GAZ = Ḫabiru is now generally accepted. See Greenberg 1955: 3-12.

12. Greenberg 1955: 10-11.

13. Greenberg 1955: 7-8; Meek 1960: 21; Bimson 1981: 227; Wood 1986: 83.

must have reference to the same episode."[14]

There is also a well-known relief from the Saqqara tomb of Horemhab, a general under Tutankhamun and Ay who later became pharaoh at the end of the Amarna Period. The tomb was constructed c. 1334 B.C., during the time covered by some of the latest letters in the Amarna archive. One of its reliefs depicts Canaanites begging Egyptian authorities to grant them permission to enter Egypt. These travelers complain that their town has been destroyed, their country is hungry, and they have had to live like the animals of the desert.[15] It is possible to see them as refugees from one of the Canaanite cities captured and destroyed by Joshua and the Israelites.[16]

It has even been claimed that an Egyptian inscription from the time of Hatshepsut actually mentions the Exodus. The text in question is the Speos Artemidos inscription carved on the wall of a temple in Middle Egypt. This text is damaged and is difficult to translate. Nevertheless, it seems to refer to Hatshepsut's anger at the actions of a group of Asiatics (the Egyptian term for people from Syria-Palestine) who lived in the Delta region of Egypt, and it announces her restoration of ruined buildings (probably temples). Immanuel Velikovsky was the first to intepret portions of this text as an Egyptian reference to events from the time of the Exodus. Velikovsky believed that the destruction of the buildings mentioned in this inscription had been due to catastrophes associated with the Exodus (which according to Velikovsky had occurred long before Hatshepsut's time).[17] Recently, however, Hans Goedicke has related the inscription to the Exodus in another way.

According to Goedicke's translation and interpretation, Hatshepsut "annulled the former privileges" that had been granted to the Asiatic immigrants, forcing them to provide labor on public building projects. They refused to perform their assigned tasks, which provoked a period of conflict. Finally, Hatshepsut allowed them to leave Egypt, but the gods punished them— "the earth swallowed up their footsteps" through an unexpected upsurge of Nun (the Egyptian name for the primeval waters).[18] Thus, Goedicke claims, the Speos Artemidos inscription provides us with an Egyptian version of the oppression of the Israelites, of their exodus from Egypt, and of

---

14. Meek 1960: 21.
15. Breasted 1909: 388 and fig. 147; Gardiner 1961: 243.
16. Horn 1977: 24.
17. Velikovsky 1952: 51-52.
18. Shanks 1981: 49-50.

the sudden flood of water at the *Yam Suph* (the "Red Sea"). The Egyptians naturally thought the flood had been sent to destroy the Asiatics, while the Israelites interpreted it as being sent by God to destroy the pursuing Egyptians.

If this inscription describes the Exodus from an Egyptian viewpoint, then Hatshepsut (c. 1503-1483), the first woman pharaoh of Egypt, was both the pharaoh of the oppression and the pharaoh of the Exodus. Obviously, if Goedicke's theory is correct, she could *not* have been Moses' adoptive mother as others have proposed; another, earlier princess would have to be found for that role. The date of the Exodus would also have to be pushed back by some thirty to fifty years, to the beginning of the fifteenth century. However, placing the Exodus during Hatshepsut's reign might allow it to be synchronized with the catastrophic eruption of the volcanic island of Thera in the Aegean, an event usually dated between c. 1500 and 1470 B.C. This eruption could be used to explain some of the miraculous events of the Exodus story, especially the wall of water that overwhelmed the Egyptians at the sea.[19]

Another Egyptian text that can be interpreted in terms of an Israelite exodus from Egypt in the fifteenth century and settlement in Canaan during the fourteenth century is the famous Merneptah stele. This inscription contains the earliest known reference to Israel in a nonbiblical source.[20] The stele was erected in the fifth year of pharaoh Merneptah's reign, c. 1208 B.C., to celebrate his victories over Libyans and Palestinians. Near its end it poetically describes the pharaoh's triumph:

> The princes are prostrate, saying: "Mercy!"
> Not one raises his head among the Nine Bows.
> Desolation is for Tehenu; Hatti is pacified;
> Plundered is the Canaan with every evil;
> Carried off is Ashkelon; seized upon is Gezer;
> Yanoam is made as that which does not exist;
> Israel is laid waste, his seed is not;
> Hurru is become a widow for Egypt!
> All lands together, they are pacified;
> Everyone who was restless, he has been bound
> by the King of Upper and Lower Egypt; Ba-en-Re Meri-Amon;

---

19. Shanks 1981: 46-48; I. Wilson 1985: 131-132, 136-137.

20. Scholars have generally agreed that the *Ysr'r* of the stele must be "Israel" (*Yishra'el* in Hebrew). The Egyptian writing system did not have an "l", so "l" is usually written with the "r" sign, making the reading of some non-Egyptian words in Egyptian texts problematic.

the Son of Re: Mer-ne-Ptah Hotep-hir-Maat, given life like
Re every day.[21]

This inscription is written in the Egyptian hieroglyphic system, which
used signs, called "determinatives," to help scribes read the text. Determinatives informed the reader about the category (a place, a tribe, a female
name, etc.) of the word to which they were attached, so that the scribe
could more easily make sense out of it. For instance, in the portion of
the Merneptah stele quoted above, the words for Hatti, Canaan, Ashkelon,
Gezer, Yanoam, and Hurru are written with the determinative for "land"
or "country" to indicate that they are the names of places. On the other
hand, Israel has the determinative for "people" rather than "place."[22] Many
have seen this as evidence that the Exodus and Conquest must have taken
place in the thirteenth century B.C., shortly before Merneptah's reign, since
the stele seems to indicate that groups of Israelites were in Canaan but
were not yet a settled people in possession of a significant portion of the
land.[23]

Another interpretation is possible, though. The stele is carelessly written,
so the scribe's use of the "people" determinative for Israel might not be
as significant as it first appears to be.[24] Secondly, it has recently been argued
that the structure of the poem requires that Israel be seen as a synonym
for Canaan.[25] Ancient Near Eastern poetry made use of parallelism—where
two lines present the same idea in slightly different words—as a compositional
device. This poetic feature often helps scholars understand the meaning
of difficult words or phrases that occur in one line by comparing them
with the elements in the parallel line. According to G. W. Ahlström and
D. Edelman, Merneptah's poem has a ring structure. That is, instead of
placing parallel statements in two successive lines, the poem parallels beginning with end and works in toward the middle. Line 1 of the composition
would parallel the last line, line 2 would parallel the penultimate line, etc.
In Merneptah's poem, they argue, line 3 ("Desolation is for Tehenu; . . .")
is paralleled by line 8 ("Hurru has become a widow . . ."), line 4 ("Plundered
is the Canaan . . .") is paralleled by line 7 ("Israel is laid waste . . ."), and
the two middle lines, listing cities in Palestine (5 and 6, which they make
into three lines), are parallel. If this analysis is correct, then "Israel" on

21. J. Wilson 1955: 378.
22. J. Wilson 1955: 378.
23. For example, see G. Anderson 1966: 28; McKenzie 1966: 28; Soggin 1984: 39.
24. J. Wilson 1955: 378; de Vaux 1978: 390.
25. Ahlström and Edelman 1985.

the stele must be an inclusive term like "Canaan." Either each term represents half of the area of Palestine (Canaan the coastal plains and Israel the hilly interior) or both terms are used as roughly synonymous names for the entire area of Palestine.[26] It could be argued that such a usage indicates that by Merneptah's reign Israelites were a significant portion of the population of Palestine and that they controlled at least the hill country, if not the entire land. This position of prominence would be consistent with a fifteenth-century-B.C. Exodus from Egypt and a fourteenth-century-B.C. Conquest of Palestine.

For many years, the most persuasive piece of evidence for a fifteenth-century-B.C. Exodus was the claim that archaeological excavations proved that Jericho had fallen to Joshua c. 1400 B.C. John Garstang made this claim on the basis of his excavations at Tell es-Sultan (the site of Old Testament Jericho) in the early 1930s. Garstang found a double defensive wall that had fallen outward (presumably as the result of an earthquake) and that showed the effects of a tremendous fire. On the basis of vessels found in tombs and of sherds (broken pieces of pottery) found at the base of the mound and in a few houses built over portions of the destroyed fortifications, Garstang dated the destruction c. 1400-1385 B.C.[27] As we have seen, this is the very time when Joshua and the Israelites would have been entering Canaan if they had left Egypt c. 1450-1440 B.C. and wandered in the wilderness for forty years.

Later excavations at Jericho by Kathleen Kenyon, however, have indicated that Garstang's interpretation of the archaeological evidence had been incorrect. The walls he thought belonged to the Late Bronze Age city of Joshua's time turned out to be Early Bronze Age fortifications destroyed c. 2300 B.C.[28] The only Late Bronze remains Kenyon could find consisted of a portion of one wall, an oven, and a small section of floor with a dipper juglet lying on it.[29] There was no trace to be found of Late Bronze Age city walls. Some of the burned walls and buildings Garstang had uncovered belonged to the Early Bronze Age destruction, while others dated to the destruction that occurred at the end of the Middle Bronze Age. For about a century after the end of the Middle Bronze Age city and before the sparse Late Bronze II reoccupation, Jericho was uninhabited. The meager evidence of Late Bronze occupation that Kenyon and Garstang

---

26. Ahlström and Edelman 1985: 60-61.
27. Garstang 1931: 145-147; Garstang and Garstang 1940: 125, 133-136.
28. Kenyon 1957: 170-171, 262; 1967: 265-267; 1978: 36.
29. Kenyon 1957: 261; 1978: 38-39.

excavated seems to have belonged to a settlement that only *began* during the fourteenth century B.C., not to a great flourishing city that was destroyed at that time.[30]

Today virtually all archaeologists agree with Kenyon's interpretation of the pottery evidence for the Middle Bronze II date of Jericho's destruction. However, a few conservative or fundamentalist scholars continue to support Garstang's view that the city continued to exist until the end of the Late Bronze Age I, being destroyed c. 1400-1385. The small amount of Late Bronze II material found by Kenyon they credit to the brief reoccupation of the site by Eglon, King of Moab, during the time of the "judges" (Judges 3:13).[31]

Problems with a Fifteenth-Century Exodus

The evidence for a fifteenth-century Exodus *seems* to be very strong. But when this evidence is examined closely, significant problems appear. The biblical chronology for the Exodus is not totally consistent or reliable, and more is claimed for the extrabiblical evidence than it, in fact, can deliver.

The biblical dates for this early material seem to be the work of the Deuteronomistic historian, who put together various traditions about the occupation of Canaan to create the Books of Joshua and Judges. For the period of the divided monarchy following the death of Solomon, the biblical authors seem to have had detailed and reasonably accurate chronological sources, including official annals of the kings of Israel and Judah. But this does not appear to have been true for the earlier period. The frequent occurrence of twenty- and forty-year periods (or of multiples thereof) in the chronology of the Judges, the wilderness wanderings, and the reigns of David and Solomon is highly suspicious. Because forty years was the time traditionally allotted for a generation in the Bible, we can suspect that the dates are probably schematic, not to be taken literally. In fact, seven of the eighteen chronological references in Judges are stereotyped figures, their totals adding up to 280 years of the 410-year total for the entire period.[32]

The "judges" were local heroes whose activities, confined to different parts of Palestine, seldom involved more than two or three of the Israelite

---

30. Kenyon 1957: 260-261; 1967: 265, 271-273; 1978: 39-40; 1981: 1-2.
31. Wood 1970: 69-73; 1986: 74-78; Waltke 1972: 40-42.
32. Soggin 1981: 9-10.

tribes. So it is possible that some of them were contemporaries, whose stories were placed schematically in a chronological sequence in order to make their actions as "saviors" relevant for *all* Israel. Just as we cannot be sure that the events recounted in the stories were *successive,* neither do we know whether they have been placed in the *correct* chronological order.[33]

The Books of Kings were written by the same person, "the Deuteronomistic historian," who compiled and organized the traditional materials in Joshua and Judges, so it is not surprising that the 480 years between the Exodus and the fourth year of Solomon in I Kings 6:1 is another one of these schematic dates—twelve times forty years.[34] If the Deuteronomistic historian intended this figure to indicate that twelve generations had passed between Solomon's reign and the Exodus, the figure could be used to point to a *thirteenth century* Exodus. A generation (the period of time from the birth of a father to the birth of his son) is really closer to twenty-five than to forty years. And twelve generations of twenty-five years each would add up to a three-hundred-year figure for the time between the Exodus and Solomon's fourth year. If the fourth year of Solomon occurred between c. 967-958 B.C., the Exodus would have taken place c. 1267-1258 B.C.[35] However, despite attempts to show that this reference in I Kings embodies genuine chronological data that is independent of the chronology for the "judges,"[36] it more likely represents the Deuteronomistic editors' schematic summary of chronological material given in Joshua, Judges, and I and II Samuel.[37]

The artificial or schematic nature of the date in I Kings 6:1 is also suggested by another interesting fact: The total number of years that the Deuteronomistic History indicates for the period from the founding of the Temple in Solomon's fourth year to the last year of the last king in Jerusalem is 430 years. Fifty years later, Cyrus, king of Persia, issued a decree allowing the Israelites who had been carried off into exile near Babylon to return to Palestine and rebuild the Temple. So, the total number of years from the building of the Temple under Solomon to Cyrus' declaration authorizing its restoration was 480![38] "In other words, by having Solomon's Temple

---

33. McKenzie 1966: 8; de Vaux 1978: 692-693; Soggin 1981: 7-12.
34. Gray 1970: 159
35. McKenzie 1966: 32; Bright 1981: 123.
36. Rowley 1950a: 86-98; Bimson 1981: 81-84.
37. Boling 1975: 23; De Vries 1976: 162; Mayes 1977: 289-290; de Vaux 1978: 389, 689-692; Soggin 1981: 10-12.
38. Miller 1977a: 241; Sarna 1986: 9.

building occur in the four hundred eightieth year after the Exodus, the biblical historiosopher may have been making that event the central point in the history of biblical Israel."[39]

In any case, the statement in I Kings 6:1 is *not* an absolutely trustworthy source for determining the date of the Exodus. The biblical chronology for the period of the Exodus, Conquest, and time of the "judges" is much too questionable for it to serve as the main support for theories of a fifteenth-century Exodus.

The unreliability of biblical chronological data relating to the pre-monarchic period is indicated by a comparison of the information given in I Chronicles 6:33-37 with that in Ruth 4:20-22 and of the chronological statement in Exodus 12:40-41 with the genealogy in Exodus 6:16-20. The passage in I Chronicles places Heman, a priest who served in the sanctuary in David's time, in the eighteenth generation after Korah, a contemporary of Moses. But the genealogy in Ruth indicates that Solomon belonged to the *seventh* generation after Nahshon, another contemporary of Moses (Numbers 1:7).[40] Exodus 12:40-41 states that there was a period of 430 years between the Israelite entrance into Egypt and the exodus from Egypt. But Genesis 15:13-16 and the genealogy in Exodus 6:16-20 indicates that only *four* generatons spanned the period from the entrance into Egypt to the Exodus. Even if one accepts the biblical statements about the advanced ages at which the ancestors of Moses died, the genealogical and chronological data given in Exodus 6 cannot be stretched over the four hundred (Genesis 15:13) or 430 (Exodus 12:40-41) years of the sojourn in Egypt.[41] The chronological and genealogical traditions of the premonarchic period are simply not trustworthy pillars upon which a chronology of the Exodus and the settlement of Palestine can be erected.

The extrabiblical textual evidence for a fifteenth-century-B.C. Exodus

---

39. Sarna 1986: 9.

40. Ramsey 1981: 76. Other inconsistencies between the Bible's genealogical data and the four hundred or 430 years cited for the period Israel stayed in Egypt are pointed out by Nahum Sarna (1986: 7-8).

41. The genealogy of Moses, as given in Exodus 6, is: Levi (died at 137 years of age), Kohath (died at 133 years of age), Amram (died at 137 years of age), and Moses (who was 80 years old at the time of the Exodus). Jacob's sons, however, were adults when they entered Egypt, and they already had children. Genesis 46:11 indicates that Levi's son, Kohath (the grandfather of Moses), had been born before Jacob and his sons entered Egypt. Actually, then, only *three* generations can be used to span the four hundred years allotted to the sojourn in Egypt, and only eighty years of the total belongs to Moses. That leaves 320 years to be split between Kohath and Amram. Yet, according to Exodus 6, their total lifespans (with no overlap) amount only to 270 years (133 + 137)! Obviously, the Bible's genealogical traditions disagree with the chronology constructed by its later editors.

is even weaker. Professor Goedicke's attempt to read the Speos Artemidos inscription of Hatshepsut as an account of the oppression and Exodus depends on his very questionable translation of a difficult text.[42] It is likely that the Asiatics mentioned in the inscription are the Hyksos who had ruled Egypt about a century before Hatshepsut's time. The inscription accuses them of neglecting the cult of Re, principal god of Egypt. But other Egyptologists find no clear references to an annulment of the Asiatics' former privileges, nor to their disregarding their assigned building tasks, nor to a destruction by Nun, god of the primeval waters. The "father of fathers" who has ordered the earth to carry off their footprints is probably Re, not Nun.[43] Only by a very idiosyncratic translation and a number of unlikely interpretations can this text be seen as related to the Israelite exodus from Egypt.

It is also unlikely that the Exodus can be dated by connecting it with the volcanic eruption of Thera in the Aegean. This question will be reviewed at length below (Chapter 4). But here it is sufficient to say that the evidence does not show that the eruption would have had the disastrous effects in the Nile Delta that Goedicke and others claim.[44] Furthermore, such an eruption does not really explain the miracles associated with the Exodus.

The argument that "Israel" in the Merneptah stele is used as a parallel for "Canaan" is also not without problems. Perhaps the use of the determinative for "people" with Israel is due to carelessness on the part of the scribe, but elsewhere in the stele the country determinative is used for settled populations like the Rebu, and places like Hatti and Ashkelon, while the determinative for people is used with the names of seminomadic groups like the Madjoi, Nau, and Tekten.[45] As the late Egyptologist John A. Wilson stated, "Determinatives should have meaning, and a contrast between determinatives in the same context should be significant."[46] And the "people" determinative for Israel would seem to indicate a seminomadic group rather than a settled population.

Even if one accepts the view of Ahlström and Edelman that on the stele Israel is used as a parallel to Canaan, one need not conclude that

---

42. Compare Goedicke's translation in Shanks 1981: 49 with that of A. H. Gardiner (1946) or John A. Wilson (1955: 231). Gardiner's and Goedicke's translations are printed side by side in I. Wilson 1985: 136.

43. See J. Wilson 1955: 231; Krahmalkov 1981: 51; Oren 1981: 49-50, 52; and Van Seters 1982.

44. See below, pp. 109-111.

45. J. Wilson 1955: 378.

46. J. Wilson 1955: 378.

it is a term for all of Palestine. As Ahlström and Edelman themselves point out, the use of the people determinative with Israel

> could be an accurate record of Israel's primary association with the hill country's population, which has been used here to represent its geographical sense as well, paralleling the term Canaan. This would suggest that the Egyptian scribe composing the coda did not know of any specific geographical term for the hill country of Palestine, such as "Ephraim," but that he did know that a group of people called Israel lived in this area.[47]

This could have been true even if Israel had not as yet gained control of more than the central hill area. The Israelites could thus have been only partially settled, entering Palestine soon after the middle of the thirteenth century, as little as twenty or thirty years before Merneptah's reign.

Furthermore, Ahlström and Edelman's analysis of the ring structure of the poem may be faulty. For Israel to parallel Canaan, Hurru would have to parallel Tehenu and Hatti. But this does not fit normal Egyptian usage. Tehenu was a term for Libya, and Hatti is the name used for the Hittite Empire of Asia Minor. On the other hand, Hurru (or Kharu) is one of the terms that, since the Eighteenth Dynasty, Egyptians had applied to the Syro-Palestinian area. Djahi, Retenu, Canaan, and Hurru were all roughly synonymous terms in New Kingdom texts.[48] Thus, in Merneptah's poem, Hurru (line 8) should be the parallel to Canaan (line 4).

The foreign countries of line 3 ("Desolation is for Tehenu; Hatti is pacified") would then be paralleled by line 9 ("All lands together, they are pacified"). Line 5 has two parts that are parallel ("Carried off is Ashkelon; seized upon is Gezer") and should perhaps be treated as two separate lines. Line 7 ("Israel is laid waste, his seed is not") then makes an excellent parallel for line 6 ("Yanoam is made as that which does not exist").

The ring structure does not seem to begin until line 3. The first two lines ("The princes are prostrate, saying: 'Mercy!'/Not one raises his head among the Nine Bows.") are parallel and function as a general introduction to the rest of the poem. Line 10 is also outside of the ring structure and leads into the concluding titulary (the official names and titles) of Merneptah.[49]

---

47. Ahlström and Edelman 1985: 60-61.

48. Wilson 1955: 235, 258, 261; Drower 1973: 432.

49. Still another possible interpretation is that line 1 is a general introduction to the poem, not part of the ring structure. Line 2 ("Not one raises his head among the Nine Bows" [a term for very ancient enemies of Egypt]) would then be parallel to line 10 ("Everyone who was restless, he has been bound").

If Israel parallels Yanoam instead of Canaan, it must be the term for a tribal group of people occupying only a small part of Canaan. Ashkelon and Gezer were in southern Palestine and Yanoam was in northern Palestine. If Israel is included with them as part of an enumeration of the parts of Canaan/Hurru, then at the time of Merneptah Israel must have been located in northern or central Palestine.[50] Furthermore, there is no way to determine whether in this stele the term "Israel" refers to a group of tribes, as it does in the biblical traditions, or merely to one tribe or one component of the many various population groups that seem to have later made up Israel.

The evidence favoring a fifteenth-century-B.C. Exodus is clearly not compelling. However, the main reason many scholars have rejected the fifteenth-century date for the Exodus is its poor "fit" into the historical and archaeological picture of the time. In the biblical story, Moses and Aaron make frequent trips from the Israelite encampments to the court of pharaoh, which implies that the residence of the pharaoh was in the delta area at the time. But in the fifteenth century B.C. the capital of Egypt was at *Thebes,* more than four hundred miles up the Nile from the delta. Thebes was also the focal point for the building activities of Eighteenth Dynasty rulers. But some of the pharaohs of the early Eighteenth Dynasty mustered troops at forts in the delta in preparation for their campaigns in Syria-Palestine (though none of these kings seem to have stayed in the delta for very long), and some spent much of their time at the old royal palace at Memphis, an earlier capital of Egypt.[51] Memphis was located at the point where the Nile begins branching into the delta, so it would fit the Exodus story's requirements much better than Thebes. But, even if during the Exodus events the pharaoh was at Memphis, Moses and Aaron would have had a journey of sixty miles or more, each way, every time they went from Goshen (in the area of Wadi Tumilat) to see him.

This objection to a fifteenth-century-B.C. Exodus is not insuperable, because the biblical account is not very precise. For example, if one supposes that the Israelites were being forced to labor in Memphis at the time of Moses and that pharaoh was staying there, the problem all but disappears. But the itinerary of the Exodus given in Exodus 12:37 and Numbers 33

---

50. de Vaux 1978: 390-391.

51. Redford 1984: 44, J. W. Jack (1925: 250), and L. J. Wood (1970: 81; 1986: 81-82) note that Amenhotep II, the prime candidate for the pharaoh of the Exodus if it is placed in the fifteenth century B.C., was born at Memphis and spent much time in the palace there during his reign.

starts in the delta, not at Memphis, which seems to indicate that all of the events narrated, from the beginning of the oppression to the Exodus, took place in the delta area. And this would make an Eighteenth Dynasty date for the Exodus very unlikely.

A fifteenth-century-B.C. Exodus from Egypt and an early fourteenth-century Conquest of Canaan would also make the period of the settlement and of the "judges" coincide with the time of maximum Egyptian control over Palestine. During the fifteenth through the thirteenth centuries B.C., Syro-Palestinian kings were tribute-paying vassals of Egypt, and the pharaohs of the Eighteenth and Nineteenth Dynasties undertook frequent military campaigns to punish cities whose rulers rebelled. Egyptian governors watched over the area, and some cities contained small garrisons of Egyptian troops.[52] So complete was Egyptian control that when a Babylonian baggage train was attacked by bandits in Canaan during the Amarna Period, the Babylonian king complained to the Egyptian pharaoh, holding him responsible and demanding that he pay compensation![53] Yet the Books of Joshua and Judges do not mention Egyptian activities in Canaan or conflict between Israel and Egyptian troops after the crossing of the *Yam Suph.*

How could the Israelites have destroyed cities and taken control of much of the land of Canaan in the fourteenth century B.C. without a major military confrontation with the armies of Egypt? Why do accounts of the "judges" correctly preserve descriptions of the various peoples of Syria-Palestine (Amorites, Canaanites, Hurrians, Ammonites, and the Philistines, for example) yet totally ignore the Egyptians, who controlled the major cities and roads throughout that area?

The Amarna Letters, once seen as a contemporaneous description of the Israelite conquest, can no longer be so regarded. Study of the terms SA.GAZ and Ḫabiru have shown that they are not ethnic terms. Ḫabiru (or better, 'Apiru) was the appellation for people of diverse ethnic backgrounds who shared a generally inferior social status. They were uprooted, propertyless individuals, refugees who might be mercenaries or bandits, settled retainers or renegades, hired laborers or freebooters—depending on circumstances. They do not seem to have been organized into tribes, and there is no indication that they invaded Palestine from outside. Furthermore, during the Amarna Period 'Apiru were also causing trouble in Syria and Phoenicia, far beyond the areas invaded by the Israelites.[54] Thus, biblical

---

52. Drower 1973: 467-483; Albright 1975a: 102-107; Redford 1985: 192-194.
53. Knudtzon 1915: No. 8, lines 16-29.
54. Greenberg 1955: 86-96.

scholars have come to realize that while some of Israel's ancestors may have been 'Apiru, not all (or even most) 'Apiru were related to the later Israelites.

The kings who ruled the cities of Jerusalem, Lachish, and Gezer at the time of the Conquest are named in Joshua 10:3 and 33, but the rulers of these cities in the Amarna Letters bear quite different names. Moreover, Joshua 10:32 claims that when the Israelites conquered Lachish they killed all its citizens. Yet the Amarna Letters show that, at the time of Akhenaton, Lachish was a flourishing Canaanite city ruled by a non-Israelite king who was a vassal of Egypt. By the beginning of Akhenaton's reign (c. 1350 B.C.), the Israelites should have completed their conquest of southern Canaan, including Lachish, if the chronology of events in the Book of Joshua is accurate and if the Conquest had begun c. 1400 B.C. Plainly, it is difficult to square the biblical narratives about these cities with the information in the Amarna archives. Anson Rainey, an Israeli archaeologist, biblical scholar, and an expert on the Amarna Letters, has observed that "the society and political situation in the el-Amarna tablets leave no room for the Israelites as we know them from the Book of Judges. There is not a single contact, but many contrasts, between the el-Amarna texts and the Bible."[55]

Some supporters of a fifteenth-century-B.C. date for the Exodus have dealt with the lack of references to Egypt during the time of the "judges" by arguing "that the Book of Judges was not intended as a full history of the period,"[56] but rather as a listing of Israel's failures to obey Yahweh and of the resulting periods of punishment. Encounters with Egypt might have been omitted from the account because they did not serve as God's punishment for Israelite disobedience.[57] Defenders of a fifteenth-century-B.C. Exodus also point out that the Bible does not mention campaigns in Palestine by Merneptah and Ramesses III in the thirteenth and twelfth centuries B.C., when Israel was settling Canaan according to the advocates of the late date for the Exodus.[58]

It is true that Joshua and Judges are primarily theological works rather than historical ones and that traditions chosen for inclusion in these books were selected and organized according to theological principles. But this is a strange defense to come from individuals who generally support the essential historicity of the biblical accounts of the Exodus and Conquest.

---

55. Rainey 1980: 251.
56. Bimson 1981: 70.
57. L. Wood 1970: 78; 1986: 86; Bimson 1981: 70-71.
58. L. Wood 1970: 78; 1986:85-86; Bimson 1981: 69-71.

Furthermore, it is not simply a question of the Bible's failure to report one or two instances of Egyptian penetration into Palestine. Rather, it is a matter of the incompatibility between the total picture of Palestine as given in Joshua and Judges and what is found in the Egyptian texts of the Eighteenth and Nineteenth Dynasties. There are *no* Egyptian garrisons at major Canaanite cities in the Book of Judges. Envoys of the Hittites are *not* stirring up trouble. Canaanite rulers do *not* appeal to Egypt for help when facing threats from Israelite forces. And *no* Egyptian armies arrive to bring the situation back under control. Invasions from northern Mesopotamia (Aram Naharaim), Moab, and Ammon occur with *no* response from Egypt and *no* indication that such a response might have been expected. Despite attempts to explain it away, this lack of agreement between the realities of fifteenth-thirteenth century B.C. Palestine and the accounts in Joshua and Judges is still a major stumbling block for anyone who supports both the historical accuracy of the events related in Joshua and Judges *and* the Bible's fifteenth-century-B.C. date for the Exodus.

Of course, if the biblical accounts of the Exodus and settlement are *not* historically accurate, their failure to agree with Egyptian historical records is not a problem. Or, it could be argued, if the Israelites were just entering Palestine and trying to gain a foothold in the hill country during the late thirteenth and early twelfth centuries, the failure of their traditions to mention the somewhat minor campaigns of Merneptah and Ramesses III (which were taking place in other parts of Palestine at the same time) might be understandable. The Egyptian empire was weakening at that time, and soon after the reign of Ramesses III Egypt gave up its attempts to control Palestine. But, if the Conquest took place much earlier, at the beginning of the fourteenth century B.C., and if the Bible's early history is at all trustworthy, how can *all* Egyptian activity go unmentioned simply because it was not seen as a means of God's judgment?

This is why in recent years most scholars have rejected a fifteenth-century-B.C. date for the Exodus. Clearly, the picture of Palestine in the Books of Joshua and Judges agrees much better with the chaotic situation at the end of the Bronze Age and the beginning of the Iron Age (c. 1200-1050)—when "everyone did what was right in his own sight" (Judges 17:1)—than it does with the earlier era of Egyptian control over Canaan.

DATING THE EXODUS AND SETTLEMENT

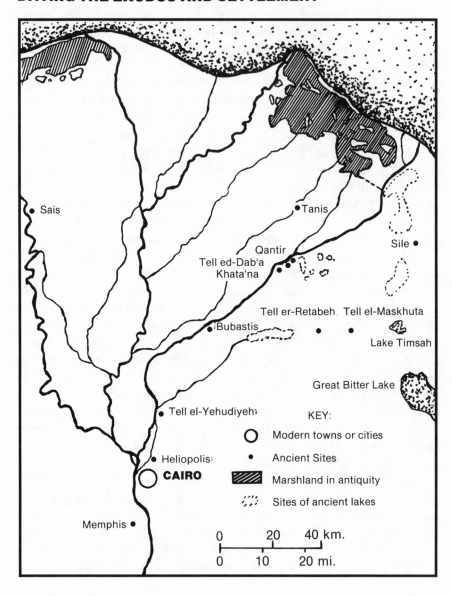

FIGURE 1: THE EASTERN NILE DELTA IN ANTIQUITY

Pithom and Ra'amses

Not only does the Bible make explicit statements concerning the date of the Exodus, it also provides implicit chronological clues within the Exodus and Conquest narratives. Probably the most important of these internal dating aids is the reference to the Israelites being forced to help construct the Egyptian store-cities of Pithom and Ra'amses (Exodus 1:11). If this passage is historically reliable, and if these cities could be identified, their archaeological strata might provide a chronological framework into which the Israelites' oppression and exodus could be set.

According to the Bible, the Israelites were living in a part of Egypt called *Goshen* (Genesis 45:10, 46:28, etc.). This area was in the eastern delta of Egypt (see Figure 1), for in Genesis 47:11 it is equated with the land of Ramses (or Ramesses), the Egyptian name for much of the eastern delta after Ramesses II (c. 1279-1212) built his capital there and named it after himself. Of course, the use of the name "land of Ramesses" in Genesis is anachronistic. But it shows that later biblical authors understood the old term *Goshen* to refer to the area that in their time was still called the land of Ramesses.

Pithom is the Hebrew transcription of the Egyptian *pr-'itm* (Per-Atum or Pi-Atum), "House of Atum." Atum was a creator god and solar deity in the Egyptian pantheon. His primary place of worship was in Heliopolis, but during the Nineteenth Dynasty his cult was also established in the eastern delta. There a border town seems to have been named Per-Atum because it contained an important temple of Atum.[59] From the references to Per-Atum/Pithom in ancient texts it is clear that it must have been located near the eastern end of the Wadi Tumilat in the area the Egyptians called *Tjeku,* or *Theku.* Tjeku may also have been the name of a town or city within the general area of the same name (possibly to be identified with the place called Succoth in Exodus 12:37 and 13:20).[60] In the report of a Nineteenth Dynasty frontier official we read the following:

> [We] have finished letting the Bedouin tribes of Edom pass the Fortress [of] Mer-ne-Ptah . . . which is in Tjeku, to the pools of Per-Atum [of] Mer-[ne]-

---

59. E. P. Uphill (1968, 1969) has argued that the "House of Atum" (Pithom) referred to in the Bible was the temple of Atum at Heliopolis. Few scholars have agreed with him, though. Both Egyptian and biblical data seem to require that Pithom be located in the eastern delta near the frontier of Egyptian territory.

60. Finegan 1963: 10-14; Aharoni 1979: 196; Soggin 1984: 111. For an argument against the equation of Egyptian Tjeku with biblical Succoth, see Peet 1923: 88-89.

Ptah . . . which are [in] Tjeku, to keep them alive and to keep their cattle alive. . . .[61]

There are two major ancient sites near the eastern end of Wadi Tumilat, Tell er-Retabeh and Tell el-Maskhuta (see Figure 1). They are only eight and one-half miles apart, and each of them has had its supporters as the site of Pithom.[62] The evidence, however, now clearly favors equating Tell er-Retabeh with Pithom. Most significant is a Roman milestone found at Tell el-Maskhuta, which indicates that Ero (the Roman name for Pithom) was nine miles west of that point. Tell er-Retabeh lies almost exactly nine Roman miles west of Tell el-Maskhuta.[63]

In excavations at Tell el-Maskhuta in 1883 Eduard Naville found a number of monuments and statues from the Nineteenth Dynasty and later, but nothing earlier than the reign of Ramesses II (c. 1279-1212 B.C.). He also uncovered a number of rectangular brick chambers of varying sizes, which he claimed were storehouses. This, he felt, clinched the identification of Tell el-Maskhuta with Pithom and proved that the oppression and Exodus occurred in the thirteenth century B.C.[64]

However, the "storehouses" Naville found were almost certainly the foundation walls of a late period fortress,[65] and the remains from the time of Ramesses II were probably moved to Tell el-Maskhuta from other sites during the Saite Period, long after the time of the Exodus. Recent excavations at Tell el-Maskhuta by John S. Holladay of the University of Toronto have shown that after a small-scale settlement during the Second Intermediate Period (c. 1786-1560 B.C.), the site remained unoccupied until c. 609 B.C.[66] There was no city at Tell el-Maskhuta during either the fifteenth or the thirteenth centuries B.C.

The evidence from the other possible site for Pithom is much more promising. Occasional finds at Tell er-Retabeh over the years had indicated that it was occupied during the Middle Kingdom and Hyksos Period, then abandoned until the Nineteenth Dynasty.[67] This site has also been excavated

61. J. Wilson 1955: 259.

62. Tell el-Maskhuta was the choice of E. Naville (1885; 1924: 32-36), W. M. F. Petrie (1906; 1911: 33-34), D. Redford (1963: 407-408), M. Haran (1976: 305), R. de Vaux (1978: 302), and others. Tell er-Retabeh has been backed by A. Gardiner (1918: 267-269; 1924: 95-96), W. F. Albright (1957: 255), M. Noth (1962: 22), G. E. Wright (1962a: 58), J. Finegan (1963: 12-15), O. Eissfeldt (1975: 322), Y. Aharoni (1979: Map 13, p. 196), J. Bright (1981: 121), and others.

63. Gardiner 1918: 269; Finegan 1963: 12-13.

64. Naville 1903: 11-13.

65. Peet 1923: 86.

66. Holladay 1982: 18-23, 44-47.

67. Petrie 1906:28.

in recent years. While the results of these excavations have not yet been published, they seem to have verified the pattern of occupation deduced from earlier finds at the site.[68] Egyptian texts indicate that Pithom existed during the Nineteenth Dynasty, and excavations have shown that Tell er-Retabeh *did* exist at that time—while Tell el-Maskhuta did not. This archaeological evidence, combined with the Roman milestone found at Tell el-Maskhuta, indicates that Tell er-Retabeh was probably the site of ancient Pithom.

The second of the "store-cities" built by the Israelites can now be identified with more certainty. Ra'amses is a shortened version of Egyptian *pr-r'mssw* (Per-Ramesses, or Pi-Ramesses, Piramesse, etc.), "House of Ramesses." This was the name of the capital city established by Ramesses II in the eastern delta. Ramesses II actually completed the work begun by his father Seti I (c. 1291-1279 B.C.), who seems to have started rebuilding Avaris, the earlier capital of the Hyksos. Avaris was destroyed by Ahmose early in his reign (c. 1560 B.C.), then abandoned for most of the Eighteenth Dynasty. But, with the rise of the Nineteenth Dynasty, there was a revival of the cult of Seth, who had been one of the most important Egyptian deities worshipped by the Hyksos. The task of rebuilding Avaris was finished by Ramesses II, who then gave his name to the city and made it his capital.[69]

The use of the name *Ra'amses* for the city built by the Israelites seems to preclude a date for the Exodus before the time of Ramesses II, when the city *received* that name.[70] And the "Israel Stele" indicating that Israel was in Canaan by the fifth year of Merneptah, successor to Ramesses II, seems to eliminate the possibility of an exodus much *later* than Ramesses' reign. On this basis, most scholars have concluded that Ramesses II (or possibly Merneptah) was the pharaoh of the Exodus.[71] The evidence of Exodus 1:11, then, would seem clearly to place the Exodus in the thirteenth rather than the mid-fifteenth century B.C.

Unfortunately, the question cannot be resolved that easily. The use of the names Pithom and Ra'amses for the cities built by the Israelites may be anachronistic (as the use of "land of Ramesses" is in Genesis 47:11).

---

68. Oren 1981: 50.

69. J. Wilson 1955: 252-253.

70. Some conservative biblical scholars have suggested that there was a place called "Ra'amses" during Hyksos times (see L. Wood 1970: 80; 1986: 73-74), but there is absolutely no evidence to support this. The only known Egyptian city named Ra'amses or something similar was built during the Nineteenth Dynasty.

71. See Albright 1957: 255-256; Eissfeldt 1975: 321-322; de Vaux 1978: 325, 389; Bright 1981: 123.

Pithom and Ra'amses could have been the names in general use when the account of the Exodus was written down, but the names of these two cities at the time of the oppression could have been quite different.[72] So we must depend on the archaeological evidence from the sites for an indication of the date of the Exodus.

Later biblical tradition (Psalm 78:12, 43) identified Avaris/Per-Ramesses with Zo'an (or Zoan), the Hebrew transcription of the Egyptian name D'nt (Dja'anet, which in Greek became Tanis).[73] It was at Tanis that the stele celebrating Seth's rule in Avaris/Per-Ramesses was found. Thus, for many years Tanis was considered to be Avaris/Per-Ramesses. Since no material earlier than the time of Ramesses II was found at Tanis, the thirteenth century date for the Exodus seemed certain. However, a few scholars argued that the stele and other Ramesside artifacts found at Tanis were not in situ—that is, not in their original archaeological contexts. They could have been taken to Tanis from Per-Ramesses, which was located somewhere else. These scholars claimed that the area between Khata'na and Qantir (see Figure 1) was really the location of Avaris and Per-Ramesses.[74]

Over the past twenty years, Austrian excavations at Tell ed-Dab'a, one of the Khata'na/Qantir complex of mounds, have proved to the satisfaction of most scholars that this was indeed the location of Avaris and Per-Ramesses. There was occupation at the site as early as the Middle Kingdom, but the area became densely settled only at the beginning of the Hyksos Period (c. 1675 B.C.). During the Hyksos era, Tell ed-Dab'a was a very large city with temples, cemeteries, and mortuary areas. And, most importantly, the archaeological evidence indicates that its population was primarily Syro-Palestinian rather than Egyptian.[75] The city was abandoned abruptly c. 1560-1540 B.C., that is, at the end of the Hyksos Period and the beginning of the Eighteenth Dynasty. A massive wall, possibly part of a fortification, was built across the site in the early part of the Eighteenth Dynasty, but it seems to have been used for only a short period of time, and the site remained largely unoccupied throughout most of the Eighteenth Dynasty. Settlement resumed during the reign of Horemheb (c. 1321-1293 B.C.) and continued into the early Twenty-first Dynasty. Then the city was again abandoned until Hellenistic times.[76] This pattern of

---

72. Jack 1925: 24-25; L. Wood 1970: 80.
73. Finegan 1963: 31-32.
74. See Van Seters 1966: 127-151 and Bietak 1981: 226-231 for summaries of the scholarly debate with full bibliographies.
75. Bietak 1981: 241-268.
76. Bietak 1981: 268-271.

settlement fits the textual information on Avaris and Per-Ramesses perfectly.

On the other hand, excavations at Tanis have not produced an archaeo-logical stratum that can be dated before the Twenty-first Dynasty. Many statues, inscriptions, and parts of buildings belonging to the time of Ramesses II and later pharaohs of the Nineteenth and Twentieth Dynasties *were* found at Tanis, but they were not *in situ.* They had almost certainly been transferred to Tanis from other sites (principally from Qantir) during the Twenty-second Dynasty.[77]

Studies of the ancient geography of the eastern delta indicate not only that the Pelusiac branch of the Nile flowed past Tell ed-Dabʻa-Qantir, but that there were also lakes in the area that have since dried up. These former lakes match descriptions of bodies of water to be found in the vicinity of Per-Ramesses in antiquity. When the Pelusiac branch of the Nile became too silted up at its mouth for ships to enter it, the capital had to be shifted to Tanis. This seems to have occurred at the end of the Twenty-first or the beginning of the Twenty-second Dynasty.[78]

Not only were statues and monuments from Per-Ramesses (Tell ed-Dabʻa-Qantir) moved to Tanis, Bubastis, and other sites in the delta, but the cults of the gods of Per-Ramesses were shifted to these cities as well. The fact that cults of the gods of Per-Ramesses continued to exist in Tanis and Bubastis into the fourth century B.C. and later explains why, during the late period, some Egyptians identified Per-Ramesses with Tanis while others identified it with Bubastis. It also makes understandable Psalm 78's equation of Raʻamses, the city mentioned in the Exodus account, with Zoʻan, the Hebrew name for Tanis.[79]

What information about the chronology of the Exodus can we gather, then, from the archaeological evidence from Pithom and Raʻamses? If Tell el-Maskhuta was Pithom, as some scholars still contend, then the reference to the Israelites building Pithom and Raʻamses in Exodus 1:11 would seem to be late and totally unhistorical.[80] Since Tell el-Maskhuta did not exist between the Hyksos Period and the late seventh century B.C., it is argued, the Israelites could not have built it, and the biblical author of these lines could not have created his account before c. 600 B.C.

There is a problem with this view, however. In the late period, after 600 B.C., Ramesses was still used as the name for an area of the delta,

---

77. Van Seters 1966: 128-131; Bietak 1981: 278-279.
78. Bietak 1981: 274-282.
79. Bietak 1981: 279.
80. See Van Seters 1982.

and Egyptians remembered there had been a city by that name. Cults of the various gods of Per-Ramesses were still active. But the Egyptians themselves do not seem to have been sure where Per-Ramesses had been located.[81] It was not the common name for Tanis or any other city in Egypt at that time. As Psalm 78 indicates, later Israelites thought Zoʻan was the city the Israelites had built. If the tradition of the building of the store-cities was not created until after 600 B.C., during the Babylonian Exile or Persian Period, one wonders why the author of Exodus 1:11 did not use the name of a city from his own time. Why didn't he locate the Exodus events at Zoʻan (as the author of Psalm 78 did) instead of resurrecting the name of an ancient city, Raʻamses, whose location was a mystery even to the Egyptians? It is more likely that the reference to a city named Raʻamses would have been made only during or soon after the period when the city was in existence and its name was in common use (that is, before or soon after c. 1070 B.C., when the Twenty-first Dynasty began).[82]

There is no need to date Exodus 1:11 (or the tradition behind it) as late as 600 B.C., though, if Tell er-Retabeh, rather than Tell el-Maskhuta, was the site of ancient Pithom/Per-Atum. The settlement pattern at Tell er-Retabeh seems to be almost identical to that of Tell ed-Dabʻa and Qantir, the mounds that comprised Avaris/Per-Ramesses. Both sites were initially occupied during the Middle Kingdom. They flourished during the Hyksos Period, then were abandoned early in the Eighteenth Dynasty. There is a gap in occupation at both sites that lasted throughout most of the Eighteenth Dynasty. Settlement resumed late in the Eighteenth or early in the Nineteenth Dynasty with widespread building activity during the reigns of Seti I and Ramesses II in the thirteenth century B.C. Thus, if Exodus 1:11 is historical and the Israelites worked on the cities of Per-Atum and Per-Ramesses, the oppression would seem to have taken place in the Nineteenth Dynasty. And Hatshepsut or Thutmose III of the fifteenth century would be ruled out as possible candidates for the pharaoh of the oppression.

The absence of occupation at Per-Ramesses during part of the sixteenth and all of the fifteenth centuries B.C. is obviously a problem for those who believe that the Exodus occurred c. 1450 B.C. However, some backers of a fifteenth-century Exodus note that the Bible does not say that the building

---

81. Bietak 1981: 279.

82. Albright 1957: 255; de Vaux 1978: 325; Bright 1981: 123. If, as some think (see below), the Israelites were forced to work on the city under the Hyksos when it was called Avaris, the use of the name Raʻamses for it would still indicate that the tradition behind Exodus 1:11 was formulated between c. 1300 and 1070 B.C., when that name was current.

of the store-cities of Pithom and Ra'amses occurred shortly before the Exodus. The building of the cities is mentioned at the *beginning* of the oppression, before the birth of Moses is described. Since the Bible claims that Moses was eighty years old at the time of the Exodus (Exodus 7:7), the building of Pithom and Ra'amses might have occurred a century or more before the Exodus. If the Exodus took place c. 1450 B.C., then, the beginning of the oppression could be placed during the Hyksos Period, a time when Tell ed-Dab'a, Tell er-Retabeh, and Tell el-Maskhuta were all occupied.[83]

There is some logic to this view, but it is certainly not without problems. The biblical tradition (at least that part of it usually assigned to the J version of the Exodus) indicates that Ra'amses was still in existence at the time of the Exodus. The Israelites gather at Ra'amses, the capital where the Egyptian pharaoh is in residence, and begin the Exodus from that point (Exodus 12:37; Numbers 33:3, 5).[84] They would not have gathered at a city that had been in ruins for almost a century at a time when the capital was at Thebes and the pharaoh's residence was either at Thebes or Memphis.

If there is any historicity to the biblical accounts of the events of the Exodus, the archaeological evidence from Per-Ramesses indicates that the story should probably be placed in the context of Nineteenth Dynasty Egypt when the pharaohs were undertaking major building operations in the delta, when Tell er-Retabeh (Per-Atum/Pithom) and Tell ed-Dab'a/Qantir (Per-Ramesses/Ra'amses) were rebuilt, when the capital was moved to the delta and the pharaoh was in residence there, and when the name Ramesses was so prominent that it could become an integral part of the oral traditions about the event. According to the Egyptian evidence, then, the most likely time for the Exodus was in the mid-thirteenth century during the long reign of Ramesses II.

---

83. Bimson 1981: 39-40, 43.

84. Both passages mention Ra'mses as the starting point of the Exodus. This is almost certainly the city mentioned in Exodus 1:11 (where it is spelled *Ra'amses*). If the author had wanted to indicate the delta region in general as the place from which the Exodus began, he probably would have used the phrase "land of Ra'mses" rather than just Ra'mses.

3

Archaeology and a Late Bronze Age Exodus

One generation (or "forty years") after their exodus from Egypt, according to the Bible, the Israelites entered Canaan and forceably took control of most of the land. Since the biblical evidence for the date of the Exodus is not clear or conclusive, many scholars have hoped that archaeological indications of the conquest of Canaan would provide a firm date for the Exodus events. Excavations during the 1930s at Bethel, Lachish, and Tell Beit Mirsim (which at the time was thought to be Debir/Kirjath-Sepher) revealed that all three sites were destroyed near the end of the Late Bronze Age, during the thirteenth century B.C.[1] At about the same time as these excavations, Nelson Glueck surveyed sites in Transjordan and concluded that "from the end of Middle Bronze Age I to the very beginning of Iron Age I, most of Transjordan was peopled largely by bedouin."[2] So the wandering Israelites' experiences with the kingdoms of Edom, Moab, and the Amorites of South Gilead could not have taken place between c. 1900 B.C. (the end of the Middle Bronze Age I) and c. 1300 B.C. (the date for the beginning of the Transjordanian Iron Age I settlements, according to Glueck).

---

1. Albright 1957:278.
2. Glueck 1967: 443. For the survey reports, see Glueck 1934, 1935, 1939, and 1951.

Archaeologists also noted new features in the material culture of Iron Age I Palestine and interpreted these as evidence of the arrival of a new people—the Israelite tribes. Around 1200 B.C. many new settlements appeared in portions of the Palestinian hill country that had not been occupied extensively during the Late Bronze period. In these villages were found two new types of pottery: a cooking pot with a vertical rim (rather than an outward-turned rim) and a "collared rim" storage jar. A new style of residential architecture, the so-called "four-room house," was also introduced at this time.[3] These new features were regarded as characteristically "Israelite," signs that the settlement of the Israelite tribes took place at the beginning of the Iron Age, c. 1200 B.C., which meant that the Exodus must have occurred just prior to that date. This archaeological evidence, coupled with the reference to Pithom and Ra'amses in the biblical account, convinced the vast majority of scholars that the Exodus must have taken place sometime between c. 1280 and 1240 B.C., with the conquest of Canaan occurring about forty years later.

In recent years, however, the archaeological evidence for the Israelite conquest of Canaan has been challenged repeatedly. Glueck's conclusions have been questioned on the basis of new discoveries, and excavations of a number of sites in Palestine have failed to produce evidence of a thirteenth-century-B.C. Israelite conquest. Instead of clarifying the date of the Conquest, archaeological research has made the issue even more complicated and confusing. Let us review the archaeological evidence, following the sequence in which the cities are mentioned in the biblical Conquest narratives.

The Negeb

The extreme southern portion of Palestine, stretching from Beer-sheba southward to the deserts of Sinai (see Figure 2), is known as the Negeb or Negev ("the dry land"). According to Numbers 15-19 (usually credited to the Priestly account of the Exodus) the Israelites spent most of their "forty years" of "wandering" in this area on the fringe of Canaan, settled at the oasis of Kadesh-Barnea. From Kadesh-Barnea they tried to invade Palestine from the south, but they were defeated at Hormah (Numbers 14:44-45). Later, however, after the Canaanite king of Arad had attacked them and taken some prisoners, the Israelites succeeded in destroying the Canaanites and their cities in this area. They then named the place *Hormah,* which

---

3. See Aharoni 1978: 160-163, 174-176.

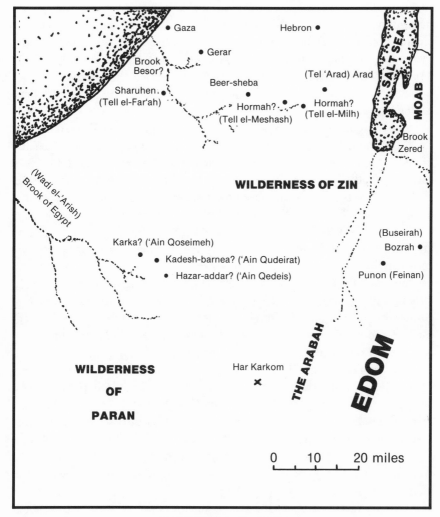

FIGURE 2: THE NEGEB

means "destruction" (Numbers 21:1-3). On the other hand, the Book of Judges (1:17-18) credits the conquest of Hormah (formerly Zephath) and its renaming to later activity "after the death of Joshua" by the tribes of Judah and Simeon.

Beer-sheba, the best-known city of the region, is not mentioned in the list of cities conquered by Israel. But it does appear in the lists of territory allotted to the various tribes. In Joshua 15:28 Beer-sheba is among the cities given to Judah, and in Joshua 19:2 it is allotted to Simeon, whose patrimony was included within that of "greater Judah" (which also included territory of the Calebites, Korahites, and other groups).[4] Beer-sheba is also mentioned in biblical stories about the patriarchs (Genesis 21:25-31; 26:32-33). Thus, the biblical authors seem to have believed that Beer-sheba was in existence at the time of the Conquest and passed into Israelite hands during that era.

On the basis of various geographical and topographical references in the Bible and other ancient sources, scholars can identify the probable sites of ancient Kadesh-Barnea, Arad, Hormah, and Beer-sheba. The Bible indicates that Kadesh-Barnea (also known as *Meribath-Kadesh,* "waters of strife in Kadesh") was an oasis on the southern frontier of later Israelite territory, in the region where the Wilderness of Paran blended into the Wilderness of Zin (Numbers 34:4-5; Ezekiel 47:19, 48:28). It was also between Edom and the Brook of Egypt (the Wadi el-'Arish). There are four springs in this general area, but two of them ('Ain Qoseimeh and 'Ain Muweilih) are too small to represent such an important settlement as Kadesh-Barnea, although they may be the sites for the smaller settlements of Azmon ('Ain Muweilih) and Karka ('Ain Qoseimeh) mentioned in Joshua 15:3.[5] However, each of the other two springs, 'Ain Qedeis and 'Ain Qudeirat, has been proposed at one time or another as the site of Kadesh-Barnea.

The biblical name "Kadesh" seems to be preserved in "Qedeis," the Arabic name of the southernmost of these springs. This similarity in names has led many scholars, starting with Henry Clay Trumbull in 1884, to identify 'Ain Qedeis as Kadesh-Barnea. This identification also seems to suit the description of the southern border of Judah given in Numbers 34:4 and Joshua 15:3, where Kadesh-Barnea is mentioned before Addar, Karka, and Azmon in a list that seems to proceed from southeast to northwest and then west.

But the fact that 'Ain Qedeis is a shallow pool of water surrounded by desert has led most modern scholars to reject it as the site of Kadesh in favor of 'Ain Qudeirat, the most abundant spring in northern Sinai, the only one in the region that flows all year, and the only one surrounded by a suitable amount of rich grazing land. 'Ain Qedeis is possibly the site of Addar or Hazar-Addar (Numbers 34:4; Joshua 15:3). Since 'Ain Qedeis is only some six miles southeast of 'Ain Qudeirat, these identifications would also fit the references in Numbers and Joshua that place the border of

---

4. See Miller and Hayes 1986: 103-105.

5. Aharoni 1979: 70-72. Some scholars—see Simon Cohen (1962: 327)—locate Azmon at 'Ain Qoseimeh instead of at 'Ain Muweilih.

Judah south of Kadesh-Barnea from Hezron and Addar (or Hazar-Addar) turning to Karka and passing by Azmon to the Brook of Egypt.

Archaeological investigations have been conducted at 'Ain Qedeis and, more extensively, at 'Ain Qudeirat. One of these two springs is almost certainly the site of Kadesh-Barnea, yet there is no evidence that either place was occupied during the Late Bronze Age, the time when most scholars think the Exodus took place. Large quantities of "Negeb ware"—crude, handmade pottery attributed to seminomads (probably the Kenites)—were found at 'Ain Qudeirat, but this pottery has such a wide chronological range that it is useless for dating purposes. Negeb ware must itself be dated by the wheel-made pottery found with it. The earliest context in which Negeb ware has been found elsewhere belongs to the thirteenth or twelfth centuries B.C.[6] The earliest datable remains uncovered at 'Ain Qedeis and 'Ain Qudeirat consisted of tenth century B.C. oval fortresses, probably built during the reign of King Solomon. No Bronze Age material (that is, nothing from the times of Abraham, the Exodus, or the "judges") was found.[7]

It is possible, of course, that the site has been incorrectly identified and that Kadesh-Barnea was located elsewhere. It is also possible that the remains from the premonarchic periods are under the mounds in places left unexcavated by archaeologists. Finally, it is possible that the early inhabitants were seminomads who left no physical remains or that the Negeb pottery that was found belongs to the premonarchic periods.[8]

However, each of these possibilities is unlikely. Other than 'Ain Qudeirat (or, to a lesser extent, 'Ain Qedeis) there is no site in northern Sinai suitable as the location of Kadesh. And while seminomads generally leave less imposing remains than sedentary populations, if they had been settled at Kadesh-Barnea as long as the Bible indicates that the Israelites were, they would have left *some* remains archaeologists could identify. Also, if the Israelite occupation of Kadesh during the Exodus period was as extensive and long-lasting as the Bible says, then it is improbable indeed that its only traces are under unexcavated parts of the site. At these sites, there also does not seem to be *any* pre-Iron Age strata containing only Negeb ware as there should be if this crude, handmade pottery derived from the Israelites of the Exodus. The Negeb ware that was found at both springs almost certainly belongs with the forts from the period of the monarchy that archaeologists have excavated there. It is very difficult to reconcile

---

6. R. Cohen 1981: 32-33.
7. M. Dothan 1977: 697; R. Cohen 1981: 30, 33.
8. R. Cohen 1981: 33.

FIGURE 3: *'RD* ("ARAD") ON FRAGMENTS OF A BOWL FROM TEL 'ARAD

The Hebrew letters for Arad were incised on this bowl a number of times (possibly as practice by someone learning to write—the letters for "r" and "d" are written backwards and the example on the left side of the bottom sherd is written from left to right instead of the normal right to left direction for Hebrew). This late ninth-century B.C. bowl supports the identifications of Tel 'Arad as biblical Arad. (Drawn from a photograph in Pritchard 1969: Fig. 806)

this evidence with the view that the biblical account of the Exodus and Conquest is accurate and that these events occurred during the Late Bronze Age.

The situation is much the same elsewhere in the Negeb. The location of ancient Beer-sheba is virtually certain. It is Tell es-Saba' (Arabic), or Tel Beer-sheba (Hebrew). Not only has the ancient name remained associated with the site, but there is no other mound in the vicinity that fits the ancient textual descriptions. Tell es-Saba'/Tel Beer-sheba was extensively excavated from 1969 through 1976, and much of the site was dug down to bedrock.[9] It is extremely unlikely that remains from the earliest settlement at the site could have been missed. Yet, except for a few sherds from the fourth millennium B.C., the excavations failed to turn up any evidence of occupation earlier than the beginning of the Iron Age, c. 1200 B.C.[10] If the Israelite conquest of Canaan took place during the Late Bronze Age, there was no city of Beer-sheba to allot to either Judah or Simeon.

The location of ancient Arad at Tel 'Arad is also well established. Eusebius, a Christian historian of the fourth century A.D., described the location of a village of Arad in his day that exactly fits the position of Tel 'Arad, and sherds of a bowl found in an Iron Age layer at Tel 'Arad are inscribed with the name of Arad (see Figure 3).[11] Tel 'Arad was excavated from 1962 through 1967. A series of fortresses from the Iron Age and the Persian, Hellenistic, Roman, and early Arab periods were uncovered. These fortresses had been preceded by a large city of the Early Bronze Age II (c. 2900-2700 B.C.). But, as at Beer-sheba, no remains from the Middle or Late Bronze Age were found.[12]

To explain the lack of Late Bronze Age material at Arad, Benjamin Mazar argued that in Canaanite times Arad was not the name of a city but of a whole district. The "King of Arad" mentioned in the Conquest account would have resided at the main city of the district, Hormah, which Mazar identified with Tel Malhata (Tell el-Milh in Arabic), less than ten miles southeast of Tel 'Arad.[13]

A different solution has been proposed by Yohanan Aharoni, the excavator of both Beer-sheba and Arad. Aharoni suggested that Canaanite Arad was located at Tel Malhata (Tell el-Milh), since Egyptian texts from the tenth century B.C. mention *two* Arads—"Great Arad" and "Arad of the House of Yeroham." Canaanite Arad (Tel Malhata) would be "Arad of the House of Yeroham" (the biblical Jerahmeelites) while "Great Arad" would represent the fort at Tel 'Arad, first built during Solomon's reign.[14] According to this theory, Hormah would be located at nearby Tel Masos (Khirbet Meshash).

---

9. Herzog 1980: 15.
10. Aharoni 1975b: 161-162; Herzog 1980: 15-18. Excavations at the nearby site of Bir es-Saba' (where modern Beer-sheba is located) have also failed to produce any evidence of Middle Bronze or Late Bronze Age occupation (see Gophna 1975).
11. Aharoni 1975a: 88; 1976b: 38-39.
12. Aharoni 1975a: 75-83; 1976b: 38-39.
13. Mazar 1965: 298-299.
14. Aharoni 1979: 201; 1975a: 88; 1976b: 39.

It is generally agreed that Hormah should be identified with either Tel Malhata or Tel Masos. There are no other likely candidates in proximity to Tel 'Arad, the site of later Arad. Excavations conducted at both sites have revealed that they both were occupied during the Middle Bronze Age II, but neither one was settled in the Late Bronze Age.[15] So, neither Mazar's nor Aharoni's theory would help proponents of a Late Bronze Age Exodus and Conquest. There are simply no Late Bronze Age settlements in the area that could represent the Arad and Hormah supposedly conquered by the Israelites.

It is difficult to believe that *all* of the major Negeb sites associated with stories about the premonarchic period (Kadesh-Barnea, Beer-sheba, Arad, and Hormah) have been incorrectly identified. Yet at none of the likely sites of these cities is there evidence of occupation during the Late Bronze Age. Obviously, this fact provides problems for supporters of biblical accuracy—regardless of whether they accept a fifteenth- or a thirteenth-century-B.C. date for the Exodus.

Transjordan

The Bible indicates that Moses led the Israelites from Kadesh-Barnea into Canaan by way of Transjordan. But there are two different traditions about the route the Israelites took from Kadesh-Barnea to the area of Transjordan opposite Jericho (see Figure 4). Numbers 20:14-21, 21:4-9, 12-20 relates that Moses sent envoys from Kadesh-Barnea to the king of Edom seeking permission for the Israelites to travel through his land. The delegation promised to remain on the King's Highway, not to trespass on fields or vineyards, and to pay for any water the Israelites used. However, the king did not accede to their request and massed his forces on the border of Edom. Thereupon Moses decided to go around the flanks of Edom instead of directly through that kingdom. The Israelites proceeded to Mount Hor, then turned southward toward the Gulf of Aqaba. Moses seems to have led them around the southern border of Edom, then past that kingdom on its eastern side to the Brook Zered. They continued northward to the River Arnon, bypassing Moab on the eastern side as well. They turned westward only when they came to the cleft in the Moabite plateau, which led them to the area of Mount Nebo and Mount Pisgah. Messengers were sent to Sihon, the Amorite king who ruled the area north of the Arnon

---

15. Kempinski 1977: 817; Kochavi 1977: 772.

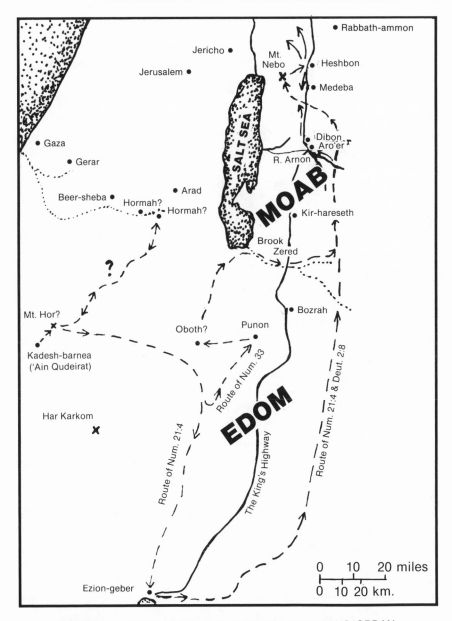

FIGURE 4:   ISRAELITE ROUTES THROUGH THE TRANSJORDAN

at the time, to seek permission to travel peacefully through his territory. But he refused, as the Edomite king had, and mustered his forces to attack the Israelites. Israel won the battle, however, and occupied Sihon's land (all the territory between the Arnon and the Jabbok), including his capital city, Heshbon.

The stages of the journey given in Numbers 21:10-11 and 33:37-48 (usually attributed to P), however, are quite different. After leaving Kadesh and Mount Hor, the Israelites stopped at Punon and Oboth in Edom before reaching Iye-abarim on the eastern side of Edom. This itinerary seems to have taken them through occupied portions of Edom, yet there is no account of conflict with Edomite military forces. There is no indication in Numbers 33 about whether the Israelites traveled around Moab on the east, as Numbers 21 indicates, or whether they went directly through Moabite territory.[16] The next stop listed is Dibon, a city located on the King's Highway just north of the Arnon River. From Dibon they traveled to the area across the Jordan from Jericho. In this account there is no mention of a conquest of Heshbon.

On the basis of his surveys of Transjordanian sites in the 1930s, Nelson Glueck concluded that the area had no settled population between c. 1900 and 1300 B.C. This evidence has often been used to bolster arguments for a thirteenth-century Exodus, for the biblical accounts seem to assume established kingdoms with urban centers. In addition to Punon, Dibon, and Heshbon, other cities mentioned in the biblical narratives whose sites can be identified with some certainty are Medeba (Numbers 21:30) and Aroer (Numbers 32:34, Deuteronomy 4:48, and Joshua 12:2). If there were no cities or kingdoms in Transjordan for six hundred years before the thirteenth century, then the Exodus could not have occurred during that span.

In recent years, however, Glueck's conclusions have been modified, as more Middle Bronze Age II and Late Bronze Age remains have been noted in Transjordan. Middle Bronze II glacis fortifications (steep beaten-earth embankments) have been uncovered at Amman, Tell Safut (a site a few miles northwest of Amman), and Sahab, while Middle Bronze II B-C tomb groups have been found at a number of sites, including Amman, Irbid, and Mount Nebo.[17] The most extensive Late Bronze Age material from Transjordan has come from an LB II "temple" excavated at Amman and from LB tombs at Amman, Irbid, Pella, and Tell es-Sa'idiyeh. But there is also evidence of Late Bronze occupation at Tell el-Husn, Tabaqat Fahl, Tell el-Mazar, Deir 'Alla, Sahab, Tell Safut, Jalul, and possibly Aroer.[18]

---

16. Y. Aharoni (1979: 201-204) and R. de Vaux (1978: 561-562) interpret Numbers 33 as implying that the Israelites proceeded straight up the King's Highway through the heart of both Edom and Moab.

17. Dornemann 1983: 15-19; Sauer 1985: 209.

18. Dornemann 1983: 20-22; Sauer 1985: 209.

In addition, a number of Middle Bronze II and Late Bronze Age sites not noted at all in Glueck's survey were found during more recent surveys of Transjordan,[19] which has led a number of scholars (including Glueck himself, shortly before he died) to conclude that some urban civilization continued to exist in portions of Transjordan during the Middle and Late Bronze Ages, though the number of sites seems to have decreased after the end of the Early Bronze Age.[20]

Those who accept the veracity of the biblical Exodus and Conquest narratives have hailed these modifications of Glueck's survey results, claiming that they remove a major problem for the fifteenth-century-B.C. date for the Exodus.[21] But, in fact, the new evidence has really supported neither the accuracy of the biblical date for the Exodus nor the historicity of the accounts of Israel's travels through Transjordan. Almost all of the evidence for Middle and Late Bronze urban occupation in Transjordan exists in the area north of the Arnon, especially around Amman. Surface surveys in southern Transjordan have found Middle and Late Bronze Age sherds at a number of sites, though pottery from these periods was not as common as that from the Early Bronze or Iron Age periods. It is clear that southern Transjordan was not as heavily populated in the Middle and Late Bronze Ages as it was in the Early Bronze or Iron Ages—out of more than 1,500 sites surveyed in recent years, only about two hundred contained Middle or Late Bronze Age sherds.[22] Whether this limited Middle and Late Bronze material is the product of true sedentary occupation only future excavation can show. So far, though, excavated sites in the areas of ancient Edom and Moab have failed to turn up evidence of Middle or Late Bronze Age urbanization.

Crystal Bennett has excavated three sites in Edom: Umm el-Biyara, Tawilan, and Buseirah (almost certainly the site of Bozrah, the city mentioned in Genesis 36:33 and the later capital of Edom mentioned in Amos 1:12, Isaiah 34:6, and other biblical passages).[23] Sedentary occupation at each of these sites seems to have begun only in the ninth century B.C. And Punon, an ancient Edomite mining center located at modern Feinan,[24] seems

19. Mittmann 1970; MacDonald 1983; Hart and Falkner 1985; Hart 1986; McGovern 1986.

20. Harding 1958: 12; Glueck 1970: 140-144; Ward 1973: 45-46; Bimson 1981: 64-65; Dornemann 1983: 165; Sauer 1985: 209-210.

21. Wood 1986: 80-81.

22. Mattingly 1983: 256; 1987: 9-10; Hart and Falkner 1985; Sauer 1985: 209-210; Hart 1986.

23. For the Umm el-Biyara excavations, see Bennett 1964; 1966; for Tawilan, see Bennett 1969; 1970; and for Buseirah, see Bennett 1972; 1973; 1974; 1975; 1977.

24. Eusebius mentions that Punon existed in his own day (the early fourth century A.D.) and writes the name *Phinon* or *Phainon* in Greek. Arabic *Feinan* continues the Greek version of the site's name. Archaeological finds at Feinan indicate that it was occupied in the Roman, Byzantine, and Medieval Arabic periods in addition to earlier times (see Gold 1962).

to have lain abandoned for centuries after c. 1800 B.C., not to be reoccupied until the Iron Age, probably during the ninth century B.C.[25] The picture is much the same for Moab. None of the sites that have been excavated in the area between the Arnon and Zered (Balu'a, 'Ader, Medeiyineh, Lejjun, Khirbet el-Fityan, and Shuqairah) were occupied in the Middle or Late Bronze periods.[26]

But does it matter if Edom and Moab were urbanized in the Middle and Late Bronze Ages? Some scholars think not, arguing that the "kingdoms" of Edom and Moab, through which the Israelites were not allowed to pass, need not have been sedentary states with numerous urban centers. The "king" of Edom, mentioned in Numbers 20:14, and Balak, the "king of Moab" (Numbers 22:4), could have been powerful chieftains leading semi-nomadic forces intent on preserving their monopoly of their portions of the Transjordanian pastureland.[27] The biblical narrative, it is claimed, mentions major cities and requires sedentary kingdoms only north of the Arnon, where Sihon was king of the Amorites (Numbers 21:21) and Og was king of Bashan (Numbers 21:33). And it is in the territories of Sihon and Og that archaeologists have discovered evidence of at least a degree of urbanization during the Middle and Late Bronze Ages.[28]

Unfortunately, this argument is still not sufficient to allow one to assert the essential historicity of the biblical account of the Transjordanian activities of Moses and Israel. The narrative does not just mention "kings" of Edom, Moab, the Amorites, and Bashan. It also mentions a number of cities, some of which it claims became Israelite possessions during this period. We have already seen that Punon, listed as a stage in the journey through Edom in Numbers 33, was not occupied during the Middle and Late Bronze Ages. Of the other cities whose identification with modern sites is almost certain (Aroer, Dibon, Medeba, and Heshbon), two (and possibly three)

---

25. Glueck 1934: 32-35. The site seems to have been abandoned throughout most of the Middle and Late Bronze periods. Glueck dated the reoccupation of the site to the thirteenth century B.C., his date for the beginning of the Iron Age in Transjordan. However, Glueck's thirteenth-century date seems to have been based on his belief that the renewal of sedentary occupation in Edom and Moab must have occurred *before* the Israelite Exodus. In Palestine and Syria, related Iron Age I wares do not appear before c. 1200 B.C. or a little later. M. Weippert's reexamination of the Iron Age pottery Glueck collected at forty sites has indicated that material that Glueck loosely designated "Early Iron I/II" usually turned out to belong to the early Iron Age II (the ninth to seventh centuries B.C.). See Weippert as quoted in Miller 1977a: 259 and also Sauer 1985: 210. The evidence seems to show that Punon was reoccupied no earlier than c. 1200 B.C. and probably remained abandoned until the ninth century B.C.

26. Mattingly 1987: 9.

27. de Vaux 1978: 518; Bimson 1981: 62-64.

28. Bimson 1981: 64.

out of four raise similar problems.

The Aroer ('Aro'er in Hebrew) mentioned in Deuteronomy 2:36, Joshua 12:2 and 13:16 is located at Khirbet 'Ara'ir on the Wadi el-Mojib (the Arnon River). Three seasons of excavations at this site in the middle 1960s revealed its occupational history.[29] After a period of limited settlement with only rudimentary constructions during the Early Bronze IV and Middle Bronze I periods, Aroer was abandoned. It lay unoccupied from c. 1900 B.C. until the latter part of the Late Bronze Age. There were no remains found from the Middle Bronze Age II or Late Bronze I periods.[30] Occupation resumed at the end of the Late Bronze Age and the beginning of the Iron Age, but the major building phase at the site did not occur until the ninth century B.C., when Mesha of Moab built a strong fortress there. Thus, the archaeological evidence from Aroer possibly could be used to support arguments for the historicity of a late-thirteenth-century-B.C. Israelite march through Transjordan, but not for an earlier one. There does not seem to have been even a temporary encampment on the site around 1400 B.C., the time that the Israelites would have been defeating Sihon and Og if the Exodus had taken place in the mid-fifteenth century B.C.

Dibon's identification with Dhiban (about three miles northwest of 'Ara'ir) was confirmed by the 1868 discovery of the mound of the Mesha stele, also known as the Moabite Stone.[31] Dhiban was excavated by the American Schools of Oriental Research from 1950-53, 1955-56, and 1965, and evidence of occupation in the Early Bronze Age (principally in Early Bronze III) was uncovered. Then there was a gap in occupation from the end of the Early Bronze Age (c. 2300 B.C.) until the beginning of the Iron Age I (c. 1200 B.C.). There was no evidence of occupation of any kind during the Middle Bronze or Late Bronze periods.[32]Therefore, the finds

---

29. Olavarri 1965; 1969; 1975.

30. Olavarri 1975: 99. Olavarri identified some of the stratified sherds he found as belonging to the Late Bronze II period (c. 1300-1200 B.C.), but James Sauer (1986: 8) has questioned the accuracy of this dating. Aroer was probably reoccupied only at the beginning of the Iron Age I.

31. See Silberman 1982: 100-111 or Horn 1986: 50-53 for an account of the discovery of the stele. A translation of the text can be found in Albright 1955: 320-321 or Horn 1986: 59. On the stele Mesha, king of Moab in the mid-ninth century B.C., calls himself "the Dibonite" and Dibon his "loyal dependency." The text makes it appear likely that the stele was erected in Dibon. That it was found on a site that is still called Dhiban clinched the identification of this mound with ancient Dibon.

32. Reed and Winnett 1964; Tushingham 1975. K. A. Kitchen (1964: 47-50) and Donald Redford (1982: 118-119) find references to Moab and Dibon in an Egyptian topographical list from the reign of Ramesses II. This reference, if valid, would require that the earliest Iron I remains at Dhiban be dated to the thirteenth century (the time of Ramesses II), that the Late Bronze remains of Dibon had not yet been found, or that Dhiban could not be Dibon. However,

from Dibon call into question the historicity of the biblical account of the Exodus *regardless* of whether one dates the Exodus to the fifteenth or the thirteenth century B.C.

Medeba (modern Madeba) was on the King's Highway between Dibon and Heshbon. It is still occupied and has not been excavated. The only remains from pre-Roman periods so far found at Medeba came from a tomb that dated from the end of the Late Bronze Age II into the early part of the Iron Age, c. 1200-1100 B.C.[33] However, this was a chance find. There is no firm evidence for or against earlier occupation of this site. We must await the results of future archaeological excavations here.

The identification of Tell Hesban, five and one-half miles north of Medeba, with the Heshbon of the time of the Israelite monarchy and the Roman period is virtually certain.[34] However, four seasons of excavations at this site between 1968 and 1974 have found no material earlier than the Iron Age I (twelfth to tenth centuries B.C.).[35] Sigfried Horn, excavator of Heshbon, believes that the city of King Sihon must have been located elsewhere, and he has suggested that "Jalul, the only important site in the vicinity which contains Late Bronze Age pottery, is a good candidate."[36] The fact remains, however, that the site accepted as Heshbon by the Israelite prophets and later writers was not occupied during the Middle or Late Bronze Ages.

The archaeological evidence from Heshbon seems to support the positions of those scholars whose literary analysis of the biblical text has led them to conclude that the story of Israel's defeat of Sihon and Og is late, being the work of either the Deuteronomistic historian or of a later editor.[37] It also justifies J. Maxwell Miller's assertion that "the claim that Israel gained immediate and full possession of the central and northern Transjordan by defeating Sihon and Og is probably an exaggeration or entirely fanciful."[38]

---

the claim of Kitchen and Redford that this Egyptian text mentions Dibon in Moab is very questionable (see Ahituv 1972 and Kafafi 1985). The text was written over an earlier inscription, making the signs difficult to read. Kitchen also had to resort to some reconstruction of the text (Miller 1977a: 250-251). The text is simply too unclear to prove that Dibon must have existed in the thirteenth century B.C. Kitchen's interpretation of the text would force a reevaluation of the archaeological evidence from Dibon. The archaeological evidence, however, is much more clear, and it can be used to argue that Kitchen's reading of "Dibon" in the Egyptian text must be incorrect.

33. Avi-Yonah 1977: 820; Dornemann 1983: 34-35.

34. Horn 1976a: 510.

35. Horn 1976b: 410.

36. Horn 1976b: 410. L. T. Geraty (1983: 247) agrees with Horn that Late Bronze Heshbon was located at Jalul rather than Hesban.

37. Van Seters 1972 (Bartlett 1978 attempts to refute Van Seters' arguments, but does not succeed—see Van Seters 1980); Miller 1977a: 225-227.

38. Miller 1977a: 227.

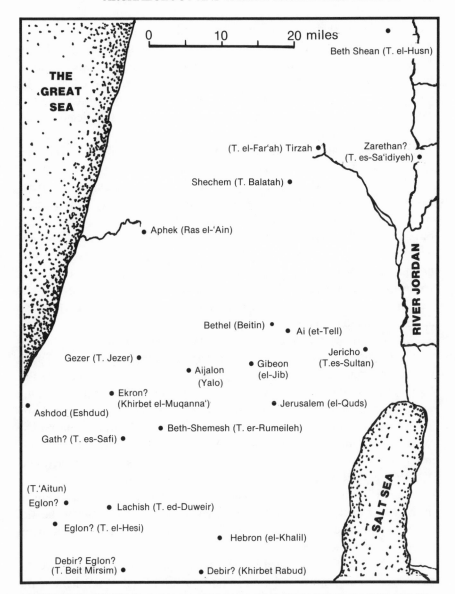

FIGURE 5: CENTRAL CANAAN AT THE TIME OF THE ISRAELITE CONQUEST

Jericho, Ai, and Gibeon

The Bible tells us that after the conquest of the kingdoms of Sihon and Og, Moses died. Joshua then led the warriors of all twelve of the Israelite tribes (even those belonging to the tribes that had been given the conquered Transjordanian territory) across the Jordan River near Jericho (see Figure 5). The account of Jericho's destruction is one of the best known stories from the Bible. The Israelites marched once around Jericho each day for six days, then seven times on the seventh day. Finally, with a blast of ram's horns and a shout from the people, the strong fortification walls of the city collapsed. Except for a harlot (who had helped the Israelites) and her family, all living creatures in Jericho were slaughtered and the city, with all of its contents, was put to the torch (Joshua 6).

Jericho is another city whose archaeological identification is virtually unquestionable. Jericho was located in the lower Jordan valley, across from the most important southern ford of the river. And it was a city of palm trees (Deuteronomy 34:3). The only suitable location is the spring-fed oasis around the modern town of Jericho. There are two mounds in this oasis near the spring, Tell es-Sultan and Tulul Abu el-'Alayiq. Excavations have shown that the first is the site of prehistoric and Old Testament Jericho while the second was the location for the Herodian and New Testament city.

Because of its major role in the story of the Conquest, Jericho was one of the first Palestinian sites to be examined archaeologically. Captain Charles Warren made a few soundings into Tell es-Sultan for the Palestine Exploration Fund as early as 1867. Then between 1908 and 1911 more widespread excavations were undertaken by an Austro-German expedition led by Ernst Sellin and Karl Watzinger. However, Warren's inadequate excavation techniques and Sellin and Watzinger's failure to appreciate the importance of pottery for archaeological chronology has rendered the results of these early expeditions practically useless today. John Garstang's excavations at Tell es-Sultan between 1930 and 1936 were a major improvement over these earlier investigations, but even his results have had to be significantly modified after the careful stratigraphical work of Kathleen Kenyon from 1952 through 1958.

Jericho was first occupied c. 7000 B.C., making it the earliest city yet discovered. It continued to be an important urban center throughout the Neolithic Period (c. 7000-3100 B.C.) and the Early Bronze Age (c. 3100-2300 B.C.). During the Early Bronze Age Jericho was surrounded by very impressive fortification walls, which were repaired and rebuilt a number of times.[39] At the end of the Early Bronze III period Jericho was destroyed and only partially reoccupied—by people without a strong architectural

---

39. Kenyon 1957: 173-182; 1967: 266-267.

tradition. During the succeeding Middle Bronze Age I (the period Kenyon called "Intermediate Early Bronze-Middle Bronze"), which lasted from c. 2300 to c. 1950 B.C., only a few flimsy buildings were constructed on the *tell*.[40] Town life resumed with the advent of the Middle Bronze Age II (c. 1950-1500 B.C.). During this period the city prospered and once more was protected by a strong fortification wall. Like Early Bronze Jericho, however, the final Middle Bronze Age city was destroyed in a great conflagration.[41]

John Garstang claimed to have uncovered evidence that the Middle Bronze Age city had continued to exist into the Late Bronze Age, down to about 1400 B.C. This was the city he thought had fallen to Joshua and the Israelites (see Chapter 2, above). However, Kenyon's excavations showed that the walls Garstang thought belonged to the time of Joshua were actually Early Bronze Age, c. 2300 B.C. She also revised some of Garstang's dates for the Late Bronze Age material he found on the *tell* and in tombs, arguing that it belonged to the fourteenth rather than the fifteenth century B.C. Kenyon asserted that Jericho was destroyed at the end of the Middle Bronze Age II (c. 1500 B.C.)[42] and lay abandoned for a considerable amount of time. During this period of abandonment there was extensive erosion of the Middle Bronze Age layers of the site. Jericho was at least partially reoccupied in the Late Bronze Age II A (c. 1400-1300 B.C.). This settlement came to an end around 1300 B.C., and once again the *tell* was heavily eroded.[43] The site then seems to have remained abandoned until the seventh century B.C. (Iron Age II).

Kathleen Kenyon found very little evidence from the Late Bronze period at Jericho, so she speculated that the extensive Late Bronze Age city described in the Book of Joshua must have been eroded away.[44] But the remains of the eroded buildings and the abundance of pottery sherds they should have contained had to go somewhere—they should have washed down the slopes of the site and been present at the base of the mound. However,

---

40. Kenyon 1957: 192; 1967: 268.

41. Kenyon 1957: 229; 1967: 271: 1973a: 92-93.

42. Kenyon 1981: 2. Kenyon used the traditional date of c. 1550 B.C. for the end the MB II C period, and thus for the destruction of Jericho. However, Manfred Bietak's excavations at Tell ed-Dab'a (the Hyksos capital of Avaris) in Egypt have indicated that the end of MB II B corresponds to the end of Hyksos rule, c. 1560-1540 B.C. The end of MB II C in Palestine would have to be lowered accordingly to c. 1500-1475 B.C. See Bietak 1984: 482-483.

43. Kenyon 1957: 259-263; 1967: 266-267, 269-273; 1973b: 544. Kenyon originally dated the end of the Late Bronze city to c. 1325 B.C. (1957: 262), but she later lowered this date to "soon after 1300 B.C." (1973b: 545).

44. Kenyon 1957: 261-262; 1967: 273.

while trenches dug at three different locations around the base of the *tell* uncovered vast amounts of material from the eroded Middle Bronze Age city,[45] no trace of the expected Late Bronze debris was found.[46]

Kenyon also hypothesized that her failure to find evidence of Late Bronze city walls at Jericho might have been due to the Late Bronze population's reuse of the Middle Bronze Age fortifications.[47] But the amount of erosion the Middle Bronze levels had undergone during the period the site was abandoned following its Middle Bronze Age II destruction makes it very unlikely that the Middle Bronze walls remained standing to any degree around the *tell*. If the walls had survived to a height sufficient for them to be used later, they would have acted as a dam around the circuit of the mound, keeping the Middle Bronze Age remains within them. The extensive erosion Kenyon noted should not have been able to occur. The only viable conclusion seems to be that there was no fortified town at Jericho for Joshua to destroy during the Late Bronze Age.

Leon Wood and B. K. Waltke, conservative biblical scholars who support the fifteenth century date for the Exodus, have tried to dispute Kenyon's conclusions and reinstate Garstang's date of c. 1400 B.C. for the destruction of Late Bronze Age Jericho.[48] Their strongest argument is based on Egyptian scarabs that Garstang found, the latest of which belonged to the reign of Amenhotep III, c. 1400 B.C.[49] Kenyon claimed that scarabs were usually unreliable for dating purposes because they were often kept for generations as family heirlooms.[50] But Wood found it difficult to accept this reason for rejecting Garstang's dating evidence. "If they were heirlooms," Wood protested, "they would have had to be sometime after c. 1400 B.C., and those found seem to appear in context only with pre-1400 B.C. pottery."[51]

This argument would be valid if the scarabs Garstang found had been buried on the *tell,* sealed beneath the ash layer that marks the destruction of the Middle Bronze Age city. But this was not the case. The scarabs came from Middle Bronze II tombs, some of which clearly had been reused in the Late Bronze Age. So the scarabs with the names of fifteenth-century Egyptian rulers on them could have been heirlooms buried with people from the fourteenth-century occupation of the site who reused earlier tombs,

---

45. Kenyon 1957: 259-260; 1967: 271.
46. Tushingham 1953: 64; 1954: 103; Kenyon 1978: 42-43.
47. Kenyon 1978: 38.
48. Wood 1970: 69-73; 1986: 76-77; Waltke 1972: 40-42.
49. Wood 1970: 72; 1986: 77; Waltke 1972: 40-41.
50. Kenyon 1957: 260.
51. Wood 1986: 77.

as Kenyon argued. By themselves these scarabs cannot prove that Jericho was inhabited in the fifteenth century, nor can the fact that they were found in Middle Bronze Age tombs prove that the *tell* was continuously occupied from the Middle Bronze Age to about 1400 B.C.[52] Other arguments Wood and Waltke make for a fifteenth-century occupation of Jericho are equally flawed.[53] Their attempts to rehabilitate a c. 1400 B.C. date for Jericho's destruction are based on a serious misunderstanding of the archaeological evidence and have no validity.

However, Bryant G. Wood has recently used a different argument to support Garstang's date for the destruction of Jericho. He has analyzed the pottery from City IV at Jericho (the layer whose destruction Kenyon dated to MB II C) and claims that it is actually characteristic of the last phase of the Late Bronze I period. Kenyon incorrectly placed this domestic pottery from Jericho's City IV in the MB II period, he asserts, because she did not find any of the inported Cypriot Basering, White Slip, or Bichrome wares characteristic of the LB I era. But Wood claims that Jericho was a cultural backwater at this time, so the absence of such imported pottery is not surprising. He also notes that the only radiocarbon date for material from the destruction layer was 1410 ± 40 B.C., indicating that Jericho was destroyed in the latter part of the LB I period.[54]

If Bryant Wood's analysis of the pottery of Jericho City IV proves to be correct, the archaeological evidence from Jericho might be in agreement with the biblical account of its fifteenth-century-B.C. destruction by Joshua. It is possible that the last phase of City IV at Jericho lasted into LB I, but whether it continued to exist until the *end* of LB I (c. 1400 B.C.) remains to be seen. On the other hand, there seems to have been no settlement at Tell es-Sultan during the thirteenth century B.C., the period in which most scholars place the Exodus and Conquest.

---

52. See Bimson 1981: 118.

53. Wood and Waltke also misinterpreted the stratigraphical relationships between the Middle Bronze II destruction layer and the Late Bronze buildings and pottery Garstang and Kenyon found on the *tell*. J. Bimson (1981: 115-117) has detailed their errors in this regard.

54. B. Wood 1987. Another recent analysis of the Jericho material (Bienkowski 1986) has concluded that the destruction of City IV occurred at the end of MB II C, as Kenyon claimed. It should also be noted that the radiocarbon date for material from City IV (1410 ± 40 B.C.) does *not* mean that the destruction date for Jericho must be close to 1400 B.C., as Wood infers. It simply means that there is a 67 per cent chance that the destruction occurred between 1450 B.C. and 1370 B.C., and *any* date within that range is as probable as any other. Thus, the date for the destruction is as likely to be 1450 B.C. as 1400 B.C. There is also a 33 per cent chance that the true date for the destruction falls outside the 1450-1370 B.C. range. Nonetheless, there is a 95 per cent probability that the destruction occurred between 1490 B.C. and 1330 B.C. (i.e., within two standard deviations from the mean date of 1410 B.C.).

Following the destruction of Jericho, the Bible relates that the Israelites advanced against the fortified city of Ai. After an initial defeat (which Joshua 7 blames on a sin committed by an Israelite), Joshua captured the city by a ruse. He left a strong force hidden to the west of Ai, then stationed the rest of his force in front of the city. The defenders of Ai attacked and Joshua retreated, leading the Canaanite army further and further from the city. When Ai was defenseless the second Israelite contingent left its hiding place and advanced, capturing the city and setting it on fire. These Israelite warriors then attacked the forces of Ai from the rear, while the men with Joshua turned and attacked from the front. The entire population of Ai was put to the sword, and the city was utterly destroyed (Joshua 8:1-29).

Since the early twentieth century almost all biblical scholars have located Ai at Khirbet et-Tell, a mound two miles east-southeast of Beitin, thought to be ancient Bethel. Investigation of other sites near et-Tell and located east or southeast of Beitin has shown that none of them was occupied earlier than the late Hellenistic Period.[55] So, if Beitin is Bethel, as most archaeologists and biblical scholars think, et-Tell is the only viable site for Ai.

Et-Tell was excavated by Judith Marquet-Krause from 1933 to 1935, Samuel Yeivin in 1936, and Joseph Callaway between 1964 and 1976. These extensive archaeological excavations uncovered a series of Early Bronze Age cities protected by a strong defensive wall. The last of these cities was destroyed at the end of the Early Bronze III period, c. 2300 B.C. The site then lay abandoned for more than a thousand years until a small unwalled twelfth century B.C. (Iron Age I) village was built above the Early Bronze Age ruins. About 1125 B.C. this village was remodeled and expanded, with numerous silo granaries being dug into the village's cobblestone streets and into the ruins of the earlier city. But, after a little more than a hundred years, this second Iron Age I village was abandoned.[56]

There was no evidence of any settlement at et-Tell during the Middle Bronze or Late Bronze Ages, which means that there was no city at Ai to be destroyed by the Israelites in either the fifteenth or the thirteenth century B.C. The nearby city at Beitin (Bethel), though, *was* destroyed toward the end of the thirteenth century B.C.[57] This fact led William F. Albright to propose that, originally, the tradition behind Joshua 8 had described

55. Callaway 1976:14.
56. Callaway 1975; 1976. Also see Zevit 1985a: 58.
57. Kelso 1968: 30-31, 48.

the destruction of Bethel and that later retellings of the story had shifted the event to Ai.[58] Geographical details in the story in Joshua, however, fit et-Tell, not Beitin. The account in Joshua 7-8 must have been composed with the site of Ai in mind.[59]

Other scholars have tried to deal with the problem of Ai by suggesting that the ruins there were serving as a temporary lookout post for a small contingent of troops from Bethel. After routing the soldiers who were guarding the approach to Bethel, Joshua went on to destroy the city of Bethel.[60] Such a theory assumes that Bethel was the real object of the attack, and this is not what the biblical account says. Moreover, the Septuagint (the ancient Greek translation of the Hebrew Scriptures) does not mention that troops from Bethel joined those from Ai in the battle, as the Hebrew text does. This discrepancy suggests that the brief mention of Bethel in the account may be a later addition to the Hebrew text.[61] Furthermore, the story in Joshua mentions a king of Ai and "all his army," refers to the city gate, describes the capture and burning of a "city" (not an outpost already in ruins), and the slaughter of both the men and *women* of Ai after the victory.[62] The "outpost" theory does not account for these particulars in the biblical account.

Joseph Callaway, the most recent excavator of et-Tell, originally suggested that the earliest Iron Age I village at the site might have been the Canaanite city conquered by Joshua. The later Iron I town, with its numerous silos dug into the earlier streets, seemed to be the work of different people— the Israelites.[63] The small unwalled Iron I village at et-Tell, though, certainly did not fit the Book of Joshua's descriptions of Ai with its city gate, king, and army. There was also no indication of a violent destruction of the early Iron I village at Ai. Callaway has since abandoned the theory that Joshua attacked the small Iron I settlement at Ai, and he has concluded that the story of the conquest of Ai is unhistorical.[64]

Callaway is not alone in this assessment. The great German biblical scholar Martin Noth and others have argued that the story of the destruction of Ai was *etiological,* not historical.[65] (An etiological story is one that explains

---

58. Albright 1934: 11; 1939: 17. See also Wright 1962: 80 and Bright 1981: 131.
59. Zevit 1985a: 65.
60. Vincent 1937: 262; Harrison 1969: 121, 327-329; Chadwick and Lomond 1985.
61. Callaway 1985b; Zevit 1985b: 23.
62. Zevit 1985b.
63. Callaway 1968: 316-320; 1976: 15-16.
64. Callaway 1985a.
65. Noth 1935; 1960: 149. See also de Vaux 1978: 618-619.

the origins of some custom or physical object.) In this case, the story supposedly originated to explain the existence of the ruins at et-Tell, which were plainly visible to the early Israelites. The Hebrew name of the city (*ha-'Ai*), which Noth claimed meant "the ruin," was evidence that the city had already been destroyed before the Israelites encountered it. Ziony Zevit has shown that this linguistic support for Noth's theory is probably invalid— the city name, Ai, does not seem to be etymologically connected with the Hebrew word for "ruin."[66] But the idea that the story may have been created in the Iron Age to explain the ruins of the ancient city is still possible.[67]

The implications of this research are clear: The biblical text is either at least partially unhistorical or in error. The city Joshua supposedly destroyed did not exist. The only way to maintain that the story of the destruction of Ai in Joshua 7-8 is historically reliable is to assert that et-Tell is *not* where Ai was located. Yet Ai is fixed by biblical references to its position vis-a-vis Bethel. And since et-Tell is the only pre-Hellenistic site that bears the proper geographical relationship to Beitin, the generally accepted site of Bethel, those who want to relocate Ai must also relocate Bethel. David Livingston has done just that, proposing that el-Bireh was Bethel and Khirbet Nisya, a mound just to the southeast of Bireh, was Ai.[68] Khirbet Nisya seems to have been at least partially occupied in the Middle Bronze Age II and Late Bronze Age I. But no buildings or walls of those periods have been found, only pottery sherds.[69]

Anson Rainey has attacked Livingston's arguments and supported the traditional identification of Beitin as Bethel.[70] Unfortunately, while Rainey's arguments are provocative, they are not absolutely decisive. He points out, for example, that the Arabic *Beitin* is derived from the Hebrew *Beth-'el,* in accordance with philological rules observed at work in a number of other cases.[71] But such an argument cannot prove that the name of Bethel

---

66. Zevit 1985a: 62-63.

67. Zevit 1985a: 66-69.

68. Livingston 1970; 1971. Livingston's position has been adopted by other conservative biblical scholars. See, for example, Bimson 1981: 204-211; Wood 1986: 144; Bimson and Livingston 1987: 46-51.

69. Bimson 1985; I. Wilson 1986: 173. Some sherds from the early part of LB I were found, but these have been interpreted as indicating a destruction of the MB II settlement at the end of MB II and the beginning of LB I (Bimson and Livingston 1987: 51). However, no building-remains, town wall, or destruction layer has been found for MB II. Because the LB I sherds are not stratified under an ash layer with the MB II material, they might indicate continued occupation of the site into the LB I period. It would seem, though, that Khirbet Nisya was always only a small unwalled village, not a fortified city—as the Bible says Ai was.

70. Rainey 1971.

71. Rainey 1971: 177; 1980: 250.

was not transferred to Beitin from another nearby site like el-Bireh. Rainey's topographical arguments are equally inconclusive—they show that el-Bireh does not *have* to be Bethel, as Livingston argued, and that Beitin fits the evidence just as well, but they don't *prove* that el-Bireh *can't* be Bethel.[72] Archaeological evidence, however, does seem to indicate that Beitin is to be preferred over el-Bireh as the site of Bethel. For while Beitin was occupied throughout the Bronze and Iron Ages, brief soundings at el-Bireh have turned up no Middle or Late Bronze Age remains.[73] Thus, if one accepts el-Bireh as Bethel in order to find another site for Ai and save the historicity of Joshua 7-8, one must give up the historicity of Judges 1:22-25, which describes the conquest of Bethel by the House of Joseph.

After the destruction of Ai, the Book of Joshua says that the inhabitants of Gibeon, fearing for their lives, tricked Israel into entering into an alliance with them (Joshua 9). When five of the Amorite kings in the area learned of this, they joined together in an attack on Gibeon, a city that was "large enough for a royal city, larger even than the city of Ai" (Joshua 10:2). Joshua hastened to the aid of Gibeon and defeated the army of the five Amorite kings in that famous battle during which the sun stood still (Joshua 10:7-15).

Gibeon, like Jericho and Ai, plays an important role in the account of the Israelite conquest of Canaan. But, also like those cities, the archaeology of this site presents problems for the biblical interpreter. The site of ancient Gibeon is now called el-Jib. The preservation of part of the ancient name at the site was enough to convince most scholars that el-Jib was Gibeon, but archaeological evidence from this site has proved the identification beyond a reasonable doubt. During excavations that took place in 1956, 1957, 1959, 1960, and 1962, James B. Pritchard found thirty-one jar handles inscribed with the Hebrew letters *gb'n,* "Gibeon." He also found evidence of a winery at the site, indicating that the jars originated at el-Jib—they were not sent there from a Gibeon located somewhere else.[74]

Gibeon proved to have been occupied extensively in the Early Bronze Age I and again in the Middle Bronze Age II and in the Iron Age. But the only Late Bronze pottery found was in eight tombs reused in the fourteenth century B.C. (Late Bronze II A). There was no evidence of settlement on the site during either the fifteenth or thirteenth centuries B.C. There was also no trace of a city wall at Gibeon before the Iron Age

72. See Bimson 1981: 206-211.
73. Rainey 1980: 250; Zevit 1985c: 80.
74. Pritchard 1959: 1-7, 17; 1964: 24-27; 1976: 446; Reed 1967: 237-238.

I.[75] The fourteenth-century-B.C. Late Bronze pottery in the tombs must have belonged to a very small, unwalled settlement on the site or to tent-dwelling people living only temporarily in the area.[76] Regardless of whether one places the Exodus and Conquest in the fifteenth or the thirteenth century B.C., no trace was found of the supposedly large and populous Gibeon of Joshua's time.

Other Conquest Accounts

The Book of Joshua tells us that the five kings who were defeated by Israel at Gibeon hid in a cave at Makkedah, but they were soon discovered and executed. Joshua and his army then conquered Makkedah, putting all its citizens to the sword. The Israelites went on to conquer Libnah, Lachish, Eglon, Hebron, and Debir, leaving no survivors in any of these cities. The king of Gezer and his entire army were also totally destroyed when they tried to aid Lachish. The entire southern portion of Canaan had been conquered and most of its population butchered (Joshua 10: 16-43).

When news of Joshua's activities reached northern Canaan, Jabin, king of Hazor, organized a coalition of city-states to defend the area against the Israelites. However, Joshua surprised the Canaanite army at the waters of Merom and totally defeated it. Hazor was captured, burned to the ground, and all its people were killed. Other cities in the area were taken and their populations put to the sword, but the cities themselves were not destroyed (Joshua 11:1-15). Later, according to Judges 18:27-29, the tribe of Dan moved to the north and destroyed the Canaanite city of Laish. The Danites then occupied it themselves, renaming it Dan.

The Bible also preserves other, somewhat different accounts of the Conquest. Joshua 15:15-17 ascribes the conquest of Debir to Othniel and the Calebites rather than to Joshua. And Judges 1 not only agrees that Othniel took Debir (1:11-13), but it credits the conquest of Hebron (1:10) and Hormah (1:17) to attacks by Judah and Simeon after Joshua's death. To complicate matters still further, Caleb (in Judges 1:20) is said to have driven the Anakim from Hebron, and the House of Joseph is given credit for the capture of Bethel (Judges 1:22-26).

There are also two Conquest narratives for Hazor. According to the

75. Pritchard 1964: 39-40; 1976: 449.
76. Pritchard 1965: 318-319.

Book of Joshua, Joshua killed Jabin, king of Hazor, and all of Hazor's citizens, and he burned the city to the ground. But soon after the Conquest (early in the period of the "judges"), Israelites fell under the power of *another* Jabin, king of Hazor (Judges 4:2). We are not told how the city was rebuilt, repopulated, or how it became powerful again in such a short time, nor is there any explanation for the fact that the name of the king of Hazor in the time of the "judges" is the same as that of the king who supposedly fought Joshua. Judges 4:23-24 says that Jabin was killed and his city captured only after Barak and Deborah had defeated his general Sisera. Finally, although Joshua 11:23 states that Joshua captured the whole country and gave it to Israel, other passages admit that large sections of Canaan were not taken. Major cities not conquered by Israel include Beth-shean, Ibleam, Acco, Dor, Taanach, and Megiddo in the north, and Jerusalem, Aijalon, Gezer, Beth-shemesh, Gaza, Ashdod, Ashkelon, Gath, and Ekron in the south (Joshua 13:1-4; 16:10; 17:11-12; Judges 1:27-35).

The locations of most of the cities discussed previously are generally agreed upon by archaeologists, but this is not true for a number of the places supposedly conquered after the battle at Gibeon. The locations of Makkedah, Libnah, Eglon, and Debir are all uncertain. Makkedah has been identified with Tell es-Safi, Khirbet el-Kheisun, or Khirbet Maqdum.[77] Libnah used to be located at Tell es-Safi, but now many scholars argue that es-Safi is either Makkedah or Gath and that Tell Bornat or Tell ej-Judeideh is Libnah.[78] Eglon has been variously located at Tell el-Hesi, Tell en-Nejileh, Tell 'Aitun, or Tell Beit Mirsim.[79] And while some scholars still support William Foxwell Albright's claim that Tell Beit Mirsim was Debir, others argue that Moshe Kochavi has shown that Debir was located at Khirbet Rabud.[80] Since the identifications of these cities are not generally agreed upon, archaeological evidence from the contending sites cannot be given much weight. Therefore, we will not consider these disputed sites. Instead, we will survey the remaining "conquered" cities—Lachish, Hebron, Hazor, and Dan—whose locations are generally accepted.

Since the 1930s virtually all Syro-Palestinian archaeologists have agreed that Tell ed-Duweir is the site of ancient Lachish. Eusebius located Lachish seven Roman miles south of Eleutheropolis (the modern Beit Jibrin) on the road to the Negeb. Tell ed-Duweir fits that description exactly and

77. May 1962: 132; Stern 1978: 1025.
78. Corney 1962 opposed by Rainey 1976b.
79. Amiran and Worrell 1976: 514 and Rose 1976 opposed by Rainey 1976a.
80. Albright 1967: 207-209, 1975b: 171-172 opposed by Kochavi 1974, 1976, and 1978.

is the largest mound in the area, a fact in keeping with the importance ancient texts ascribe to Lachish.[81]

Tell ed-Duweir has been extensively excavated, first by James Starkey from 1932 to 1938, then by David Ussishkin since 1973. The first true town to exist at Tell ed-Duweir arose in the Early Bronze Age III. This settlement came to an end c. 2300 B.C., though no ash layer has been found to prove that it was destroyed by enemy action. During the Middle Bronze Age I no buildings seem to have been constructed on the mound, though burials from this time have been found.[82] Another city was built on the site in the Middle Bronze Age II, a settlement that had a strong fortification wall protected by a steep embankment and a ditch or moat (called a "fosse"). Lachish came under Egyptian control in the Late Bronze Age, and the Middle Bronze II defenses fell into disuse. The city expanded beyond (and over) the old, crumbled walls, and a temple was built on top of the silted-up moat.[83] At least portions of this large unwalled city, including the Fosse Temple, were burned toward the end of the thirteenth century B.C., but it was quickly rebuilt, presumably by the same people who had occupied it earlier. Then, during the middle to the latter part of the twelfth century B.C., Lachish was again destroyed in a terrible fire. It remained unoccupied for more than a century before a fort was built on the site around the time of Solomon (the tenth century B.C.).[84]

Starkey's excavations in the 1930s led scholars to believe that the destruction of the last phase of the Fosse Temple (Temple III) occurred at the same time as the destruction of the final Late Bronze Age city on the *tell*. This general destruction of Lachish was dated to the end of the thirteenth century B.C. and credited variously to the Israelites under Joshua, the Philistines, or the Egyptians.[85] Ussishkin's work in the 1980s, however, has shown that this view is incorrect. Fosse Temple III was contemporaneous with the *penultimate* Late Bronze Age city on the *tell* (Level VII). The Fosse Temple was not rebuilt following its destruction, although the city on the *tell* was. This final Late Bronze Age II city is designated Level VI.[86] Level VI Lachish seems to have remained a Canaanite city—it had a temple on the acropolis, which contained a graffito portraying a Canaanite god and a plaque depicting

---

81. Tufnell 1967: 296-297.
82. Tufnell 1967: 297-298.
83. Tufnell 1967: 298-300; Ussishkin 1977: 741-742; 1987: 20-23.
84. Tufnell 1967: 302-303; Ussishkin 1987: 22-35, 39.
85. Kenyon 1960: 214-215; Hamilton 1962: 54; Tufnell 1967: 302.
86. Ussishkin 1987: 21-22.

a Canaanite goddess.[87] There is also evidence that the city of Level VI remained under Egyptian control just as its predecessor had been. The acropolis temple was built in Egyptian style; scarabs and a cartouche of Ramesses III were found in the Level VI remains; and a tomb contemporaneous with Level VI contained two Egyptian-style anthropoid clay coffins similar to those found at other Egyptianized Canaanite cities.[88] It is now clear that Egyptian control over much of Palestine did not end until sometime during or after the reign of Ramesses III (c. 1182-1151 B.C.) and in some areas not until the death of Ramesses VI (c. 1134/3 B.C.).[89]

A building on the *tell* (possibly a temple) was destroyed by fire early in the Late Bronze Age,[90] but there is no indication that there was a general destruction of the city at the end of the Late Bronze Age I, the time of the Conquest according to advocates of a fifteenth-century Exodus. The only general destructions of Lachish during the Late Bronze Age occurred in Late Bronze Age II B (Levels VII and VI). If Joshua and the Israelites are credited with the destruction of the thirteenth-century-B.C. city at Lachish (Fosse Temple III and Level VII on the *tell*), the Bible must have greatly exaggerated the results of that conquest. Joshua 10:32 says that Joshua killed every person in Lachish (and in most of the surrounding cities), but Lachish seems to have been immediately rebuilt by Canaanites after the destruction at the end of the thirteenth century B.C. In any case, it is obvious that the city did not pass into Israelite hands at that time. On the other hand, if one argues that the final Late Bronze Age city at Lachish (Level VI) was the one conquered and destroyed by Joshua, then at least part of the Israelite conquest of Canaan must be redated to the twelfth century, c. 1150-1130 B.C.[91]

Hebron is still occupied, and its Arabic name, el-Khalil ("the friend"), stresses its traditional association with Abraham, the "friend of God." Excavations undertaken at el-Khalil in the 1960s have indicated that the site was occupied in the Early Bronze Age I, Middle Bronze II, the Iron Age, Hellenistic, and Byzantine periods. The expedition uncovered some

---

87. Ussishkin 1987: 23, 28-31. The objects in the temple seem to have been associated with the Egyptian-Canaanite goddess Asherah or Astarte (also known by her appellation *Qudshu*, "holiness") and the god Resheph.

88. Ussishkin 1987: 31-35.

89. Ussishkin 1987: 35. The base of a statue of Ramesses VI was found at Megiddo and an inscription of his at Beth-shean (Aharoni 1978: 151-152, 181).

90. Ussishkin 1977: 750.

91. Ussishkin 1987: 36-39.

of the fortifications of the Middle Bronze Age city that was destroyed at the end of Middle Bronze II C. But no remains were found from the Late Bronze Age.[92] As at other sites, the absence of Late Bronze Age remains at Hebron indicates either that the Exodus and Conquest did not take place during the Late Bronze Age or that the biblical accounts of those events are not historically accurate.

One of the key archaeological supports for a thirteenth-century Israelite conquest of Canaan has been provided by Yigael Yadin's excavations (1955-58, 1968) at Tell el-Qedah (also known as Tell Waqqas), the undisputed location of ancient Hazor. A cuneiform legal text on a clay tablet found during the excavations at Tell el-Qedah deals with a conflict over real estate in Hazor, thus proving the identity of the site.[93] The *tell* proper (or acropolis) at Hazor was occupied from the Early Bronze Age II onward, but in the Middle Bronze Age II B the city expanded to cover an immense area known as "the lower city." This roughly rectangular addition to the *tell* covers some two hundred acres (as opposed to only twenty-five acres for the *tell* proper), making it one of the largest sites in the entire Near East.[94] The lower city went through two phases before being destroyed at the end of Middle Bronze II C; but it was rebuilt soon afterward and continued to be occupied until the end of the Late Bronze Age II B (c. 1200 B.C.), when it was again burned. A succession of Iron Age settlements were built atop the Late Bronze Age ruins on the *tell*, but the lower city was never reoccupied.[95]

A temple on the *tell* was destroyed at the end of the Late Bronze Age I and not rebuilt,[96] but there does not seem to have been a general destruction of the site at this time as there should have been according to the fifteenth-century Exodus hypothesis. On the other hand, the Late Bronze II B destruction of Hazor has been used to support the theory of a thirteenth-century-B.C. Exodus and Conquest. Yadin was convinced that the destruction of the last Late Bronze Age city at Hazor (Stratum XIII on the *tell* and Stratum 1a of the lower city) was caused by the Israelites under Joshua. The small, poorly built Iron Age I settlement of Level XII was, he felt, Israelite.[97]

The archaeological finds at Hazor, however, do not harmonize with

92. Hammond 1965; 1966; 1968.
93. Yadin 1975: 20
94. Yadin 1975: 21-22.
95. Yadin 1975: 252-275; 1976: 478-481, 485.
96. Yadin 1975: 259-262.
97. Yadin 1975: 249-255; 1976: 494.

the biblical account of another destruction of the city during the time of the "judges" (Judges 4). If the Late Bronze II B city at Hazor was the one destroyed by Joshua, and if the succeeding Iron I settlement is Israelite, there are no remains to belong to a Canaanite king of Hazor at the time of Deborah. Yadin has argued that the references to Hazor in the account of the battle with Sisera were glosses added by a later editor of the prose story (Joshua 4), since Hazor is not mentioned in Joshua 5, the poetical "Song of Deborah."[98] It is generally agreed that the "Song of Deborah" is a very early piece of poetry that dates from the early monarchy, if not the period of the "judges" itself. It was probably the primary source upon which the prose story was based—just as the prose account of the sun standing still at Gibeon was derived from an older poem from the lost *Book of Jashar* (Joshua 10:12-13). Thus, while the finds from Hazor do not support the biblical data for a Conquest at the end of the fifteenth century or the accuracy of the references to Hazor in Judges 4, they can be used to support those biblical passages that suggest a Conquest in the thirteenth century B.C.

The ancient city of Dan (or Laish, as it was known before its conquest by the tribe of Dan) was located at Tell el-Qadi at the foot of Mount Hermon. Since 1966 it has been excavated by Avraham Biran. Occupation at the site seems to have begun in the Early Bronze Age II and continued until the end of the Early Bronze III period, when the flourishing city was destroyed.[99] Settlement was not resumed until the Middle Bronze II A period, c. 1900 B.C. During the Middle Bronze Age II A-B, the city was surrounded with a fortification wall, which included an almost perfectly preserved arched gateway flanked by two towers.[100] This wall and gateway were later covered (and thus preserved) by a huge rampart, which was typical of Middle Bronze II B fortifications.[101] This Middle Bronze II city was destroyed by fire, but what immediately succeeded it is not clear. There does not seem to have been a significant Late Bronze I settlement on the site, for only a few pottery sherds, which possibly belong to that period, have been found. But there *was* a Late Bronze II city that was burned at the end of the thirteenth century B.C.[102] The Iron Age I settlement that

---

98. Yadin 1982: 19-23.

99. Biran 1980: 168-169; 1985: 187.

100. Laughlin 1981: 24-29; Biran 1984.

101. Laughlin 1981: 24, 29. The exact phase of the Middle Bronze Age during which the rampart was built was unknown until fairly recently. Biran is now convinced that it was constructed in Middle Bronze II B (Biran 1985: 187).

102. Except for a few sherds and a tomb, Late Bronze remains were not found in the early campaigns at Dan (Biran 1969: 123; 1975: 316 and 1980: 172-173). However, in recent years a

succeeded it consisted mainly of pits and silos, possibly indicating the semisedentary nature of the new inhabitants who, according to Biran, were members of the Israelite tribe of Dan.[103] Just as at Hazor, the archaeological evidence from Dan fits the biblical accounts quite well—if the Conquest is placed in the thirteenth century B.C.

Conclusions

There is very little support for a fifteenth-century Exodus and Conquest if the customary dating of the archaeological material is maintained. The fifteenth-century date for the Exodus places the Conquest at the end of the Late Bronze Age I and beginning of Late Bronze Age II, c. 1400 B.C. Yet very few of the sites mentioned in the Conquest narratives were destroyed or even occupied at that time (see Table 3). According to the Bible, seven cities played significant roles during the Exodus and Conquest: Kadesh-Barnea, Heshbon, Jericho, Ai, Gibeon, Hazor, and Dan. If Bryant Wood's contention that the pottery of Jericho City IV was LB I proves to be correct, then Jericho's destruction would agree with a fifteenth-century Conquest. But none of the rest of these sites has produced evidence that fits the biblical accounts, if one accepts a Late Bronze I setting for the stories.

The theory of a thirteenth-century Exodus and Conquest claims more archaeological support. There *was* widespread destruction of cities in Palestine at the end of the Late Bronze Age II B (c. 1200-1150 B.C.), and it was thought that much of this destruction could be credited to the invading Israelites. But when the remains from the particular sites mentioned in the Conquest narratives are studied, as we have seen, support for the historicity of a thirteenth-century Exodus and Conquest is only moderately better than that for a fifteenth-century one (see Table 3). The thirteenth-century-B.C. destructions of Hazor, Dan, and Bethel can be correlated with the biblical accounts fairly well, and the evidence from Aroer and Lachish can be made to fit, if not exactly. Further, if one accepts the identifications of Eglon with Tell el-Hesi and Debir with Tell Beit Mirsim, the Late Bronze Age II B destructions at those sites could also be used to support the biblical narratives.[104] But there is no evidence of a Late Bronze II B Israelite

Late Bronze II stratum, complete with floors and structures covered by a layer of ash, has been uncovered (Biran 1985: 187; 1987: 12-15).

103. Biran 1975: 316; 1985: 187; 1987: 14-16.

104. In contrast, Moshe Kochavi has argued very persuasively that Khirbet Rabud, *not* Tell Beit Mirsim, is Debir (Kochavi 1974), and most archaeologists now accept this identification.

TABLE 3

Archaeology and a Late Bronze Age Exodus and Conquest

City	Biblical Reference	Archaeological Evidence
Kadesh-Barnea	Deut. 1:19-46. The Israelites spent most of their 40 years in the wilderness at Kadesh	No LB remains at any of the possible sites for Kadesh-Barnea
Arad	Num. 21:1-3 indicates that the city was destroyed by Joshua	No LB occupation at any of the possible sites for Arad
Hormah	Num. 21:1-3 says the city was destroyed by Joshua; Judges 1:17-18 credits its conquest to later action by Judah and Simeon	No LB occupation at any of the possible sites for Hormah
Heshbon	Num. 21:25-26. Heshbon is the capital of King Sihon and is destroyed	No LB occupation
Dibon	Num. 21:30. Dibon was destroyed after Heshbon	No LB occupation
Aroer	Deut. 2:36. Aroer was conquered after Sihon's defeat	Occupied only from LB II B onward into the Iron Age
Jericho	Josh. 6 describes the total destruction of this city and its population	MB II city possibly destroyed in LB I; only slight occupation in LB II A; no LB II B remains
Ai	Josh. 7-8. The city and all of its population were destroyed	No LB occupation
Gibeon	Josh. 9-10:2. Gibeon was "a royal city, larger even than Ai" and became Israel's ally	No LB I or LB II B occupation; LB II A pottery found only in tombs—Gibeon was at best a small unwalled village at that time
Lachish	Josh. 10:32. Lachish was captured and its people killed	LB I and II occupation; LB II B destructions in the 13th and 12th centuries B.C.
Hebron	Josh. 10:36-37. Hebron was captured and its people killed	No LB occupation
Bethel	Judges 1:22-25 credits the destruction of Bethel to the House of Joseph	No LB I occupation; LB II A-B occupation with an LB II B destruction
Hazor	Josh. 11:1-11. Hazor was burned and its people killed	LB I and II A occupation, but no destruction; LB II B city destroyed
Dan	Judges 18:27-29 states that Laish was destroyed and then reoccupied by the tribe of Dan	Few definite LB I remains; LB II B occupation and destruction

Note: Underlined cities have significant stories told about their roles during the Conquest period.

encampment at Kadesh-Barnea, no Late Bronze II B Gibeon to become an Israelite subject-ally, and no Late Bronze II B destruction of Arad, Hormah, Heshbon, Dibon, Jericho, Ai, or Hebron. Of the seven sites given significant attention in the narratives, only two provide archaeological evidence to support a thirteenth-century-B.C. Exodus and Conquest. And, since the twelfth and thirteenth centuries B.C. were also a time of great turmoil, with Egyptian armies and "Sea Peoples" (including the Philistines) invading Palestine, the Late Bronze II B destructions that did occur were not necessarily the work of Joshua and the Israelites.[105]

But what of the evidence for an Israelite presence in Iron I Palestine, which would indicate that the Exodus and settlement must have occurred at the end of the Bronze Age? Yigael Yadin once made a very confident statement in this regard:

> All archaeologists agree that at the end of the Late Bronze Age . . . , the material culture we associate with this period abruptly stopped. Late Bronze agriculture was based on fortified city-states. At the end of the period, many of these cities were destroyed. The archaeological evidence shows conflagrations and destructions which cannot be attributed to famine or earthquakes. Sometime later (that is, in a later archaeological stratum), a new and completely different culture developed, sometimes on the destroyed site and sometimes on a new site. This new culture (Iron Age culture) was initially rather poor architecturally, so poor it can hardly be called urban. This culture appears to reflect the first efforts at settlement by a semi-nomadic people.[106]

Unfortunately, Yadin's contention that archaeology clearly reveals the arrival of seminomadic outsiders (the Israelites) at the beginning of the Iron Age is simply wrong. Even at the time Yadin's statement was published (1982), not "all archaeologists" agreed that the material culture of Late Bronze Age Palestine abruptly stopped and was replaced by a new and different Iron Age culture. Many archaeologists continue to agree with J. Maxwell Miller's assertion of 1977 that, with the exception of the appearance of Philistine pottery, "the techniques and styles of Iron I suggest more of a cultural continuum from LB than a cultural break." "One would not conclude from the material remains themselves," he wrote, "that newcomers entered Palestine from the outside at any particular time during LB or

---

At Khirbet Rabud the transition from the Late Bronze era to the Iron Age seems to have occurred peacefully (Kochavi 1976; 1978).

105. Miller 1977: 256-257; Kenyon 1978: 33; Bimson 1981: 48-51; Ramsey 1981: 70-71.
106. Yadin 1982: 18.

Iron I."[107] Dutch archaeologist H. J. Franken also has stated that "archaeologists would be totally unaware of any important ethnic changes at the end of the Late Bronze Age were it not for the biblical traditions."[108] Furthermore, despite Yadin's assertion to the contrary, cities *can* be destroyed as a result of famine, plague, extensive earthquakes, and climatic changes; disastrous military battles are not always necessary.[109]

The material culture of Iron Age Palestine evidences decline and impoverishment when compared to that of the Late Bronze Age, but, as Franken has pointed out, "a decline in the quality of the potter's product does not necessarily point to invasions."[110] There must be a lot of other archaeological evidence, like dramatic changes in a number of aspects of the material culture, in order to prove that newcomers took over an area. However, there is no sharp break in cultural traditions between the Late Bronze and Iron Age periods in Palestine. Imported Mycenaean ware is no longer found, indicating a decline in trade and wealth, but, except for Philistine pottery, the basic Iron Age I pottery styles clearly were developed from those of the Late Bronze Age. In fact, Palestinian pottery styles display continuity and evolutionary development, with *no* major cultural breaks, from the beginning of the Middle Bronze Age II (c. 1950 B.C.) to the end of the Iron Age (c. 500 B.C.).[111] Continuity is also evident in other aspects of culture, most notably burial practices. New elements were added to the repertoire of artifacts throughout this long time-span, but only in a gradual, evolutionary fashion. Periods when cities were destroyed and material culture declined also are noted at various times between the beginning of the Middle Bronze Age II and the end of the Iron Age, but there is little reason to associate any of these changes with the arrival of new population groups.

A connection between the Israelites and the introduction of the "four-room" house style, collared-rim storage jars, a new type of cooking pot, and the appearance of small Iron I villages in the hill country of Palestine has not been demonstrated. These features developed out of Late Bronze "Canaanite" culture; they were not introduced from outside.[112] In addition, during the Iron I period the "Israelite" four-room houses and collared-rim jars were *not* found in all areas that the Bible claims became Israelite,

---

107. Miller 1977: 255.
108. Franken 1975: 337 (see also p. 332).
109. Franken 1975: 333. See also Carpenter 1968 and Stiebing 1980.
110. Franken 1976: 7-8.
111. Amiran 1970: 90-285, especially pp. 191-192. See also Pritchard 1965: 320-321.
112. Weippert 1971: 132-134; Miller 1977: 257; Bimson 1981: 51-56; Callaway 1985c; 1985d: 75-77; Mazar 1985: 64-70.

while they *were* found in supposedly non-Israelite areas of Canaan and Jordan.[113] Even Yohanan Aharoni, who discovered many of the Iron I "Israelite" villages, admitted that the pottery he found was essentially the same kind found in the "Canaanite" settlements. His conclusion was telling: The Israelites did not have a distinctive material culture of their own but "borrowed everything from the previous inhabitants."[114] And Amihai Mazar, another prominent Israeli archaeologist, was recently forced to conclude that seminomadic Israelite tribes must have absorbed the Canaanite material-cultural traditions when they encountered them—but, he wrote, the early phase, before that absorption was complete, "has not left any archaeological evidence."[115] However, if the Israelites had no distinctive material culture, how *can* their presence be recognized archaeologically? And how can Aharoni, Mazar, or anyone else consider some Iron I remains "Israelite" and others "Canaanite"?

Israel Finkelstein solves this problem simply by defining as Israelite any "hill country people in a process of settling down," whose villages are located in Galilee or in areas that were part of the territory later ruled by Saul.[116] His solution is to use "Israelite" as a socioeconomic term rather than an ethnic one.

It *is* possible to list some distinctions between the large cities on the plains and the small villages in the hills.[117] But these distinctions are indicative of economic, social, and ecological differences rather than of differences in kind. There are no new cultural features that prove that the inhabitants of the new villages in the hills must have arrived from *outside* the area of Canaan. There is much, however, that connects them with the previous Late Bronze culture of that area.

Working backwards from correlations between biblical accounts and Assyrian records of the ninth and eighth centuries B.C., we can be fairly sure that there was a nation called Israel with a monarchical form of government by about 1000 B.C. As we have seen, though, archaeological evidence does not confirm the historicity of biblical traditions about how Israel gained control of Canaan. If there is little evidence for the Conquest in the Late Bronze Age, could it have taken place at some other time? Could our archaeological-historical correlations be erroneous? Or is the entire tradition

---

113. Miller 1981: 72; Kochavi 1985: 57-58; Mazar 1985: 66-69; Finkelstein 1988: 29, 31.
114. Aharoni 1979: 240-241. The quote is from p. 240.
115. Mazar 1985: 70.
116. Finkelstein 1988: 28.
117. Finkelstein 1988: 29-31.

of an Israelite conquest of Canaan unhistorical? The succeeding chapters will consider these questions.

4

Redating the Exodus and Conquest

Catastrophes like those mentioned in the Exodus story should surely have left their mark on ancient Egypt. But historians have found no Egyptian references to the Exodus events. The conquest of Canaan and the annihilation of much of that land's population, as recounted in the Book of Joshua, also should have left clear signs in the archaeological record. But archaeologists find little correlation between biblical accounts and the evidence from Late Bronze Age Palestinian cities. Faced with these problems, most scholars reject all or part of the biblical narratives, crediting the errors to legendary distortion during a period of oral tradition or to theological reworking of disjointed early traditions.

But what if it is our scholarly historical and archaeological synchronisms and chronologies that are erroneous? Perhaps there *is* evidence of plagues and a miracle at the *Yam Suph* in Egyptian records, which has gone unrecognized. Or possibly the conventional archaeological chronology has led scholars to look for evidence for the Israelite conquest in the wrong places. Obviously, there are many believers in biblical inerrancy who would welcome such assertions; attempts to find evidence of the Exodus catastrophes or to redate Palestinian archaeological remains have often had large popular followings. So, before concluding that the biblical Exodus and Conquest stories are largely unhistorical, we need to critically review the leading alternative historical and archaeological synchronisms that have been suggested for the Exodus and Conquest period.

REDATING THE EXODUS AND CONQUEST

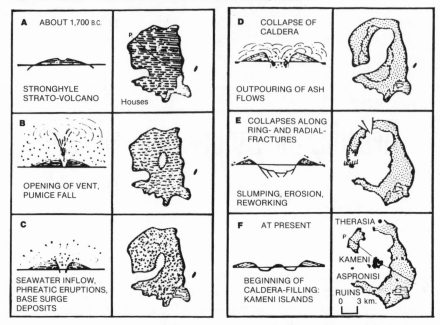

FIGURE 6: PHASES OF THE MINOAN ERUPTION OF THERA
(after Pichler and Friedrich 1980: 17)

The Volcanic Eruption of Thera and the Exodus Events

Can the biblical story of the plagues and the parting of the Red Sea be accounted for by the eruption of the volcanic island of Thera? Thera (also known as Santorini) is the southernmost island in the Greek Cyclades, lying about seventy miles north of Crete. The volcano seems to have exploded during the sixteenth century B.C., breaking it into three pieces that surround a large, deep bay (called a "caldera" by scientists), located where the center of the island had once been. This great explosion, and the subsequent collapse of large portions of the island into the sea, has often been suggested as the cause for the end of the ancient Minoan civilization on Crete and as the source of the Atlantis legend.[1] The explosion of Thera originally was thought to have occurred c. 1450 B.C., near the time the Bible gives for

---

1. For example, Marinatos 1939, 1972; Galanopoulos and Bacon 1969; Mavor 1969; Luce 1969, 1976; Platon 1971: 265-320; I. Wilson 1985: 86-114.

the Exodus. So, many have theorized that Thera's eruption can explain many of the "miracles" of the Exodus story.[2]

Excavation of a Minoan town on Thera that was buried by the eruption and scientific study of the geological evidence on the island have revealed the stages of Thera's destruction (see Figure 6). First there was a severe earthquake, which caused extensive damage in the local settlement and prompted an evacuation of the island by its population. When the tremors subsided, some of the inhabitants returned to Thera and tried to repair portions of the town. However, a vent in the volcano's ancient crater opened and the eruption began, forcing these people to flee once more. Large amounts of ash and pumice covered the island and buried the once-flourishing town (Figure 6, B). After a brief pause in activity, which lasted anywhere from a few months to two years, the volcano began erupting again. A fracture in the side of the volcano allowed sea water to pour in. "Base surges"— violent clouds of hot gases and ash that roll outward and downward from the crater at speeds of sixty miles an hour or more—redistributed the ash and pumice over the island (Figure 6, C). The influx of sea water precipitated extremely violent explosions. There was further fracturing of the vent area and a collapse of much of the central portion of Thera, which created a large bay (Figure 6, D). The crater continued to collapse, and as more of the volcano crumbled into the sea, the present-day islands of Thera, Therasia, and Aspronisi (portions of the flanks of the former volcanic cone) were left surrounding a water-filled caldera (Figure 6, E and F).[3]

The possible effects of the Bronze Age eruption of Thera have been surmised from the known effects of other eruptions, particularly those of Krakatoa (or Krakatau) in 1883 and Mount St. Helens in 1980. Krakatoa was a South Pacific volcanic island in the Sunda Strait between Java and Sumatra. As at Thera, for six or seven years before the eruption of Krakatoa there were severe earthquakes in the area. Then the eruption began. Large amounts of pumice and ash were ejected over a four-month period, climaxing in four tremendous explosions, explosions that were heard 2,000 miles away. Shock waves from the explosions damaged houses up to one hundred miles away, and a great cloud of vapor and fine ash brought darkness to much of Java and Sumatra. Two-thirds of the volcano collapsed into the sea, causing *tsunamis* (commonly known as "tidal waves") fifty to a hundred

---

2. For example, J. Bennett 1963; Galanopoulos and Bacon 1969: 193-199, Mavor 1969: 282-286; H. Goedicke's views described in Shanks 1981: 48 and Goedicke 1987; I. Wilson 1985: 112-141.

3. Luce 1969: 69-74; Pichler and Friedrich 1980.

feet high to race through the Straits. Thirty-six thousand people on nearby islands lost their lives.[4]

Mount St. Helens is located in the northwestern United States. After several minor earthquakes, internal explosions, and the appearance of steam vents, the volcano blew off much of its northern slope with the force of a ten- to fifty-megaton nuclear bomb. Seventy-two people died immediately, some as far as fourteen miles from the volcano. The explosion and collapse of Mount St. Helens occurred well inland, so there were no *tsunamis* associated with this eruption. But clouds of ash were carried some five hundred miles to the east. A pall of darkness spread over portions of the states of Washington, Idaho, Montana, and Wyoming. Up to 250 miles away from the volcano automobiles stopped running as their air filters became clogged with ash, and the process of photosynthesis was interrupted as the leaves of trees and plants became coated with dust.[5]

The Mount St. Helens eruption was not nearly as violent as that of Krakatoa. And, since Thera's caldera is four times larger than that of Krakatoa and more than thirty per cent deeper, it is often asserted that Thera's eruption must have been even more devastating. Perhaps, some have suggested, the eruption was violent enough to seriously affect life in Egypt, some 570 miles away.

Some of the plagues mentioned in the Exodus account *are* similar to features associated with major volcanic eruptions. Darkness in the middle of the day (Exodus 10:21-23) recalls the ash-cloud-induced darkness noted at Krakatoa, Mount St. Helens, and other eruptions.[6] Swarms of insects (Exodus 8:2-14, 16-18, 21-24; 10:13-15) were associated with eruptions of Mount Pelée on Martinique in the West Indies.[7] And lightning and severe hail, mentioned in the Bible (Exodus 9:23-26), can also be caused by volcanic activity, due to a build-up of static electricity in the ash clouds and to steam and ash being ejected high into the atmosphere.[8] The rain of pumice, cinders, and ash from a volcano might also be perceived as a hail storm.[9]

---

4. Luce 1969: 74-82; Vitaliano 1973: 184-187; I. Wilson 1985: 116-119.

5. I. Wilson 1985: 115-116.

6. J. Bennett 1963: 142-143; Rudman 1981: 15; I. Wilson 1985: 120-122

7. I. Wilson 1985: 123-126.

8. Galanopoulos and Bacon 1969: 198; Kemp 1988. When Vesuvius erupted in 79 A.D., heavy rains joined with vast amounts of steam from the eruption to produce hot mud-lava flows, which inundated the town of Herculaneum. Electrical storms also seem to have been a feature of this first-century catastrophe, as they were of another eruption of Vesuvius in 1779. Excavations at Pompeii and Herculaneum have uncovered evidence of a number of lightning strikes (Grant 1976: 31).

9. I. Wilson 1985: 121, 122.

Volcanic explanations have also been suggested for the turning of the Nile River "to blood" (Exodus 7:20-21), the death of Egyptian livestock (Exodus 9:6), and the plague of dust that caused boils and sores (Exodus 9:8-11). Indeed, red-brown discoloration of the water and the death of marine creatures due to underwater emissions *has* been noted in recent eruptions of Thera. It has been suggested that during the Bronze Age eruption this discoloration might have extended as far as Egypt or that pink Theran ash might have fallen heavily enough to make the water in Egypt turn red.[10] Livestock could have been smothered by heavy clouds of volcanic ash or died of starvation when most of the vegetation was destroyed. And volcanic ash has been known to produce skin irritation.[11] In fact, the Bible specifically credits the outbreak of boils and sores to "fine dust" spread over the entire land.

Even the death of the Egyptians' first-born sons (Exodus 12: 29-30) has been credited to Thera. An ancient people could easily have interpreted the series of catastrophes produced by the volcanic eruption as signs of their gods' anger. The scale of these disasters might have impelled these people to seek something more drastic than the usual animal sacrifices to propitiate the gods; nothing less than each family's first-born son would do.[12]

Finally, the "miracle at the Sea" has been seen as the result of a Theran *tsunami.* The Israelites followed "a pillar of cloud" by day and "a pillar of fire" by night (Exodus 13:21-22) out of Egypt. This, it is claimed, was Thera erupting over the horizon.[13] When they came to the edge of the *Yam Suph* Moses and his people found themselves trapped between this body of water and the Egyptian forces. But the sea parted, and the Israelites were able to cross over dry land. The Egyptian forces, though, were drowned by the returning sea, which stood "like a wall" (Exodus 14:21-29).

One account in the Book of Exodus (attributed to the Priestly author) gives four landmarks to indicate where the Israelites were camped when the Egyptians caught up with them—the *Yam Suph,* Baal-zephon, Pi-hahiroth, and Migdol. None of these places can be located with certainty today. Migdol is the Semitic word for "tower" or "fortress" and could refer to Sile (Tell Abu Seifeh), the Egyptian fortress guarding access to Egypt by way of the *Via Maris* (the road called "the Way to the land of the

---

10. Galanopoulos and Bacon 1969: 199; Rudman 1981: 15; I. Wilson 1985: 123.
11. Galanopoulos and Bacon 1969: 198; I. Wilson 1985: 121, 123.
12. I. Wilson 1985: 126-127.
13. I. Wilson 1985: 112-113.

Philistines" in Exodus 13:17). But several other forts were also located on the frontiers of the eastern delta, some of them having "Migdol" (or the Egyptian equivalent *hetem,* the Etham of Exodus 13:20) as part of their names.[14]

Baal-zephon was the name of a West Semitic god who had temples at a number of Egyptian cities in the eastern delta region, including Tahpanhes (Tell Defaneh on the ancient shoreline of Lake Menzaleh), Casium (Ras Qasrun or Mohammadiyeh on Lake Sirbonis), and Pelusium (Tell Farama on the Mediterranean coast).[15] If one of these places was the Baal-zephon of the Exodus story, it would point to Lake Menzaleh, Lake Sirbonis, or Lake Ballah (a few miles to the east of Tell Defaneh) as the *Yam Suph* (see Figure 7). On the other hand, the version of the Exodus usually credited to the combined Yahwist/Elohist source indicates that the Israelites took a route that led directly into Sinai (Exodus 13:17-18), and this tradition thus suggests that either one of the lakes north of the Gulf of Suez or the Gulf of Suez itself (the Red Sea) was the *Yam Suph.*[16]

Professor Hans Goedicke has argued that Tell Defaneh was Baal-zephon and that the Israelites had taken a position on Tell Hazzob just west of Lake Ballah (the *Yam Suph?*) to defend themselves from the approaching Egyptians. Before the expected battle took place, however, a flash flood (a *tsunami* from Thera's eruption) overwhelmed the Egyptian army. The Israelites, on the only high ground in the area, were saved.[17]

It is also possible that, if the Israelites followed the northern route out of Egypt and the *Yam Suph* was either Lake Menzaleh[18] or Lake Sirbonis[19] (see Figure 7), their crossing could have been aided by a recession of the Mediterranean due to the eruption of Thera. Then, when they tried to follow, the Egyptians were destroyed by the onrushing *tsunami.*[20]

The eruption of Thera cannot be dated exactly, but archaeological evidence from Akrotiri (the Minoan site on Thera) and from Crete indicates that Thera exploded near the end of the Late Minoan I A period. This

---

14. See the discussion and references in Finegan 1963: 84-87. See also de Vaux 1978: 378-379; Sarna 1986: 108.

15. Finegan 1963: 80-81; de Vaux 1978: 379-380; Aharoni 1979: 196; Sarna 1986: 109.

16. Finegan 1963: 83. For the division of the account about the miracle at the Sea between the J-E source and the P tradition, see Noth 1962: 102-120, Wright 1962b: 193-194, or Batto 1984: 62. These two different biblical versions of the Israelites' route out of Egypt and of the location of the *Yam Suph* that they crossed seem to be irreconcilable.

17. Shanks 1981: 44-48; I. Wilson 1985: 130-132.

18. For example, May 1962: 58-59.

19. For example, Aharoni and Avi-Yonah 1968: Map 48.

20. Galanopoulos and Bacon 1969: 193-197; Mavor 1969: 282-286; I. Wilson 1985: 132-133.

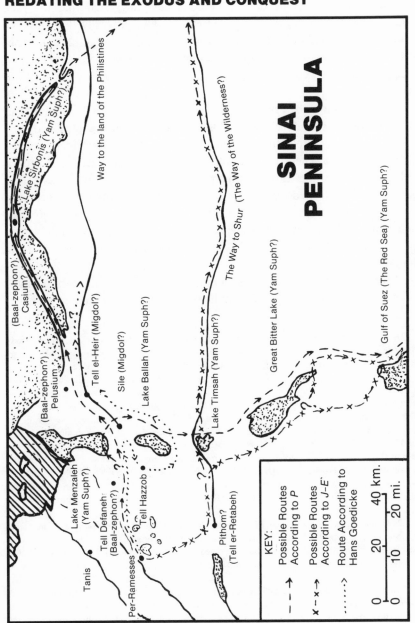

FIGURE 7: VARIOUS POSSIBLE EXODUS ROUTES

era is usually considered to have lasted from c. 1550 B.C. to c. 1500 B.C. However, recent scientific dating methods have suggested that the Late Minoan I A period began and ended earlier than generally thought. The eruption of Thera should be dated no *later* than c. 1525 B.C., and it probably took place about a century or so earlier than that date.[21] This new evidence makes it extremely difficult to connect that event with the Exodus.

Goedicke dates the eruption of Thera c. 1483 B.C.,[22] a little later than the formerly accepted date of c. 1500 B.C. But even if one accepts Goedicke's date (which is probably too late), in order for the Exodus to be related to the eruption of Thera the date of the Exodus would have to be moved back in time by some thirty to fifty years—one or two generations earlier than the date indicated by I Kings 6:1. The Exodus would have occurred during the joint reign of Thutmose III and Hatshepsut of the Egyptian Eighteenth Dynasty, with Hatshepsut (the dominant partner in this co-regency) filling the roles of both the pharaoh of the oppression and the pharaoh of the Exodus.

While providing explanations for most of the plagues and for the "miracle at the Sea," the Thera hypothesis still has all of the historical and archaeo-

---

21. See Stiebing 1984: 48-50 for evidence relating the eruption to the LM I A period. Study of acid levels in a deep ice core from Greenland has suggested that the eruption took place c. 1645 B.C. (Hammer, Clausen, Friedrich, and Tauber 1987), and frost-ring evidence in tree-ring sequences provide a date of c. 1628 B.C. for the eruption (La Marche and Hirschboeck 1984; Baillie and Munro 1988). Calibrated radiocarbon dates for short-lived samples (mostly grain) from Akrotiri on Thera yield a range of 1675-1525 B.C. (Hammer, Clausen, Friedrich and Tauber 1987: 517-518) or 1687-1575 B.C. (Betancourt and Michael 1987) at two standard deviations from the mean. This means that there is a 95 per cent chance that the date of the eruption falls within that 112- or 150-year range. The 1628 tree-ring date falls within the error limits of both of the other methods and may be correct. At present, it is hard to adjust the dates of LM I A enough to accommodate an eruption as early as 1645 or 1628 B.C. (see Warren 1987). It is clear, though, that the evidence now favors a seventeenth- or early-sixteenth-century date for Thera's explosion rather than the traditional date of c. 1500 B.C. (Betancourt and Weinstein 1976; Betancourt 1987; and Cadogan 1987).

22. Goedicke, as I've mentioned, synchronizes the Exodus and Thera eruption with the events described in Hatshepsut's Speos Artemidos inscription. He originally placed these events in Hatshepsut's thirteenth regnal year, which he dated to 1477 B.C. (Shanks 1981: 50). (Note that the Egyptian chronology, which we used in Table 2, would place Hatshepsut's thirteenth regnal year in 1492 B.C., since she dated her regnal years from the accession of Thutmose III rather than from the date when she actually became his coregent.) Recently, however, Goedicke has argued that a text found at el-Arish near Gaza mentions a catastrophe that occurred when Hatshepsut became the coregent of Thutmose III, and he now dates her assumption of power and the events of the Exodus supposedly described in the Speos Artemidos inscription to 1483 B.C., the seventh year of Thutmose III (Goedicke 1987: 19). The seventh year of Thutmose III would be 1498 B.C. according to the chronology of Wente and Van Siclen, which we have followed in this study.

logical problems of other Eighteenth Dynasty dates for the Exodus. Exodus 1:11 must be declared unhistorical, for there was no Pithom or Ra'amses for the Israelites to build during the reign of Hatshepsut.[23] One would still face the problem of having the Conquest and the period of the "judges" occur at the time of maximum Egyptian control over Palestine, when there are no references to Egyptian campaigns, governors, or garrisons in the Books of Joshua and Judges. And still there would be the archaeological problems—no Late Bronze I or II A settlement at Kadesh-Barnea, at other sites in the Negeb, or in much of Transjordan, and the lack of Late Bronze I or II A destructions at most of the sites mentioned in the Conquest accounts.

In addition, evidence from Crete and eastern Mediterranean sea cores show that it is extremely unlikely that Thera's eruption could have affected Egypt the way this theory says it did. A series of cores taken from the Mediterranean sea bottom shows that the ash-fall from Thera did extend in an east-southeast direction, *toward* Egypt (see Figure 8). Very little ash, however, actually made it that far; amounts approached zero at a distance of more than one hundred miles from the Egyptian delta. Some high atmospheric ash-clouds might have produced a darkening of the skies in Egypt and surrounding areas, but the amount of ash that would have fallen on Egypt was certainly too small to have caused the death of livestock, to have turned the Nile red, or to have been responsible for widespread destruction of crops. Only an average of one half to two and a half inches of ash fell on eastern Crete, which is much closer to Thera than Egypt is. And this ash-fall does *not* seem to have had the disastrous effects in Crete that are hypothesized for Egypt,[24] so it is highly unlikely that ash from the eruption produced *any* damage in Egypt. And it is even more improbable that a heavy rain of cinders and stones ("hail") pelted the Egyptian delta, almost six hundred miles from Thera.

Other features of volcanic eruptions—like insect infestations, lightning, change in sea color, and the death of fish—occur only in the immediate vicinity of the volcano, not hundreds of miles away. Indeed, if the Thera

---

23. Goedicke disputes the connection of biblical Ra'amses (which he transliterates as Ra'amezez) with Per-Ramesses, the capital city of Ramesses II. But he still locates the biblical store-city at Tell ed-Dab'a. He also accepts Tell er-Retabeh as Pithom (Shanks 1981: 43-44). But there is no evidence that either site was occupied at the time of Hatshepsut.

24. Vitaliano 1973: 190-191, 203-204; 1978: 151-153; Blong 1980; McCoy 1980; Doumas 1983: 148-149; Stiebing 1984: 45. Daniel J. Stanley of the Smithsonian Institution has found traces of Theran ash in Nile Delta sediments (Stanley and Sheng 1986), but the amounts are too small to indicate a major ashfall on Egypt.

REDATING THE EXODUS AND CONQUEST

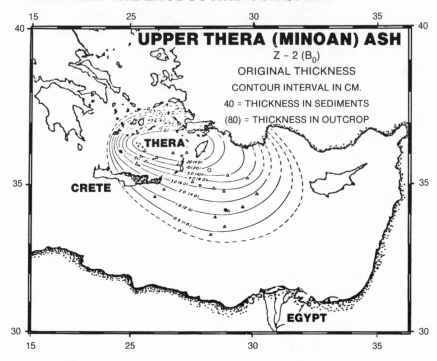

FIGURE 8: THE THERAN ASHFALL PATTERN AND ITS THICKNESS
(after McCoy 1980: 66)

eruption had caused the water around the island to turn red and marine life to die, even on a gigantic scale, only the Mediterranean would have been affected, not the Nile.

It is also unlikely, despite claims to the contrary, that the eruption of Thera would have been visible from the Nile Delta. Some have argued that, if Thera's column of ash, smoke, and vapor rose more than thirty miles, it could have been seen from Egypt.[25] Light intensity, however, is diminished over distance by scattering due to gas molecules. At a distance of some 570 miles, the visibility of Thera's ash column would have been only 7.3 per cent of its original intensity. Atmospheric dust would have reduced this visibility still more, so Thera's cloud would have been virtually *invisible* from Egypt, no matter how high it rose.[26] Furthermore, the flames

---

25. Rudman 1981: 16; I. Wilson 1985: 112-113.

26. This information was derived from a personal communication I have had from Leroy Ellenberger. He cited Weisskopf 1986 to support his calculations.

from the volcano (or the reflections of the flames on the ash cloud) would not have risen as high as thirty miles; they could not have been seen in the Nile Delta at night.[27] So the identification of the "pillar of cloud" and "pillar of fire" with the erupting Thera is difficult to sustain.

For the sake of argument, let's grant the possibility that the Israelites indeed saw a tiny cloud of smoke on the distant horizon. Much still needs explaining, because the Israelites headed in an easterly direction out of Egypt (different theories have Moses leading the Israelites along routes varying from a northeasterly to a southeasterly direction). But Thera lies *northwest* of the Egyptian delta. If the Israelites had headed toward the Theran "pillar of cloud" they would have marched directly into the Mediterranean Sea!

The main connection between the Theran eruption and the Exodus, however, is the "miracle at the Sea" supposedly caused by Thera's *tsunami.* Estimates of the size of this "wall of water" and the length of time it took to reach Egypt are partially based on pumice found at a height of one hundred and fifty feet above sea level at Anaphi, a small island near Thera, and fifteen feet above sea level just north of Tel Aviv.[28] But recent study has determined that the pumice at Anaphi was not put there by the Theran eruption, and that the height of the *tsunami* on the north coast of Crete, only seventy miles away from Thera, was only about twenty to thirty feet.[29] The central portions of Thera seem to have collapsed into the sea gradually, producing many small *tsunamis* rather than one gigantic one.[30] It is unlikely that these waves had any destructive effects by the time they reached Tell Hazzob or other sites in the Egyptian delta.

Even small waves, though, might have destroyed a group of people moving along the narrow sand spit north of Lake Sirbonis. But this route for the Exodus, though favored by some scholars, is unlikely. To get to this sand spit, the Israelites would have had to pass a number of strong Egyptian forts guarding the western end of the primary road to Canaan, the *Via Maris,* which the Bible calls the "Way to the Land of the Philistines." They would have been heading into what they must have known was the strength of the Egyptian defenses in the area. It is difficult to believe that the Israelites would have followed Moses in this direction even if he told them God had ordered it! In fact, Exodus 13:17-18 states that God did

---

27. Ellenberger 1982 contra Rudman 1981: 16. For other problems with pillar of cloud/ fire = Thera, see Oren 1981: 52.

28. Doumas 1983: 147; I. Wilson 1985: 134.

29. Pichler 1980: 324; Doumas 1983: 147-148.

30. Pichler 1980; Doumas 1983: 144.

not lead Israel out of Egypt by the "Way to the Land of the Philistines" precisely because the people might change their minds and return to Egypt when faced with the prospect of fighting their way past the strong Egyptian forts guarding this road.

Moreover, if the Israelites *had* taken this route and somehow managed to get past the Egyptian forts and to the western end of Lake Sirbonis, the main force of the Egyptians probably would not have followed them onto the sand spit north of the lake. A small detachment might have been sent along behind the fleeing Israelites, but most of the troops would have proceeded over the "Way to the Land of the Philistines" along the south shore of Lake Sirbonis. This is a shorter route, which would have enabled the pursuing Egyptians to intercept Moses and the Israelites as they tried to leave the sand spit at its eastern end. Even if a small *tsunami* would have overwhelmed the minor detachment of Egyptians on the sand spit, the major portion of the pursuing force would have escaped harm and would still have been able to attack the Israelites at the eastern end of the lake. The theory of an exodus along the sand spit north of Lake Sirbonis is untenable, yet this is the only route that could have been affected by small *tsunamis* from the eruption of Thera.

Professor Goedicke's reconstruction of events is based on a simple reading of the Exodus story as it now stands in the Book of Exodus, without any attempt to apply the methods of source and literary criticism customarily used by biblical scholars and ancient historians. He does not, for example, discuss what seems to be a contradiction between Exodus 13:17-18 and Exodus 14:1-2 regarding the route of the fleeing Israelites (see above, pp. 105-106), verses that many leading biblical scholars have attributed to two different sources (J-E on the one hand and P on the other). Nor does he deal with any of the other differences scholars have noted in the Exodus narratives. He does not *reject* previous source criticism of Exodus, he just *ignores* it.

Goedicke also dismisses without counterargument the possibility that the biblical story might have been theologically symbolic rather than historical. In a number of other biblical passages, the *Yam Suph* can certainly be identified as the Red Sea or one of its two extensions, the Gulf of Suez and the Gulf of Aqabah (Numbers 21:4, 33:10-11; I Kings 9:26; Jeremiah 49:21). But the *Yam Suph* might also have had a mythological connotation. Some scholars have claimed that it was regarded as the "Sea at the End of the World" or the "Sea of Extinction," equated with the waters of chaos that God overcame when He established order and created the world.[31] In short, the "miracle at the Sea" may not have been an objective historical event at all. The tradition of the Crossing of the Sea might have been a symbolic story that saw in the Exodus God's defeat of the powers of chaos and evil and His creation of His people, Israel. The early authors expressed this theological idea in terms of Canaanite creation myths, describing God as defeating the watery chaos in order to bring His people into existence as a nation (see, for example, Psalm 77:15-21 and Isaiah 51:9-10).[32] If this interpretation is correct, none of the real bodies of water on Figure 7 represents the *Yam Suph* the Israelites crossed in leaving Egypt, and the crossing cannot be connected to a Theran *tsunami* or any other observable occurrence.

In sum, the eruption of Thera seems to have taken place during the late seventeenth or early sixteenth century B.C.—a bit too early to allow any connections with the Israelite exodus. It is also now evident that the eruption of Thera did not destroy the Minoan civilization on Crete, as had been thought earlier. Clearly its effects were not as great as had been hypothesized.[33] So the likelihood that this eruption also had dire consequences in Egypt is exceedingly small. Except for changes in the appearance of sunsets or slight changes in weather caused by high ash and dust, the eruption probably went unnoticed in Egypt. There is no way that the Exodus can be securely related to this volcanic explosion or securely dated to c. 1483 B.C.

The Exodus and Cosmic Cataclysms

The eruption of Thera is not the only natural catastrophe that has been used to explain the Exodus events. In 1940 a psychoanalyst named Immanuel Velikovsky became convinced that a catastrophic natural event must have occurred at the time of the Israelite exodus from Egypt. His subsequent search through the texts, legends, myths, epics, and folklore of many peoples

---

31. See Snaith 1965 and Batto 1983, 1984, where the derivation of Hebrew *sûph* from Egyptian *twf(y)* (pronounced *thoof*), "papyrus (reeds)," is challenged. Snaith and Batto derive the *sûph* in *Yam Sûph* from Hebrew *sôph*, "end; extinction."

32. Batto 1983: 30-35; 1984: 60-62. See also Cross 1973: 135-144, where the mythological allusions in the Song of the Sea (Exodus 15:1b-18), Psalm 77, Isaiah 51, and other biblical references to the Exodus are noted. Cross believes that these mythological interpretations were grafted onto an original historical event that took place when Israel crossed the "Reed Sea" (1973: 143-144).

33. See Doumas 1983: 140-147 and Stiebing 1984: 44-51.

led him to identify the cause of the disaster as a comet that passed extremely close to the earth. His discovery of what he thought was an Egyptian reference to the Exodus catastrophes led him to radically revise the accepted synchronisms between Israelite and Egyptian history.[34]

Using the Bible, myths, and legends as his primary sources, Velikovsky argued that about 1450 B.C. a comet that had been ejected from the planet Jupiter came very near the Earth. As the Earth passed through the comet's tail, a rain of red meteorite dust made rivers, lakes, and seas appear to turn to blood. Fiery meteorites and ash fell from the skies like hail. Petroleum rained down also, causing fires to rage all over the world. The dust from the comet's tail produced a pall of darkness over the earth that lasted for days. Earthquakes and hurricane-force winds rocked the globe, producing *tsunamis* that destroyed many areas and uncovered some former seabeds (like the Red Sea's) for a time. The Earth's rotation was slowed and the heat thus produced melted rocks, boiled seas, and caused a furious propagation of frogs, flies, and other vermin. When the Earth emerged from the comet's tail, people saw the comet standing like a pillar of cloud during the day and a pillar of fire at night. In clouds above the Earth, reactions between carbon and hydrogen from the tail of the comet produced carbohydrates that fell to Earth and were considered "heavenly food"— manna and ambrosia.[35]

Fifty-two years later, the comet returned. On this occasion, while Joshua was fighting a battle near Gibeon, the comet's close passage caused the Earth to gradually slow its rotation to a complete stop for a time. This comet eventually collided with Mars and sent Mars into several near collisions with the Earth during the eighth and early seventh centuries B.C. At the time of the last of these near-misses (687 B.C.) the Assyrian army of Sennacherib, which was besieging Jerusalem, was destroyed. After colliding with Mars the comet's elliptical orbit became nearly circular; it is now, according to Velikovsky's theory, the planet Venus. Following their series of encounters with one another, Mars and Earth settled into their present-day orbits.[36]

An Egyptian text called the "Admonitions of Ipuwer" seemed to Velikovsky to describe the same comet-caused catastrophes recounted in the biblical story of the Exodus. The text states that grain had been destroyed, cattle abandoned in the fields, wailing pervaded the land, death was every-

---

34. See Velikovsky 1950 and 1952.
35. Velikovsky 1950: 39-104, 126-138, 172-175, 183-187.
36. Velikovsky 1950: 39-46, 202-203, 207-359.

where, and the river had become like blood.[37] However, this document was dated by Egyptologists to the beginning or the end of the Middle Kingdom, long *before* the Israelite exodus. Puzzled, Velikovsky decided that there was something radically wrong with the chronology of Egypt— Egyptian dates were about five or six hundred years older than they should be. So he synchronized the "Admonitions of Ipuwer" and the beginning of the Hyksos Period in Egypt with the Exodus, c. 1450 B.C., and worked forward from that point. The Hyksos Period was contemporaneous with the period of the "judges," he argued, and the Egyptian Eighteenth Dynasty was in power during the Israelite United and Divided Monarchies (see Table 4).[38]

Scientists, especially astronomers, have pointed out numerous problems with Velikovsky's scenario of cosmic collisions or near-collisions between Venus, Mars, and Earth.[39] Venus has a density close to that of the Earth, but Jupiter's density is much lower, which makes it unlikely that Venus originated from Jupiter.[40] The nearly circular orbits of Mars' two small moons and the fact that these satellites were not lost to the larger Earth or Venus argue against any close contacts between Mars and either Earth or Venus.[41] Scientific measurement of coral growth in tropical waters shows that there were no major catastrophes that caused the seas to boil (thus killing coral polyps and numerous other marine creatures) during recent millennia.[42] Such scientific evidence indicates that, while imaginative, Velikovsky's theory is simply preposterous.

In recent years a revised, more scientifically acceptable version of Velikovsky's cosmic catastrophism has been championed by S. V. M. Clube, an astrophysicist at Oxford University, and William M. Napier, an astronomer at the Royal Observatory in Edinburgh. Clube and Napier contend that there are giant comets that are qualitatively different from smaller, more ordinary comets. Through fragmentation these giant comets can produce meteor streams and asteroid belts whose asteroids probably encountered

---

37. Velikovsky 1952: 12-47. For a translation of the "Admonitions of Ipuwer," see J. Wilson 1955: 441-444. Egyptologists and other specialists in ancient history generally see this text as a reference to social and political upheaval and change, not to physical cataclysms.

38. Velikovsky 1952: 50-340.

39. Goldsmith 1977; Stiebing 1984: 59-69.

40. Morrison 1977: 154-155; Sagan 1977: 73-78. The atmospheres of Jupiter and Venus are also quite different (Owen 1982: Tables II and IVb).

41. Mulholland 1977: 111. It should also be noted that surface features of Venus indicate that it was not molten only a few millennia ago (Pettengill, Campbell, and Masursky 1980).

42. Stiebing 1984: 67. Study of coral growth rings also indicates that there hasn't been a change in the length of the year in recent millennia, as Velikovsky claimed (Sagan 1977: 53).

TABLE 4: Conventional Chronology Compared with Velikovsky's Revisions

DATE	CONVENTIONAL SYNCHRONISMS		ISRAELITE HISTORY	VELIKOVSKY'S SYNCHRONISMS		DATE
	OTHER AREAS	EGYPT		EGYPT	OTHER AREAS	
1500	KASSITE PERIOD IN BABYLON	DYNASTY XVIII Hatshepsut Thutmose III		MIDDLE KINGDOM		1500
1450			THE EXODUS (?) (I Kings 6:1)			1450
1400	Kadashman-Enlil Burnaburiash (II)	Amenhotep III Akhenaton				1400
1350						1350
1300	HITTITE EMPIRE MYCENAEAN PERIOD IN GREECE	DYNASTY XIX Ramesses II				1300
1250			THE EXODUS (?)	HYKSOS RULE		1250
1200	DESTRUCTION OF MYCEAN SITES AND HITTITE EMPIRE	DYNASTY XX Ramesses III defeats Sea Peoples				1200
1150			PERIOD OF THE JUDGES			1150
1100	DARK AGE IN GREECE	DYNASTY XXI				1100
1050			UNITED KINGDOM Saul	DYNASTY XVIII BEGINS		1050
1000		DYNASTY XXII	David			1000
0950		DYNASTY XXII (LIBYAN RULE) Shoshenk I (Shishak)	Solomon	Hatshepsut		0950
0900	ASSYRIAN EMPIRE Shalmaneser III		DIVIDED KINGDOM	Thutmose III (= Shishak)		0900
0850			Ahab of Israel & Jehoshaphat of Judah	Amenhotep III Akhenaton	Shalmaneser III (= Burnaburiash)	0850
0800		DYNASTY XXIII		LIBYAN DYNASTIES (XXII-XXIV)		0800
0750			Fall of Samaria Hezekiah of Judah			0750
0700	Shalmaneser V Sargon II Sennacherib	DYNASTIES XXIV-XXV DYNASTY XXVI (SAITE PERIOD) Necho II		ETHIOPIAN DYNASTY (XXV) DYNASTY XIX (=DYNASTY XXVI)	MYCENAEAN SITES DESTROYED	0700
0650	Esarhaddon Asshurbanipal					0650
0600	NEO-BABYLONIAN EMP. Nebuchadnezzar		Josiah Fall of Jerusalem THE EXILE	Ramesses II (=Necho II)	Nebuchadnezzar (=Hattusilis III)	0600
0550						0550

the Earth a number of times in the past, extinguishing many species and inducing ice-ages. They also argue that the most recent of these giant comets fragmented repeatedly between c. 3000 and 500 B.C., leaving the Taurid-Arietid meteor stream and Comet Encke as its by-products. The asteroids produced by the breakup of this comet periodically rained down upon the Earth—destroying cities, causing floods, forcing migrations, and producing dark ages. And, they claim, two especially severe episodes of fragmentation and their associated catastrophes took place around 3000 B.C. and 1300 B.C.[43]

Similar theories about asteroid collisions with Earth have been used to explain the extinction of the dinosaurs and other species in past geological ages.[44] Undoubtedly, large asteroids *have* struck the Earth, with disastrous results, many times during the four-and-a-half billion years of the Earth's history. But in their popular book on their theory, Clube and Napier, like Velikovsky, see a giant comet as the cause of the Exodus "miracles" and other major catastrophes during relatively recent *historical* times.[45] Like Velikovsky they see cometary phenomena and comet-caused cataclysms reflected in many ancient myths and legends.[46] And, like Velikovsky, they find it necessary to revise ancient Egyptian chronology and the synchronisms between Egyptian history and biblical events. According to their revised chronology, the catastrophic events associated with the Exodus occurred in 1369 B.C.[47]

Were there cometary disasters in the fifteenth, eighth, and seventh centuries B.C., as Velikovsky claims, or throughout the period from c. 3000 to 500 B.C., as Clube and Napier contend? Should the Exodus events be understood in terms of worldwide catastrophes caused by a huge comet? Are there an extra four to six hundred years in Egyptian chronology, and should the correlations between Egyptian rulers and biblical characters be radically revised? Evidence suggests not.

The methodology by which Velikovsky, Clube, and Napier find descriptions of cometary disasters in ancient myths and legends is questionable at best. Their interpretations are highly subjective, paying little attention to modern studies of myth and the myth-making mentality.[48] Moreover,

---

43. Clube and Napier 1982: 131-156; Clube 1985: 13-17; Clube and Napier 1986; Bailey, Clube, and Napier 1986: 37-42.

44. Alvarez, *et al.*, 1980 and 1984.

45. Clube and Napier 1982: 209-223, 253-272.

46. Clube and Napier 1982: 157-209.

47. Clube and Napier 1982: 224-253.

48. See Stiebing 1984: 62-66. The arguments presented there apply specifically to Velikovsky's treatment of ancient myths, but these critical comments could be directed against Clube and Napier as well, since their use of myth is so similar to Velikovsky's.

if worldwide cosmic cataclysms took place in antiquity, why have they left their mark *only* in vague myths and legends?[49] The theories of Velikovsky and of Clube and Napier would lead one to expect numerous clear references in ancient literature to catastrophe-causing comets and deadly showers of asteroids, especially in the early Mesopotamian and Chinese omen or oracle texts. Such references aren't there. And ancient astronomical and astrological texts give no indication that the early civilizations were aware of tremendous disasters produced by comets.

The Sumerians (who between 3500 and 3000 B.C. created the earliest civilization presently known) seem to have had little interest in astronomy. All they have left us is a list of about twenty-five stars.[50] The earliest real evidence we have for Mesopotamian astronomy comes from the Old Babylonian Period (c. 1800-1600 B.C.). Texts from this era include the famous observations of the appearances and disappearances of Venus made during the reign of Ammisaduqa and tablets grouping constellations, stars, and planets into three zones of the sky, each zone containing twelve sectors. From the Kassite and Assyrian Periods (c. 1600-612 B.C.) we have a collection of omen texts known as *Enuma Anu Enlil,* a number of "astrolabes" listing stars in their sectors, and the star and planet catalogue known as [mul]APIN. During the Neo-Babylonian and Persian Periods (612-331 B.C.), mathematical astronomy was developed alongside zodiacal and horoscopic astrology,[51] which provided the basis for the eventual development of Hellenistic Greek astronomy. The gradual growth of Mesopotamian astronomy and astrology over some two thousand years seems to owe nothing to terror produced by rampaging planets, gigantic comets, or asteroid bombardments.

The Egyptians may have been observing the rising of the star Sirius as early as 3000 B.C., for a First Dynasty tomb contained a plaque describing Sirius as "herald of the new year and of the flood."[52] It is not known when the Egyptians first recognized the relationship between the first visibility of Sirius in the morning sky and the beginning of the Nile flood. But, for most of their history, they do not seem to have used their observations of the heavens for much except calendrical functions and determining cardinal points of the compass for orienting buildings. The skies were generally not the source of fearful portents for the Egyptians. Indeed, there are no

---

49. Egyptians, Mesopotamians, Chinese, Hittites, and other peoples were recording historical events during the times the catastrophes were supposedly occurring.

50. Kramer 1963: 90-91.

51. Neugebauer 1957: 99-144; Van der Waerden 1974: 46-126.

52. Van der Waerden 1974: 8.

signs that Egyptians accepted astrology (and the careful astronomical observations it implies) before the Hellenistic Period when they, like the Greeks, came under the influence of Mesopotamian astronomy.[53]

The Chinese also produced early astronomical records, but little survives from the era before the fourteenth and thirteenth centuries B.C. The oldest record of a nova is found on a Chinese oracle bone from c. 1300 B.C.; stars, constellations, and lunar phenomena are also mentioned in these early texts.[54] One inscription, dated 1211 B.C., states that "the summer solstice recurs at 548 days after the winter solstice," indicating that regular and long-continuing observations were certainly being carried out by the thirteenth century B.C.[55] However, the earliest systematic Chinese records of comets and meteor showers date only from the seventh century B.C.,[56] which seems to indicate that the early Chinese did not become interested in heavenly bodies because giant comets brought great disasters.

Early Mesopotamian and Chinese astronomy developed in large measure because these cultures believed in omens and oracles. They kept records of both good and bad experiences along with notations about contemporaneous natural phenomena. It was thought that when the phenomena recurred, the results would be the same, thus allowing humans to react more quickly to the will of the gods. So, if comets and "shooting stars" were regularly associated with disasters on Earth, we would expect that fact to be noted in these texts. But in Mesopotamian omen texts the behavior of insects and animals and the appearance of clouds and other common meteorological phenomena are viewed as portents more often than are astronomical phenomena.[57] Astronomical phenomena that *are* mentioned are generally quite ordinary: comets are conspicuous only by how infrequently they are mentioned. The earliest Chinese oracle texts likewise display no special interest in comets or meteors. Even when Chinese astronomers and annalists started recording these phenomena on a regular basis, their objective descriptions gave no indication that past experience had led them to expect that the appearance of comets or "shooting stars" portend widespread catastrophes, chaos,

---

53. Neugebauer 1957: 80-91.

54. Needham 1959: 242-245, 424; Lo 1987: 283.

55. Needham 1959: 293.

56. Needham 1959: 430-434. Meteor showers and other important astronomical phenomena were mentioned at earlier dates in the Chinese *Annals* and on oracle bones, but astronomical texts devoted entirely to these phenomena did not appear before the seventh century B.C.

57. Oppenheim 1964: 217-221; Van der Waerden 1974: 59; Leichty 1975; Reiner and Pingree 1975; Culver and Ianna 1984: 15-18.

or an end to civilization.[58]

Not only does the ancient textual evidence provide little support for theories of historical cosmic disasters, but archaeological evidence also argues against such views. If Mesopotamian, biblical, and other flood myths derive from a cosmic catastrophe that occurred in ancient historical times, there must have been simultaneous flooding of extensive Near Eastern areas. But evidence of such floods is not found in the archaeological record.

When Leonard Woolley uncovered a thick flood deposit during his excavations at Ur in southern Mesopotamia in the 1920s, scholars thought they had found evidence of a great flood that had covered most of the Tigris-Euphrates Valley in ancient times. Soon afterward, flood deposits were discovered at other Mesopotamian sites and a pan-Mesopotamian flood seemed to be proved. Clube and Napier claim this great flood as evidence of the catastrophes caused by the breakup of a giant comet between 3000 and 2500 B.C.[59]

As long ago as the early 1940s, however, archaeologists came to recognize that the various prehistoric flood deposits of Mesopotamia belonged to different ages, most of them earlier than 3000 B.C. And some Mesopotamian sites, including al-'Ubaid, near Ur, exhibited no flood deposits at all.[60] The flood layers that were found at various sites were the residue of several local floods—there was no single prehistoric flood that covered most of Mesopotamia. There is also no evidence of a great flood at other Near Eastern sites occupied this early (Jericho, for example); no evidence to support the idea that a single great flood gave rise to biblical, Mesopotamian, and other early flood stories;[61] and no evidence for widespread flooding

---

58. Lo 1987: 286-287. See also, for example, Needham 1959: 433-434. Velikovsky dealt with the failure of the ancients to clearly mention cometary catastrophes by positing a "collective amnesia" through which mankind, unable to bear the horrible memories of what had happened, recorded these events only in myths and legends (1950: 298-300). Clube and Napier resort to a similar approach to explain the paucity of ancient references to comets: "This cannot be because they did not exist, so it must be because they were generally described as something else" (1982: 163). Obviously, the logic of Clube and Napier is deficient—their conclusion is *not* the only one that can be drawn from the scarcity of ancient references to comets! These speculations—"collective amnesia," describing comets as "something else"—are lame excuses for the lack of records of disastrous comets and asteroid showers among peoples who believed in omens and kept records of other natural phenomena that might presage disaster. These theories also do not explain the failure of the Mesopotamians or Chinese to record the supposed cosmic cataclysms in their annals and historical records, which were usually written on a yearly basis and which are fairly well preserved for the period from the ninth through the first centuries B.C.

59. Clube and Napier 1972: 209-210.

60. Bright 1942.

61. Stiebing 1984: 9-22.

around 1450 B.C. (Velikovsky's date for the catastrophes associated with the Exodus) or 1369 B.C. (Clube and Napier's date for the Exodus disasters).

Some of the most important evidence Velikovsky, Clube, and Napier used to support their hypotheses depends upon their revised chronology for ancient Egyptian civilization. Revisions are particularly necessary in order to make the "Admonitions of Ipuwer" contemporaneous with the Exodus (and thus a record of the same catastrophe). These chronological revisions have been rejected—with good reason—by virtually all qualified Egyptologists and Near Eastern archaeologists.

One major problem is the failure of Egyptian and other Near Eastern textual sources to match up when Egyptian dates are lowered by four to six hundred years and biblical and Mesopotamian dates remain unchanged. According to the proposed revisions, the Amarna Period (customarily dated to the mid-fourteenth century B.C.) belongs to the mid-ninth century B.C. For this chronological revision to be acceptable, conditions described in the famous Amarna Letters must "fit" into the history of the mid-ninth century B.C. as known from the Bible and Assyrian texts. Despite Velikovsky's efforts to make them fit,[62] the names of Near Eastern rulers in the Amarna Letters do not match those of ninth-century rulers mentioned in other Near Eastern texts (see Table 5).[63] Occasionally, ancient rulers were known by more than one name, but it is difficult to believe that *every* king mentioned in the Amarna Letters was referred to by a name different from the one used in ninth-century B.C. Mesopotamian and biblical sources.[64] The fact is, not one royal name in the Amarna Letters is mentioned in biblical or Assyrian accounts of the mid-ninth century.

Archaeological stratigraphy also contradicts the revised chronologies of Velikovsky, Clube, and Napier. Clube and Napier, like Velikovsky, did not attempt to revise the chronology of the Israelite monarchy, which is tied to the detailed chronology of Mesopotamia. In Palestinian archaeological terminology, the period of the Hebrew monarchies, the Assyrian Empire, and the subsequent Neo-Babylonian Empire is the Iron Age (see Table 1 in Chapter 1, above). Velikovsky, Clube, and Napier did not challenge this correlation. According to their revised chronology for Egypt, the Iron Age is also the era of the Egyptian Eighteenth and Nineteenth Dynasties. But stratified archaeological deposits in Syria-Palestine indicate that the Egyptian pharaohs of the Eighteenth and Nineteenth Dynasties lived during

---

62. Velikovsky 1952: 223-340.
63. Stiebing 1984: 72-75.
64. Storck 1986: 81-84.

TABLE 5

Near Eastern Rulers in the Amarna Letters and Ninth Century Texts

Rulers in the Amarna Letters	Place			Rulers in the Mid-Ninth Century B.C.
Abdu-Hepa	Jerusalem	}		
Milkilu, then Ba'ilu-shipli	Gezer	} Judah	Jehoshaphat
Zimreda	Lachish	}		
Lab'ayu	Shechem	}		
Biridia	Megiddo	} Israel	Ahab
Abdu-Tirshi	Hazor	}		
Rib-Addi	Byblos			
Zimreda	Sidon			Ethbaal
Abdi-Ashirta, then Azaru	Syria			Ben-Hadad (I), then Hazael
Asshur-uballit	Assyria			Shalmaneser III
Kadashman-Enlil, then Burnaburiash	Babylon			Nabu-apal-iddin, then Marduk-zakir-shumi

the Palestinian Late Bronze Age, not the Iron Age! Scarabs and other inscribed objects bearing the names of Thutmose III, Amenhotep III, Ramesses II, Merneptah, and other Egyptian New Kingdom rulers have been found with Late Bronze Age artifacts buried beneath Iron Age material at a number of Palestinian archaeological sites.[65] This stratified physical evidence will not allow one to move Egyptian chronology forward by four hundred years or more while keeping Israelite and Mesopotamian chronology unchanged.[66]

Prehistoric Greek chronology is also linked to Egypt by archaeological deposits. Large numbers of Mycenaean pottery vessels were uncovered at Tell el-Amarna, site of the Egyptian capital during the reign of Eighteenth Dynasty pharaoh Akhenaton. Mycenaean pottery is often found in Late

---

65. Stiebing 1973; 1984: 75-76; 1985: 64.

66. Velikovsky does not seem to have understood archaeological methodology, so he never fully appreciated the force of this argument. See the exchange in *Pensée:* Stiebing 1973; Velikovsky 1973b; Stiebing 1974; Velikovsky 1974.

Bronze Age deposits in Syria-Palestine as well. Such pottery is *not* found in Iron Age II layers, as it should be if Akhenaton ruled in the mid-ninth century as the revised chronologies indicate. Instead, Greek proto-Geometric and Geometric pottery is found in Palestinian and Syrian Iron Age strata. These pottery styles belong to the period *after* the Mycenaean Age in Greece. It is clear that the Greek Mycenaean Age, the Palestinian Late Bronze Age, and the Egyptian Eighteenth and Nineteenth Dynasties were all contemporaneous, while the Greek Dark Age (the era of the Geometric pottery) corresponds to the Palestinian Iron Age.

Such archaeological evidence makes it impossible for Hatshepsut to be a contemporary of Solomon, or Akhenaton a contemporary of Jehoshaphat, or Judah and Ahab of Israel, as Velikovsky, Clube, and Napier have argued. And, without their chronological revisions, there is little textual support for a fourteenth or fifteenth century B.C. cosmic cataclysm associated with the Exodus. Comet-caused catastrophes provide no better historical context for the Exodus than do the supposed disasters associated with the eruption of Thera.

Did the Exodus Occur During the Early Bronze Age?

Even if the Exodus could be correlated with the eruption of Thera or catastrophes caused by a giant comet, most of the problems that archaeological evidence has presented to the biblical account would remain. Regardless of whether the Exodus is dated to 1500, 1450, or 1369 B.C., archaeologically it would still be placed within the Late Bronze Age. And Chapter 3 has pointed out the many problems associated with the idea of a Late Bronze Age Exodus and Conquest. Because of these problems, some scholars have searched through the archaeological eras to find a period where the evidence *does* fit the biblical data. Some of them have also modified the dates of the archaeological periods to accommodate their placement of the Exodus and have produced new correlations between biblical accounts and the archaeological evidence.

The most radical of these theories places the Exodus at the end of the Early Bronze Age. The latter part of the Early Bronze Age was an era of widespread urbanization in Palestine: Large walled cities, often much larger than those of later times, flourished throughout the land, including the Negeb and Transjordan.[67] But almost every one of these cities was

---

67. Aharoni 1978: 57-80; Richard 1987: 27-34.

destroyed at the end of the Early Bronze Age III (EB III), and a nonurban pastoral society succeeded them. Unfortunately, Palestinian archaeologists have been unable to agree on a name for this post-Early Bronze III era. Early Bronze IV, Middle Bronze I, Intermediate Early Bronze/Middle Bronze, Intermediate Bronze, Middle Canaanite I, and Early Bronze IV/Middle Bronze I are among the terms that prominent archaeologists have used at various times in the past. It seems that "Early Bronze IV," or "EB IV," is winning support today, but, since most of the authors whose theories we will be reviewing call this period "Middle Bronze Age I," or "MB I", we shall continue to use that term. This era is generally dated c. 2300-2000 B.C.[68]

Until fairly recently it was customary to see the change from EB III to MB I as a total cultural break. The urban culture of EB III was succeeded by an era in which there were no true cities—only small villages consisting of a few flimsy, poorly built structures. Tombs containing only one or two burials each replaced the Early Bronze practice of multiple burials in large caves. And pottery types and other artifacts were very different in the two periods. Kathleen Kenyon and other archaeologists have argued that this evidence indicates that the EB III cities had been destroyed by seminomadic invaders, whose nonsedentary lifestyle and tribal social structure prevailed throughout MB I.[69] It is this view of an almost total destruction of the EB III culture and its replacement by that of invading seminomadic tribes that has led some scholars to place the Israelite conquest of Canaan at this point in the archaeological history of Palestine.[70]

Such an archaeological placement for the Exodus and Conquest does solve some problems. Both Ai and Jericho were occupied in EB III and were destroyed at the end of that era. There was also extensive Early Bronze occupation in the Negeb and Transjordan, as the Bible indicates for the Conquest period. And the widespread destruction of cities, as well as changes in pottery styles, burial practices, and other cultural features at the end of EB III, would be evidence that the incoming Israelites conquered virtually all of the land and massacred most of the Canaanite population, just as the Bible says.

This view has been bolstered in recent years by claims that the spread of the MB I culture into Palestine follows precisely the pattern that the Bible gives for the incoming Israelites. In a study of the Middle Bronze

68. Richard 1987: 36.
69. Kenyon 1971: 567-583; Aharoni 1978: 80-89.
70. Courville 1971: 87-91; 1985: 10-11; Vaninger 1983: 72-79.

Age I culture, Rudolph Cohen, an Israeli archaeologist, has argued that the material remains characteristic of these people first appear in the Sinai, then progress through Transjordan, cross the Jordan River near Jericho, spread through the southern hill country, and finally enter northern Palestine.[71] Cohen concluded:

> I do not necessarily mean to equate the MBI people with the Israelites, although an ethnic identification should not automatically be ruled out. But I am suggesting that at the very least the traditions incorporated into the Exodus account may have a very ancient inspiration reaching back to the MBI period. The migration of the MBI population from the southwest and their conquest of the Early Bronze civilization evidently made a very deep impression, and the memory of these events was preserved from one generation to the next. . . . The similarity between the course of the MBI migration and the route of the exodus seems too close to be coincidental.[72]

In addition, Emmanuel Anati, professor of paleo-ethnology at the University of Lecce in Italy, has connected Mount Sinai with the EB III/ MB I era. At Har Karkom, a mountain in the southern Negeb (see Figure 2 above), Anati uncovered a great concentration of rock art, much of it with what seem to be religious themes. He also found standing stones and altars, suggesting that this mountain had been a place of religious pilgrimage, which fits the Bible's description of Mount Sinai quite well.[73] The largest number of habitation sites near the mountain and the greatest volume of rock art belong to the Early Bronze Age and Middle Bronze Age I. Settlement dwindled and little rock art was produced for more than sixteen hundred years after c. 2000 B.C., indicating little activity at the mountain throughout the Middle Bronze II, Late Bronze, and Iron Ages.[74] So, if Har Karkom was the Mountain of God (Mount Sinai or Mount Horeb) described in the Exodus accounts, as Anati believes it was, then the Exodus and Conquest must have taken place at the end of the Early Bronze Age.

Anati and Cohen both accept the conventional dating for the archaeological periods of Palestine according to which the end of EB III and the beginning of MB I took place c. 2300 B.C. So, if the Exodus and Conquest are associated with the transition from EB III to MB I, they must have occurred about a thousand years *earlier* than they are usually dated. But

---

71. Cohen 1983, especially the map on p. 24.
72. Cohen 1983: 29.
73. Anati 1985 and 1987.
74. Anati 1985: 46, 48-53.

neither author deals with the question of how that thousand years can be filled.

Cohen trys to avoid the problem, suggesting that the MB I people might not have been the Israelites, that the traditions about the Exodus and Conquest might have been influenced by the memory of the MB I invasion passed down generation after generation. It seems highly unlikely, though, that a non-Israelite tribal memory or tradition from MB I times could have persisted for a thousand years in Palestine through population movements, cultural changes, conquest by the Egyptians, and the settlement of the Philistines and Israelites. It is also difficult to see why the Israelites would have adopted an ancient, foreign tradition as their own—especially if they themselves had entered Palestine from Egypt much more recently.

On the other hand, if the MB I people *were* the Israelites and Har Karkom *was* Mount Sinai, then something still must be done to account for the thousand-year gap between the new date for the Exodus and the conventional one. As I have shown earlier, synchronisms between Assyrian history and the histories of the kingdoms of Judah and Israel indicate that Solomon died between 931 and 921 B.C. This fact, in turn, makes it difficult, if not impossible, to date the beginning of the Israelite monarchy under Saul earlier than c. 1050 B.C. Thus, if the Israelite conquest of Canaan occurred at the end of EB III, the period of the "judges" must be stretched to cover an enormous expanse of time, from c. 2300 B.C. to c. 1050 or 1020 B.C.

The first three hundred years or so of this long period of the "judges" would correspond to the MB I era of Palestinian archaeology—a time during which, as we have seen, there were virtually no cities or towns in Palestine. Yet, as we have also noted, the Bible states that the Israelites did not destroy *all* of the cities in Canaan. Major urban centers such as Beth-shean, Taanach, Dor, Gezer, and Beth-shemesh were among the cities that remained in Canaanite hands during the era of the "judges," according to Scripture (Judges 1:27-29, 33). But excavations have shown that Beth-shean, Dor, and Beth-shemesh were not occupied in EB III. Taanach and Gezer seem to have been destroyed at the end of EB III, as were those cities supposedly conquered by the Israelites; and, like other Palestinian cities, they seem to have had no sedentary occupation during MB I. The EB III destruction is thus *too* widespread to represent the Israelite conquest as depicted in the biblical narratives. Moreover, various towns and cities are mentioned throughout the Book of Judges. The Bible does not describe a period like the Middle Bronze Age I, in which there was no urban occupation in Palestine.

In addition, this new dating would have to reconcile the Amarna Letters of the fourteenth century B.C. with biblical accounts in the Book of Judges, and the failure of the Bible to mention Egyptian control over much of Palestine from the sixteenth through the twelfth centuries B.C. (the latter half of the period of the "judges," according to this new chronology) would still have to be explained. This seems to be an impossible task.

Donovan Courville and Stan Vaninger, two fundamentalist Christians who support Velikovsky's chronology as well as an Early Bronze Age Exodus, have dealt with the problem by radically redating the Palestinian archaeological ages and revising the generally accepted correlations between archaeological eras and biblical history (see Table 6).[75] They accept the I Kings 6:1 date of c. 1440 for the Exodus and c. 1400 for the Conquest. So 1400 B.C. (rather than c. 2300 B.C.) becomes the date for the end of EB III and the beginning of MB I. The reappearance of cities and urban culture in the Middle Bronze II A period corresponds, they claim, to the latter part of the period of the "judges." And they argue that the renewed urbanization of MB II resulted from Israelites abandoning their nomadic way of life, settling down, and "utilizing their inherent ingenuity and abilities in the direction of creating a culture of their own."[76] Courville and Vaninger equate the Middle Bronze II B and C periods with the biblical era of the United Monarchy (c. 1020-922 B.C.) and the Late Bronze Age with the period of the Divided Monarchy (c. 922-722 B.C.), thus removing one of the archaeological objections to Velikovsky's historical synchronisms.[77] This redating makes the famous Late Bronze Age Ugaritic texts belong to the time of the Israelite monarchy, so it can be claimed that any similarities between these texts and the Bible are due to Canaanite copying of biblical material rather than the other way around.[78] According to Courville and Vaninger's chronology, the widespread destruction that wracked Palestine and Syria at the end of the Late Bronze Age was caused by the Assyrian invasions of 722 and 701 B.C.[79]

---

75. Courville 1971: II, 196; Vaninger 1984: 11-14.

76. Courville 1971: I, 91. See also Vaninger 1983: 80-82.

77. See above, pp. 121-122.

78. Courville 1971: I, 109-112.

79. Courville 1971: II, 196; Vaninger 1984: 11-14. Problems like those mentioned below (pp. 133-135) caused Courville to claim later that the Late Bronze Age was a duplicate of Middle Bronze II C and ended in the tenth century B.C. (1985: 12); the Iron I and II periods would then correspond to the era of the Divided Monarchy. But this revision reintroduces a major archaeological problem for Velikovsky's synchronisms (which are accepted by Courville): The Egyptian Eighteenth Dynasty belongs to the Late Bronze Age, while the Divided Monarchy would belong to the Iron Age, so they could not have been contemporaneous.

TABLE 6

The Courville-Vaninger Archaeological Chronology
Compared with the Conventional One

Date	Conventional Archaeo-logical Chronology	Events in Israel's History (Traditional Dates)	Chronology of Courville and Vaninger	Date
2400	EARLY BRONZE III		CHALCOLITHIC ERA	2400
2300			– – – –	2300
2200	EARLY BRONZE IV			2200
	OR		EARLY BRONZE I	
2100	MIDDLE BRONZE I			2100
2000			– – – –	2000
		PATRIARCHAL ERA		
1900	MIDDLE			1900
	BRONZE II A		EARLY BRONZE II	
1800				1800
1700	– – – – –	ISRAEL IN EGYPT	– – – –	1700
	MIDDLE BRONZE II B			
1600				1600
	MIDDLE BRONZE II C		EARLY BRONZE III	
1500	– – – –			1500
	LATE BRONZE I	THE EXODUS		
1400	– – – – –	THE CONQUEST		1400
	LATE BRONZE II A		EB IV/MB I	
1300	– – – – –		INTERMEDIATE ERA	1300
	LATE BRONZE II B			
1200	– – – – –	THE "JUDGES"	– – – –	1200
			A	
1100	IRON AGE I		MIDDLE BRONZE	1100
			II B	
1000		UNITED MONARCHY		1000
	– – – –	– – – –	C	
900			LATE BRONZE I	900
		DIVIDED MONARCHY	– – – –	
800				800
	IRON AGE II		LATE BRONZE II	
700		ASSYRIAN CONQUEST	– – – –	700
587			IRON AGE	587
		BABYLONIAN EXILE		

There is, however, a major inconsistency in this theory. The cultural changes between the EB III and MB I periods are seen as clear evidence of the entrance of new people—the Israelites. On the other hand, the differences between the MB I and MB II A cultures are supposed to have resulted simply from the Israelites settling down and improving their cultural level. But the cultural break between MB I and MB II A was even greater than that between EB III and MB I. A few types of EB III pottery vessels survived for a time into MB I, and in Transjordan a number of urban centers continued to be occupied from EB III into MB I.[80] In Palestine, however, virtually nothing of MB I survived into MB II A.

Urbanization resumed in MB II A, and multiple burial became common practice once again. With the exception of cooking pots, the styles of pottery vessels and other artifacts used in MB II A were completely different from those of MB I, and there are strong indications that these new cultural elements came into Palestine from Syro-Phoenicia and northern Mesopotamia.[81] Such evidence has led Kathleen Kenyon to declare that between MB I (her EB-MB period) and MB II A (her MB I period) "there was such a complete break in material equipment that it can only be interpreted as a cultural break introduced by the arrival of new groups."[82] And Israeli archaeologist Yohanan Aharoni agreed:

> The towns of Middle Canaanite II [his term for MB II] belong to another culture having practically nothing in common with the people of Middle Canaanite I [his term for MB I]. The general picture does not support the theory that their temporary settlements eventually developed into new towns. They disappeared and were blotted out just as they had appeared.[83]

Yet Courville and Vaninger see both of these periods—MB I and MB II A—as phases of the Israelite settlement in Palestine during the period of the "judges." Vaninger argues that the return to urban life was due to population growth, climatic change, and other factors, that the new practice of multiple burials was due to increased population, and that the new types of artifacts were due to the use of new techniques of manufacture and to influence from the north brought about by trade.[84] But he rejects the opinions of archaeologists like T. L. Thompson, William Dever,

---

80. Van Seters 1966: 11-14; Aharoni 1978: 84; Richard 1987: 35-37.
81. Van Seters 1966: 11, 20-21; Kenyon 1973a: 77-86; Aharoni 1978: 94-95.
82. Kenyon 1973a: 80.
83. Aharoni 1978: 89.
84. Vaninger 1983: 80-82.

and Suzanne Richard, who have argued for continuity between EB III and MB I on much the same grounds—that the changes reflect sociocultural fluctuations between periods of urban settlement and eras of pastoralism rather than invasions by new populations.[85]

Vaninger justifies his different treatment of the two periods of cultural change by noting that almost every major site was burned at the end of EB III while there are no destruction levels to mark the end of MB I.[86] However, climatic changes and internal strife can lead to widespread destruction and abandonment of towns and a reversion to pastoral life; the EB III destructions do not necessarily prove that an invasion of new people occurred. On the other hand, since during the MB I period there were only seminomadic encampments or villages rather than true towns or cities in Palestine, destruction levels should not be expected. Small groups of seminomadic pastoralists probably would have scattered at the approach of invaders or would have fought them in the open country rather than attempting to defend themselves within their unwalled encampments. There would have been little reason for invaders to burn the few abandoned villages they would have found in Palestine, especially since most of the MB I settlements were in the Negeb, an area the MB II A population chose not to settle. So destruction layers at the end of EB III do not prove that an invasion of newcomers took place then, nor does the lack of destruction levels at the end of MB I prove that there was no invasion at that time.

The changes between MB I and MB II A are comparable to those between EB III and MB I. If such changes signal the appearance of new population groups at the end of EB III, the abrupt change from MB I pastoralism to the new urban culture of MB II A should also be credited to invaders. Or, if one is willing to admit that the almost total change in living style and material culture that took place between the MB I and MB II A periods could have been due to climate, trade, and other factors effecting changes in the local population without a large influx of new groups, then the change from EB III to MB I should be viewed in the same way. Courville and Vaninger cannot logically claim one set of changes as proof of the Israelite invasion and the other set only as evidence of the progress of the Israelite settlement.

Their theory is beset by other problems. In order to accommodate

---

85. See Dever 1980 and Richard 1987 and the rejection of their views in Vaninger 1983:74-75.

86. Vaninger 1983: 82.

his major revision of the dates for the Palestinian archaeological periods, Courville was forced to revise Egyptian chronology in radical ways, just as Velikovsky had done before him. The occurrence of EB III objects in Egyptian tombs belonging to the Fourth through the Sixth Dynasties (the Old Kingdom), as well as the discovery of Old Kingdom Egyptian objects in the EB III temple at Ai (et-Tell) in Palestine, has demonstrated that the Palestinian EB III period and the Egyptian Old Kingdom were roughly contemporaneous.[87] Courville therefore had to date the end of the Old Kingdom around the end of the fifteenth century B.C. instead of c. 2200 B.C. Then, to fit all of the Egyptian material into the shorter time span of this new chronology, he argued that the Old and Middle Kingdom Dynasties were either contemporaneous with each other or partially overlapped.[88]

However, the sequence and lengths of the ancient Egyptian dynasties and of individual reigns within those dynasties have been painstakingly reconstructed, using Egyptian king lists (such as the Turin Canon of Kings, the Palermo Stone, the Abydos List, and the Saqqara List), as well as many individual inscriptions.[89] While the evidence indicates that there *were* periods when two or more dynasties ruled concurrently in different parts of Egypt, it is also clear that this was not going on during the reigns of the strong kings of the Old and Middle Kingdoms. There simply is no textual support for making the Sixth and Twelfth Dynasties contemporaneous, as Courville does. That EB III pottery from Syria-Palestine has often been found in tombs from the era of the Sixth Dynasty but *not* in tombs dated to the Twelfth Dynasty argues against Courville's reorganization of the Egyptian dynasties. Furthermore, developments in the style of tomb reliefs and inscriptions indicate that the Old Kingdom and Middle Kingdom were not contemporaneous.[90] Courville's arbitrary reordering and redating of Egyptian dynasties is totally untenable.

Acceptance of such a dramatic revision in Near Eastern chronology also involves the rejection of both radiocarbon dating (also known as carbon-14 or C^{14} dating) and dendrochronology (tree-ring dating).[91] Possible fluc-

---

87. Albright 1965: 51-52; Kantor 1965: 17-19; Hennessy 1967: 69-74; de Vaux 1971: 231-232.

88. Courville 1971: I, 77, 101-104, 164-210.

89. See, for example, Hayes 1970. Courville seems to hold the mistaken idea that the sequence of ancient Egyptian kings and dynasties is still almost totally dependent on the remnants of the work of Manetho, an Egyptian priest who wrote an account of Egyptian history in Greek in the mid-third century B.C. Courville does not use the Turin Canon or other ancient king lists in constructing his chronology.

90. Woldering 1963: 119-129.

91. For a brief description of the basic methodology of dendrochronology and radiocarbon

tuations in the amount of radioactive carbon (C14) present in the atmosphere in earlier times has raised questions about the accuracy of radiocarbon dating, but dendrochronology long has been recognized as an incontestably accurate dating technique. It relies on the well-known principle that trees add one ring each year. While exceptions to this rule do occur, they are very rare, altering a large tree's apparent age by only one or two years at most.

It is also significant that tree rings vary in size. In years with more than normal rainfall the rings are generally wider than usual, and in especially dry years the rings are narrower. By comparing a series of tree rings and relating their wide and narrow rings with one another scientists can construct a "sequence" of rings that stretches from a known date in the present or recent past deep into antiquity. Long-lived bristlecone pine trees in the American Southwest have allowed scholars to develop a tree-ring sequence stretching more than 7,000 years into the past.[92]

Radiocarbon tests on precisely dated rings from the bristlecone pine sequence have enabled scientists to refine and calibrate the radiocarbon dating method, making it possible to correct for past fluctuations in the amount of atmospheric carbon-14. Recently, this calibration has been validated and made even more precise by carbon-14 tests on tree rings from an Irish oak sequence covering the past 6,000 years.[93] So, despite the claims of Velikovsky and Courville to the contrary, radiocarbon dating as calibrated by tree-ring sequences can provide fairly accurate dates for past events. And the calibrated radiocarbon dates for Egyptian objects show that the Old Kingdom (and the Palestinian Early Bronze III period that is linked to it by archaeological evidence) could not have ended as late as 1400 B.C.[94] Carbon-14 dates also place the Twelfth Dynasty *later* than the Sixth Dynasty, not contemporaneous with it, and they indicate that the Eighteenth Dynasty (and the related Palestinian Late Bronze Age) came earlier than the tenth to eighth centuries B.C. (the date assigned to Dynasty XVIII by Velikovsky, Courville, and Vaninger).[95] In sum, radiocarbon dates from Egypt support the conventional chronology rather than the radical revisions we have been considering.

dating, see Champion 1980: 34-35 and 103-105. For Velikovsky's reservations about the radiocarbon dating method, see Velikovsky 1973a. And for Courville's doubts on the validity of both dendrochronology and carbon-14 dating, see Courville 1971: II, 31-46.

92. Renfrew 1979: 69-83; Shaw 1985: 295-297.
93. Shaw 1985: 297.
94. Shaw 1985, especially the Dynasty VI dates on p. 311.
95. MacKie 1978, especially p. 61; Shaw 1985, especially pp. 297-299, 303-304, and 311-312.

The chronology advocated by Courville and Vaninger also has internal problems. Its correlations between archaeology and the Bible don't mesh. While the Courville-Vaninger revisions produce a fairly good correlation between archaeological evidence and biblical accounts of the Conquest, they create major conflicts between the Bible and the archaeological material from later periods. For example, by equating the end of EB III with Joshua's invasion, the chronology of Courville and Vaninger eliminates the problems that Jericho, Ai, and Dibon have presented to supporters of the accuracy of the biblical text of the Conquest. All of these places were occupied in EB III. But, according to the Bible, after its destruction Jericho was cursed and remained unoccupied until it was rebuilt during the time of the Divided Monarchy (Joshua 6:26; I Kings 16:34). Therefore, according to Courville and Vaninger's archaeological correlations there should be no remains at Jericho from the Middle Bronze I and II periods (the era of the "judges" and the United Monarchy in their system). However, large numbers of MB I tombs were found at Jericho and some limited materials were found on the *tell;* there also was a flourishing walled city on the site throughout the MB II period! The major Middle Bronze II city at Jericho is difficult to reconcile with biblical accounts if Courville and Vaninger's chronology is correct.

We have already seen that the EB III destructions are too extensive to represent the Israelite conquest as depicted in the Bible. In addition to the sites mentioned above, Gaza and Shiloh present major problems for theories of an EB III conquest. Gaza (Tell Harube) was a Philistine city that plays an important role in the stories about Samson (Judges 13-16) during the period of the "judges," and Shiloh (Khirbet Seilun) was one of the centers of Israelite activity during that time (Joshua 18:1-10; Judges 21:12, 19; etc.). Yet Shiloh was occupied for the first time in MB II B (which begins just before the time of Saul, according to the Courville/ Vaninger chronology), while Gaza was not occupied until the Late Bronze Age.[96] There was thus no Shiloh at which Joshua and the Israelite tribes could meet at the end of EB III or early in MB I, and there was no Gaza to serve as a Philistine center in MB I and MB II, as required by the Courville/Vaninger archaeological dating scheme.

Courville and Vaninger equate the Late Bronze Age with the period of the Divided Monarchy of the ninth and eighth centuries B.C. For this era the biblical accounts correlate well with Assyrian records; even scholars who are skeptical about the accuracy of early biblical history admit that

96. Finkelstein 1986: 24-27; 1988a: 212.

the Bible is generally reliable for the time of the Divided Monarchy. Yet there are no Late Bronze Age layers at a number of sites mentioned prominently in biblical texts from the ninth and eighth centuries B.C., including places such as Beer-sheba (I Kings 19:1-3; II Kings 12:1; 23:8; and Amos 5:5), Heshbon (Isaiah 15:4; 16:8-9), Dibon (Isaiah 15:2), and Bozrah (Amos 1:12; Isaiah 34:6).

The most important discrepancy between the Bible and archaeology, however, would come from Samaria. This city was founded by King Omri and made the capital of the northern kingdom of Israel about 879 B.C., and it remained Israel's capital until its destruction by the Assyrians in 722/721 B.C. If the Courville-Vaninger archaeological chronology were correct, Samaria should exhibit extensive Late Bronze Age remains and a major destruction layer at the end of the Late Bronze era. But major excavations at Sebastiyeh, the site of ancient Samaria, by George Reisner from 1908 to 1910 and by J. W. Crowfoot from 1931 to 1935 failed to turn up *any* Late Bronze Age strata or artifacts.[97] The earliest buildings uncovered on the site belonged to the Iron Age, a fact that agrees quite well with traditional synchronisms between archaeology and the Bible, but that cannot be reconciled with the Courville-Vaninger revision.[98]

Finally, there is archaeological evidence that the end of the Late Bronze Age and the beginning of the Iron Age cannot be placed as late as 722-700 B.C. (the date given by Courville and Vaninger). Pottery from the earliest levels of Greek cities in Sicily (which Greek sources indicate were built between 750 and 700 B.C.) belonged to styles of Greek wares called late Geometric and Corinthian.[99] So, these Greek pottery types were in use in the latter half of the eighth century B.C., a period when the Late Bronze Age was ending in Palestine, according to the Courville-Vaninger chronology. But, as I have shown, Greek Geometric pottery has been found in Palestine in *Iron II* strata rather than in strata representing the transition between

---

97. For detailed descriptions of the excavation results, see Reisner, Fisher, and Lyon 1924; Crowfoot, Kenyon, and Sukenik 1942; and Crowfoot and Kenyon 1957. Shorter summaries of the evidence can be found in Ackroyd 1967 and Avigad 1978.

98. Courville questions the excavators' interpretations of the archaeological evidence for the earliest city at Samaria (1971: II, 215-220). He claims that similarities between the walls of the earliest buildings at Samaria and those of structures at Late Bronze Age Ugarit show that Samaria was first occupied in the Late Bronze Age (1971: II, 220-221). However, if Samaria had been extensively occupied in the Late Bronze Age, there should have been a considerable number of pottery sherds from that era found in the excavations. The lack of Late Bronze Age pottery sherds at Samaria and the association of Iron Age sherds with the earliest building layers there dooms Courville's attempt to make Samaria fit into his chronology.

99. Boardman 1964: 178-184, 187-189.

the Late Bronze and Iron I periods.[100] Greek Mycenaean pottery is found stratified with Late Bronze material in Palestine and Syria, and the stratified evidence from Greece shows that this Mycenaean pottery is earlier than the Greek Geometric wares. Such interlocking evidence indicates that the end of the Palestinian Late Bronze Age must be placed earlier than the era of the Greek Geometric pottery, which was coming to an end in the latter half of the eighth century B.C. So, the end of the Palestinian Late Bronze Age must have occurred much earlier than the 722-700 date given to it by Courville and Vaninger. Furthermore, both the Greek and Palestinian archaeological evidence make it unlikely that the Palestinian Iron Age can be shortened to a mere hundred and twenty or so years (c. 722-600 B.C.), as Courville and Vaninger suggest.[101]

Placing the Exodus at the end of the Early Bronze Age does solve some problems, especially those related to Jericho and Ai. But it does not produce perfect harmony between the biblical accounts and archaeological evidence (see Table 7). The EB III archaeological finds from Dibon, Jericho, Ai, Lachish, Bethel, Hazor, and Dan can be reconciled with the biblical accounts of the conquest of those cities. The same cannot be said for Kadesh-Barnea, Arad, Hormah, Heshbon, Aroer, Gibeon, and Hebron, which do not seem to have been occupied in the EB III period. The finds from seven identifiable cities fit the biblical narratives if the Exodus and Conquest occurred at the end of the Early Bronze Age III, but the finds from seven sites do not. This score (seven to seven) is better than those for a Late Bronze Age Exodus and Conquest (a maximum of three for, eleven against for an LB I conquest and five to nine for an LB II B conquest), but it is still not very good. The Bible and archaeological evidence would agree only half of the time. This "score" would decline for an EB III conquest (but increase for a Late Bronze conquest) if we included Dor, Beth-shemesh, Gaza, Shiloh, and other sites that were supposed to be occupied during the era of the "judges" but which had no EB III or MB I sedentary occupation.

In order to produce this slight improvement in the agreement between the Bible and archaeology, the theory of an Early Bronze Age exodus and conquest creates problems that are even more serious than the ones it solves. Agreement between the Bible and archaeology in the post-Conquest period declines substantially when the Exodus is placed at the end of EB III. Neither the theories of Anati and Cohen nor the more radical revisions

---

100. For example, see Woolley 1953: 172-173, Plates 19b and 20b; Boardman 1964: 61-70; Pritchard 1975: 67-70, 94-96.

101. See Stiebing 1985: 66-67.

TABLE 7: Archaeology and an Early Bronze III Exodus and Conquest

CITY	BIBLICAL REFERENCE	ARCHAEOLOGICAL EVIDENCE
Kadesh-Barnea	Deut. 1:19-46. The Israelites spent most of their 40 years in the wilderness at Kadesh	No EB III occupation at any of the possible sites for Kadesh-Barnea, but EB II sites nearby
Arad	Num. 21:1-3 indicates that the city was destroyed by Joshua	Tel Arad destroyed near the end of EB II; no EB III occupation. No EB III at other possible sites for Arad.
Hormah	Num. 21:1-3 says the city was destroyed by Joshua; Judges 1:17-18 credits its conquest to later action by Judah & Simeon	Only Chalcolithic-EB I material at Malhata; no EB at Tel Masos (the two possible sites of Hormah)
Heshbon	Num. 21:25-26. Heshbon is the capital of King Sihon and is destroyed	No EB occupation
Dibon	Num. 21:30. Dibon was destroyed after Heshbon	Occupied in EB III
Aroer	Deut. 2:36. Aroer was conquered after Sihon's defeat	No EB III occupation; only limited MB I remains
Jericho	Josh. 6 describes the total destruction of this city and its population	Large city destroyed at the end of EB III
Ai	Josh. 7-8. The city and all of its population was destroyed	Large city destroyed at the end of EB III
Gibeon	Josh. 9-10:2. Gibeon was "a royal city, larger even than Ai" and became Israel's ally	Unwalled village in EB I, but little or no EB III occupation
Lachish	Josh. 10:32. Lachish was captured and its people killed	EB occupation, but extent and exact period unknown
Hebron	Josh. 10:36-37. Hebron was captured and its people killed	No EB III occupation
Bethel	Judges 1:22-25 credits the destruction of Bethel to the house of Joseph	EB III occupation
Hazor	Josh. 11:1-11. Hazor was burned and its people killed	EB III city seems to have been destroyed
Dan	Judges 18:27-29 states that Laish was destroyed and then reoccupied by the Tribe of Dan	EB III occupation

Note: Underlined cities have significant stories told about their roles during the Conquest period.

of Courville and Vaninger, therefore, have much to recommend them. They are not to be preferred over the conventional Late Bronze dates for the Exodus and Conquest.

Placing the Exodus at the End of the Middle Bronze Age

Urban settlements were reestablished in Palestine during the Middle Bronze II A period, and they continued to develop and flourish throughout the Middle Bronze Age. A peak of prosperity and urbanization seems to have been attained during the MB II B-C era, when massive fortifications, often consisting of a ditch, a beaten-earth or plaster-coated glacis with a wall on top, and well-protected gateways were erected at many sites. In the past, scholars often claimed that these new features were introduced by Hyksos invaders on their way to Egypt, but it is now recognized that this view is erroneous. The new fortification systems, like other aspects of MB II B-C culture, developed out of elements introduced during the MB II A period.[102]

At the end of MB II C a wave of destruction swept over the land once again. Most of the cities occupied in MB II C were destroyed at the end of that period, and many were not reoccupied for a century or more, if at all. The material culture of the succeeding Late Bronze I period is derived from that of the Middle Bronze Age II, so there is no severe cultural break between the periods, as there was at the end of EB III and again at the end of MB I. But the LB I period exhibits a decline in wealth and culture, with fewer and smaller towns and cities. Many towns seem to have been unfortified, and even when the number of cities began to increase again in LB II, new fortification walls were rarely built.[103] These facts, coupled with the discrepancies between the Late Bronze Age remains and the biblical account of the Conquest, have led John Bimson, a British biblical scholar and archaeologist, to relate the MB II C destructions in Palestine to the Israelite invasion.[104]

Like Courville and Vaninger, Bimson believes that the date for the Exodus in I Kings 6:1 is approximately correct (he dates the Exodus to c. 1470 B.C., during the time Thutmose III reigned alone). The Conquest

---

102. Aharoni 1978: 97-112. On the non-Hyksos nature of MB II culture, see Van Seters 1966, Parr 1968, and Stiebing 1971.

103. Aharoni 1978: 115-119., Gonen 1984.

104. Bimson 1981; I. Wilson 1985: 170-173; Bimson and Livingston 1987.

would have taken place forty years later, c. 1430 B.C. So he redates the end of the MB II period (usually placed at 1550 B.C.) to c. 1430 B.C.[105] For a time, he also proposed extending the Late Bronze I period to cover all of the time from the end of the fifteenth century to 950 B.C. and changing the date for the end of the Late Bronze II period to c. 733-700 B.C.,[106] which would have made the LB II era contemporaneous with the divided kingdom—as Courville and Vaninger suggested. This chronology would have been subject to the same problems that their scheme encounters— lack of LB occupation at Heshbon, Dibon, Beer-sheba, and Samaria, all of which were important in the period of the divided kingdom.[107] Because of such problems, Bimson has abandoned his attempts to radically alter Late Bronze and Iron Age chronology.[108] The only change in the standard archaeological chronology he still makes is to move up the date for the end of MB II by seventy to one hundred and twenty years, from c. 1550-1500 B.C. to c. 1430 B.C., and thus place the Exodus in MB II C and the Conquest at the end of the MB II period.

Manfred Bietak's excavations at Tell ed-Dab'a in Egypt have shown that the end of the Hyksos era coincided with the end of the Middle Bronze II B period, not the end of Middle Bronze II C, as had been thought. Thus, the date for the end of MB II B must be moved up to c. 1550 B.C.[109] and the end of MB II C to c. 1500-1475 B.C. This discovery has made John Bimson's suggestion that the date for the end of MB II be moved up another forty-five or seventy years to c. 1430 B.C. seem much more plausible.[110]

An MB II date for the Conquest would eliminate problems at Jericho, where a large walled city *was* destroyed at the end of MB II C.[111] Bimson claims it would also solve some of the problems that Late Bronze I or LB II B dates for the Conquest have with Arad, Hormah, Gibeon, and Hebron. None of these sites were occupied in LB I or LB II B, but all of them had MB II settlements (if one follows Aharoni's suggestion and places Bronze Age Arad at Tel Malhata instead of at Tel Arad and Hormah

105. Bimson 1981: 119-223; Bimson and Livingston 1987.

106. Bimson 1978.

107. For more detailed criticism, see Stiebing 1984: 76-80.

108. See the editorial note in Stiebing 1985: 67. Conventional dates for the end of LB II and for the Iron Age are given in Bimson and Livingston 1987: 45-47.

109. Bietak 1984: 474-485. A number of Egyptologists now favor a later chronology for the Eighteenth Dynasty, beginning the reign of Ahmose c. 1540 B.C. rather than 1570 B.C. (see Bietak 1988).

110. Shea 1986: 34-35.

111. Bimson 1981: 110-136.

at Tel Masos).[112] However, a number of problems would still exist. It is rather firmly established that the Late Bronze II A period began about 1400 B.C. or very soon afterward. This date is based primarily on finds that show that LB II A pottery and imported Mycenaean III A wares were already widespread by the time of the Amarna Period (c. 1350-1321 B.C.) in Egypt. But if LB II begins c. 1400 B.C. and MB II C ends c. 1430-1420 B.C., as Bimson argues, only twenty to thirty years are left for the Late Bronze I period. This is far too short a span for this period.[113] LB I may have begun c. 1500 or even 1475 B.C. rather than 1550 B.C., but it is almost impossible to make it start as recently as 1430 or 1420 B.C.

Ai also would continue to present difficulties, for there was no MB II occupation at et-Tell, just as there was no Late Bronze settlement there. As we have seen, Bimson adopts Livingston's identification of Khirbet Nisya as Ai and el-Bireh as Bethel in order to eliminate this discrepancy between the Bible and archaeology. Six seasons of excavations at Khirbet Nisya have produced some MB II and LB I pottery sherds, but no building remains or city walls, from those periods. The excavations have also failed to turn up an ash layer or any other evidence of destruction at the end of the MB II period.[114] Livingston has suggested that the buildings from the MB II era were destroyed by later builders who went down to bedrock for the foundations of their structures. The mud-brick superstructures of the city wall and gates, he argues, would have been destroyed by erosion and the stone base of the wall might have been dismantled to construct later buildings or terrace walls.[115] This explanation, while possible, is not very likely. Even on a largely denuded site, some traces of the gates, city wall, and building remains from a flourishing era should have remained.[116] The excavation evidence from Nisya seems to indicate that it was never more than a small unwalled village. Furthermore, el-Bireh, according to Livingston and Bimson the supposed site of Bethel, does not seem to have been a walled town in the Middle and Late Bronze periods either.[117] So, Ai remains a problem

112. Bimson 1981: 188-193.
113. Halpern 1987: 57-58. Halpern's attempts to show that LB I must begin c. 1550 B.C. are not as persuasive as his arguments that LB I was longer than twenty or thirty years. The use of thirty-seven and a half years as an average for each level at various sites is arbitrary. LB I could have begun later than 1550 B.C., though not much later than c. 1500-1475 B.C. (Bietak 1988). Recently Bimson has disputed the 1400 B.C. date for the end of LB I, arguing that LB I could end and LB II A begin as late as 1360 B.C. (1988: 52-53). This *is* possible, but not very likely.
114. Bimson 1985; Livingston 1987: 6; Bimson and Livingston 1987: 48.
115. Livingston 1987: 6; Bimson and Livingston 1987: 48-50.
116. See Halpern 1987: 58.
117. Rainey 1980: 250; Zevit 1985c: 80 contra Bimson and Livingston 1987: 47-48, where Kochavi 1972: 178 is cited.

for a Middle Bronze conquest just as it is for a Late Bronze conquest.

Archaeological evidence from Gibeon does not fit a Middle Bronze II conquest as well as Bimson claims either. According to Joshua 9 the Gibeonites tricked the Israelites into making a treaty with them, and thus they avoided having their town destroyed by Joshua. But Joshua forced them to become hewers of wood and drawers of water for the Israelites, a role they continued to perform into later times (Joshua 9:22-27). The biblical narrative presumes that Gibeon continued to be occupied throughout the time of the "judges" and into the monarchical period. But there is no evidence that Gibeon was occupied during LB I or LB II B, and there seems to have been only limited occupation during LB II A. If the Conquest took place at the end of MB II C, there would have been virtually no occupation at Gibeon throughout most of the period of the "judges."

The Negeb and Transjordanian sites would also remain problematic. Bimson claims that the evidence from Hormah (Tel Masos) fits an MB II C conquest but not an LB Israelite invasion; for, while no LB remains were found at Tel Masos, "the remains of an earth rampart dating from MB II are evidence that a fortified town existed here at that time."[118] However, Bimson fails to point out that the Middle Bronze II settlement at Tel Masos was short-lived, being founded in MB II A and destroyed during or at the end of MB II B, not at the end of MB II C![119] This destruction came at least 120 years earlier than Bimson's date for the Conquest. Hormah could be identified with nearby Tel Malhata, which was destroyed at the end of MB II C, but then Arad would have to be located at Tel 'Arad, which was not occupied in MB II. So if the Conquest is placed at the end of MB II, either Arad or Hormah does not agree with the biblical narratives. There also was no MB II occupation at Beer-sheba or at any of the possible sites for Kadesh-Barnea, where the Israelites are said to have camped for almost forty years.

Nor is there evidence that the nations of Edom, Moab, and Ammon in Transjordan existed in the Middle Bronze II period. As Baruch Halpern has noted, the personal names from Iron Age Edom, Moab, and Ammon are quite distinctive, often containing the names of Transjordanian national gods such as Qaus or Chemosh. But no evidence of the existence of these characteristic names is found earlier than the twelfth century B.C. (the Iron Age I).[120] Furthermore, Aroer, Dibon, and Heshbon—sites supposedly

---

118. Bimson 1981: 190.
119. Kempinski 1977: 818.
120. Halpern 1987: 60.

conquered by the Israelites—were not even occupied during the Middle Bronze Age II (see Table 8). An MB II date for the Conquest thus produces *some* agreement between the Bible and the archaeological finds at eight major sites (though Gibeon's "fit" is very questionable), but significant discrepancies continue for six sites.

The archaeological finds at Shiloh (Khirbet Seilun) and Dor also present some difficulties for Bimson's proposal, just as they do for the theory of an EB III conquest. Shiloh, an important city from the time of Joshua into the early monarchy, was not occupied during the Late Bronze Age (which corresponds to the first two-thirds of the period of the "judges," according to Bimson's chronology). It was burned to the ground at the end of MB II C (though the Bible does not indicate that Shiloh was destroyed by the Israelites), and it was not rebuilt as a town until the Iron Age I. Some Late Bronze pottery sherds have been found with ashes and animal bones there, which indicates that some activity (probably cultic) continued to take place at Shiloh during the Late Bronze Age; but no architectural remains from that era have been uncovered.[121] So, as is the case with Gibeon, a place that according to Bimson's placement of the Conquest should have been occupied during the Late Bronze Age was not.

The king of Dor was conquered by Joshua and his land taken by Israel according to Joshua 12:23. On the other hand, Judges 1:27 states that the tribe of Manasseh could not dislodge the inhabitants of Dor and its dependent towns. However one attempts to reconcile those two passages, it is clear that the various biblical traditions regarded Dor as a city that was in existence at the time of the Conquest. Yet excavations at Dor have indicated that the site was first occupied in the Late Bronze Age I.[122] If the Conquest occurred at the end of MB II C, then, there was no Dor in Joshua's time. This city was just being founded when the Israelites were settling down, so it is difficult to see why Manasseh would have had trouble conquering it. They should have been able to attack and defeat the citizens of Dor as soon as they began to build their city, before the walls were erected or the city strong enough to defend itself. Clearly, Bimson's redating of the Exodus and Conquest does not produce perfect harmony between the biblical narratives and the archaeological remains at a number of sites.

The most important discrepancy between archaeology and the Bible, if Bimson's view is adopted, comes from the excavations at Tell ed-Dabʿa in Egypt. As we have seen in Chapter 2, this site was almost certainly

121. Finkelstein 1986: 34-35; 1988a: 216-220.
122. Foerster 1975: 335.

TABLE 8: Archaeology and a Middle Bronze II C Exodus and Conquest

CITY	BIBLICAL REFERENCE	ARCHAEOLOGICAL EVIDENCE
Kadesh-Barnea	Deut. 1:19-46. The Israelites spent most of their 40 years in the wilderness at Kadesh	No MB II occupation at any of the possible sites for Kadesh-Barnea
Arad	Num. 21:1-3 indicates that the city was destroyed by Joshua	No MB occupation at Tel Arad; MB II city at Tel Malhata destroyed at end of MB II C
Hormah	Num. 21:1-3 says the city was destroyed by Joshua; Judges 1:17-18 credits its conquest to later action by Judah & Simeon	MB II city at Tel Masos destroyed at end of MB II B; MB II city at Tel Malhata destroyed at end of MB II C
Heshbon	Num. 21:25-26. Heshbon is the capital of King Sihon and is destroyed	No MB II occupation
Dibon	Num. 21:30. Dibon was destroyed after Heshbon	No MB II occupation
Aroer	Deut. 2:36. Aroer was conquered after Sihon's defeat	No MB II occupation
Jericho	Josh. 6 describes the total destruction of this city and its population	Fortified city destroyed at the end of MB II C (or possibly early in LB I)
Ai	Josh. 7-8. The city and all of its population was destroyed	No MB occupation at et-Tell; limited MB II settlement at Khirbet Nisya
Gibeon	Josh. 9-10:2. Gibeon was "a royal city, larger even than Ai" and became Israel's ally	An unwalled town existed at el-Jib in MB II; no LB I occupation
Lachish	Josh. 10:32. Lachish was captured and its people killed	Fortified city in MB II, but no destruction at end of MB II C
Hebron	Josh. 10:36-37. Hebron was captured and its people killed	Fortified city destroyed at the end of MB II C
Bethel	Judges 1:22-25 credits the destruction of Bethel to the house of Joseph	Beitin destroyed at end of MB II C; el-Bireh does not seem to have been occupied in MB II
Hazor	Josh. 11:1-11. Hazor was burned and its people killed	Fortified city destroyed at the end of MB II C
Dan	Judges 18:27-29 states that Laish was destroyed and then reoccupied by the Tribe of Dan	Fortified city destroyed at the end of MB II C

Note: Underlined cities have significant stories told about their roles during the Conquest period.

the location of Avaris, capital of the Hyksos, and (along with Qantir) of Per-Ramesses, delta capital of Ramesses II. Manfred Bietak's excavations here have revealed that Avaris/Per-Ramesses (the Ra'amses of the Exodus narrative) was not occupied during most of the Eighteenth Dynasty. We have already noted that this fact causes problems for supporters of an LB I fifteenth century Exodus as well as for those who favor Goedicke's link between the Exodus and the eruption of Thera. It is just as problematic for Bimson's theory. The Bible indicates that Ra'amses (by whatever name it was known in Moses' day) was in existence from the time of the oppression through the time of the Exodus. So it is difficult to defend the historicity of the biblical account of the Exodus and Conquest (as Bimson does) if there was no Ra'amses at which the Israelites could gather and from which they could begin their journey out of Egypt. Furthermore, there was no city at Tell ed-Dab'a at the time of Hatshepsut, Thutmose III, or Amenhotep II, one of whom *must* have been the pharaoh of the Exodus if it took place in the fifteenth century B.C.

Bimson was aware of this evidence from Tell ed-Dab'a when he wrote *Redating the Exodus and Conquest* in 1978. But he argued that the date for the start of the occupation gap at this site could be significantly moved up from Bietak's date of c. 1550 B.C. Bichrome ware was found in Stratum D at Tell ed-Dab'a (the last stratum before the gap in occupation); and, according to Bimson's revised pottery chronology, bichrome ware did not appear in Palestine until c. 1450 B.C. So, he felt, Tell ed-Dab'a must have remained occupied until shortly after the time of the Exodus (which took place in 1470 B.C., according to Bimson).[123]

This argument is seriously flawed. It ignores the fact that Bietak's dates for the strata at Tell ed-Dab'a are based primarily on data drawn from Egyptian sources. It is generally agreed that the Syro-Palestinian culture characteristic of Strata D/2, D/3, E, and F at Tell ed-Dab'a is that of the Hyksos rulers of Egypt. Settlement at the site ceased for a time at the end of Stratum D/2, and all the graves of this stratum were plundered. Stratum D/1 is represented by a single massive filling wall across the *tell*, which was in use only for a very short time and which can be dated by Egyptian pottery to the early Eighteenth Dynasty. The site was reoccupied in Stratum B, which bore inscriptions from the reign of Horemheb, last king of the Eighteenth Dynasty.[124] Evidence from this excavation thus tells

---

123. Bimson 1981: 250-251.

124. Bietak 1979: 268-270; 1984: 477. Bimson and Livingston (1987: 43) state that in a letter to Bimson in March 1987 Bietak mentions finding Eighteenth Dynasty material at Tell ed-Dab'a. The extent of this new material and the exact period of the Eighteenth Dynasty to which it

us that Tell ed-Dab'a was abandoned as an urban center at the end of Stratum D/2 and not rebuilt as a city until Stratum B.

This archaeological evidence must be correlated with what we know from textual sources. A tomb biography of an Egyptian soldier states that Ahmose I, first pharaoh of the Eighteenth Dynasty, captured Avaris and drove the Hyksos from Egypt. It also mentions that Avaris was looted by the Egyptian army.[125] This event can be dated c. 1560-1530 B.C., depending on which chronology for Egypt one follows. In any case, around 1550 B.C. Avaris and Hyksos rule in Egypt came to an end. So the end of Stratum D/2 can be dated to c. 1550 B.C. with some confidence. And the gap in occupation at the site can be dated from the first reign or two of the Eighteenth Dynasty to the reign of Horemheb, when the reoccupation of Stratum B took place.

The dates for Strata D/2 and B at Tell ed-Dab'a are much more secure than the dates for the MB II phases in Palestine, which are largely based on Egyptian scarabs and destructions hypothetically related to Egyptian military campaigns. So, despite William Dever's opposition,[126] Palestinian Middle Bronze chronology must be modified to fit the evidence from Tell ed-Dab'a. If bichrome ware is indeed found in Tell ed-Dab'a Stratum D, this would indicate that bichrome ware began to circulate before 1550 B.C., not that the end of Stratum D must be redated to c. 1450 B.C.!

No Palestinian MB II C material has been found at Tell ed-Dab'a or anywhere in the eastern delta, so this phase of the Middle Bronze Age must represent the continued development of the MB culture in Palestine after the Hyksos were defeated and driven out of Egypt.[127] The Egyptian evidence does not seem to allow a fifteenth-century-B.C. or an MB II C occupation at Avaris/Per-Ramesses or at Pithom (Tell er-Retabeh)—or an MB II C exodus from the eastern delta region. And if there was no

---

belongs is not mentioned, however. Since this evidence has not yet been published, it is difficult to judge how much it will modify Bietak's published claims for a gap in occupation at Tell ed-Dab'a throughout most of the Eighteenth Dynasty. The published evidence indicates that much of the site was abandoned during the fifteenth century B.C., though Bietak 1988 mentions a religious installation (a temple?) on the site during the reign of Amenhotep III. This is still too late for a c. 1470-1450 B.C. exodus.

125. J. Wilson 1955: 233.

126. Dever 1985: 76-78.

127. Bietak 1984: 482-485. Bichrome ware was found in Stratum D/2 (MB II B/C) at Tell ed-Dab'a, as it was in strata from MB II C in Palestine, so Stratum D/2 at Avaris (Tell ed-Dab'a) possibly overlaps somewhat with the MB II C era in Palestine and Syria. Bietak argues that the Egyptian campaigns of Ahmose and his immediate successors caused the end of MB II C and the beginning of the Late Bronze Age in Palestine around 1500 B.C. (Bietak 1988).

Exodus in MB II C, there could have been no Conquest at the end of MB II C—at least not if one is trying to stick fairly closely to the biblical narrative. The evidence from Egypt, when considered along with the problematic sites in Palestine, shows that an MB II C date for the Exodus and Conquest does not really preserve the accuracy of the biblical account any more than a Late Bronze placement of the Exodus and Conquest does.

An Iron Age Date for the Conquest?

If destructions of Palestinian sites at the end of the Early Bronze Age, Middle Bronze Age II, or Late Bronze Age do not correlate very well with the biblical accounts of the Israelite conquest of Canaan, what of a later date? As we have seen, the beginning of the United Monarchy under King Saul must be dated c. 1050-1020 B.C., which in archaeological terms is the latter part of the Iron Age I. So, an Israelite conquest of Canaan could not have taken place any later than the *early* part of the Iron I period. An early Iron I date for the Conquest has been suggested by archaeologist Joseph Callaway, the excavator of et-Tell, the generally accepted site of biblical Ai. Callaway found that, while et-Tell had not been inhabited in the Middle or Late Bronze Ages, *two* phases of occupation had taken place on the site in the Iron I period. The first of these Iron Age villages, he argued, was probably Canaanite Ai, while the second represented the settlement of the Israelites.[128]

No Iron I settlements have been found at Jericho, Heshbon, or Lachish,[129] so these sites would continue to be problematic. But Iron I remains have been uncovered at Kadesh-Barnea, Arad, Hormah, Dibon, Aroer, Gibeon, Hebron, Bethel, Hazor, and Dan, in addition to Ai.[130] Thus, all but three of the identifiable cities that play a part in the Conquest narratives were occupied in the early part of the Iron Age. No other archaeological placement of the Conquest can match this record of agreement.

---

128. Callaway 1968: 316-320; 1976: 14-16.

129. Kenyon 1967: 273-274; Horn 1976: 513; Ussishkin 1977: 743-744. Since the Late Bronze II city at Lachish does not seem to have been finally destroyed until the twelfth century B.C. (Ussishkin 1987: 35), it still might be possible to reconcile its evidence with the theory of an Iron I Conquest.

130. Dothan 1977: 692; Aharoni 1975: 82-83; Kempinski 1977: 818; Tushingham 1975: 332; Olivarri 1975: 99; Pritchard 1976: 449-450; Kelso 1975: 192; Yadin 1976: 487, 495; Biran 1975: 316.

Despite its initial attractiveness, the idea of an Iron I Conquest has so many difficulties that even Callaway has abandoned it in recent years.[131] The first problem, of course, is that it severely shortens the period of the "judges." A common complaint against the theory of a thirteenth-century-B.C. (LB II) Exodus and Conquest is that it reduces the length of the period of the "judges" to only about two hundred years or so—while the Bible assigns this era more than four hundred years. Placing the Conquest in the early part of Iron I would reduce that period still further, leaving only about a century or a century and a quarter for the activities of the various "judges." Also, the earliest settlement at Kadesh-Barnea is dated to the tenth and ninth centuries B.C., not the *beginning* of the Iron I period (the twelfth century B.C.).[132] In order for Kadesh-Barnea to be included in a list of sites agreeing with the biblical account of the Conquest, the Israelite entrance into Canaan would have to be placed at the very end of Iron I (the mid-tenth century B.C.), practically eliminating the period of the "judges" altogether.

Furthermore, the Iron I occupations at some of the Conquest "cities" do not seem to fit the biblical accounts very well. Arad, Ai, Bethel, Hazor, and Dan seem to have been only small unwalled villages in Iron I.[133] They are quite unlike the strongly fortified Canaanite cities that threw fear into the Israelites' hearts according to the Bible (Numbers 13:28). And at Aroer, Hazor, and Callaway's own site of Ai there were no signs of destruction during the Iron I period.[134] So, all in all, there is little substantive agreement between the archaeological evidence from Iron I Palestine and the biblical accounts of Israel's conquest of Canaan (see Table 9).

Almost all of the sites mentioned in the biblical Conquest stories were settled in the Iron Age, while many were often not occupied in earlier periods. What might this mean? Perhaps the biblical accounts say more about when the stories began to take shape than they do about the Conquest itself. There does not seem to be a point in the archaeological sequence in Palestine where the physical evidence revealed by the spade closely matches the biblical Exodus and Conquest narratives. Whether the Exodus and Conquest are placed at the end of EB III or MB II or in Iron Age I, there are still serious discrepancies, just as there are with the more common

---

131. Callaway 1985a.

132. Dothan 1977: 697.

133. Aharoni 1975: 82-83; Callaway 1976: 14-16; Kelso 1975: 192; Yadin 1975: 253-257; 1976: 487, 495; Biran 1987: 14-16.

134. Olivarri 1975: 99., Yadin 1975: 253-257; Callaway 1975: 39, 52, 1976: 15-16.

TABLE 9: Archaeology and an Iron Age I Exodus and Conquest

CITY	BIBLICAL REFERENCE	ARCHAEOLOGICAL EVIDENCE
Kadesh-Barnea	Deut. 1:19-46. The Israelites spent most of their 40 years in the wilderness at Kadesh	Fortresses were constructed at 'Ain Qudeirat and 'Ain Qedeis only at the *end* of Iron I
Arad	Num. 21:1-3 indicates that the city was destroyed by Joshua	Small unwalled village at Arad in Iron I
Hormah	Num. 21:1-3 says the city was destroyed by Joshua; Judges 1:17-18 credits its conquest to later action by Judah & Simeon	Unwalled Iron I villages at Tel Masos and Tel Malhata; Tel Masos destroyed at end of Iron I period
Heshbon	Num. 21:25-26. Heshbon is the capital of King Sihon and is destroyed	Occupied in Iron I
Dibon	Num. 21:30. Dibon was destroyed after Heshbon	Occupied in Iron I
Aroer	Deut. 2:36. Aroer was conquered after Sihon's defeat	Occupied in Iron I; apparently it was a small unwalled village
Jericho	Josh. 6 describes the total destruction of this city and its population	No Iron I occupation
Ai	Josh. 7-8. The city and all of its population was destroyed	Small unwalled village in Iron I; no Iron I destruction
Gibeon	Josh. 9-10:2. Gibeon was "a royal city, larger even than Ai" and became Israel's ally	El-Jib was a walled town in Iron I
Lachish	Josh. 10:32. Lachish was captured and its people killed	Unoccupied for most of Iron I; rebuilt at the end of that era
Hebron	Josh. 10:36-37. Hebron was captured and its people killed	Occupied in Iron I
Bethel	Judges 1:22-25 credits the destruction of Bethel to the house of Joseph	Apparently Beitin was a small unwalled village in Iron I
Hazor	Josh. 11:1-11. Hazor was burned and its people killed	Apparently Hazor was a small unwalled village in Iron I; no evidence of destruction
Dan	Judges 18:27-29 states that Laish was destroyed and then reoccupied by the Tribe of Dan	Apparently Dan was a small unwalled village in Iron I

Note: Underlined cities have significant stories told about their roles during the Conquest period.

Late Bronze placements for these events. Obviously, the lack of correspondence between biblical accounts of the Exodus/Conquest period and archaeological remains must be solved in some way other than shifting the archaeological date for the Israelite entrance into Canaan.

5

Interpretations of the Israelite Settlement in Canaan

Over the years, a number of different theories, or "models," have been proposed to explain how ancient Israel emerged in Palestine. These fall into three categories: the theory that Israelite armies conquered Canaan; the theory that Israelites settled by peaceful infiltration; and the theory that the Israelites were indigenous to Canaan and formed their nation through an "internal revolt."[1] There have been many variations on each of these models, and sometimes elements of the first two categories have been joined into one theory. We could, perhaps, treat this composite theory as a separate category called something like "multiple tribal movements and invasions." However, since individual variations on this theme usually emphasize either the conquest element or the peaceful-infiltration aspect, we can consider multiple exodus and settlement theories as variations of one or the other of the first two models.

Recently two additional models have emerged that combine elements from both the peaceful-infiltration and internal-revolt theories. However, these new theories are different enough to merit a separate discussion. The

1. For other surveys and criticisms of these schools of thought, see Weippert 1971: 5-62; Miller 1977: 268-279; Gottwald 1979: 192-219; Ramsey 1981: 65-98; Chaney 1983: 41-61; Finkelstein 1988: 295-314.

first of these reconstructions is "the Frontier Development Model," while the second can be called "the Symbiosis Hypothesis" or "the Internal Nomadic Settlement Model." (They will be treated below in the section on "Recent Hybrid Models.")

All scholarly attempts to reconstruct the historical circumstances concerning Israel's origins have to deal with the evidence we have already discussed—the biblical accounts, nonbiblical Near Eastern texts, and the archaeological record. But the various theoretical models differ in the weight they give to each type of evidence and in the way they interpret the evidence. The pictures they provide of the Israelite settlement can therefore differ quite radically.

An Israelite Military Conquest of Canaan

The view that Israelite control of Canaan was achieved by means of a military invasion by a unified group of twelve tribes and that this invasion resulted in the conquest of most of the Canaanite cities and the destruction of their population is, of course, that of the biblical Book of Joshua (though sections of Judges and of Joshua itself indicate a less organized and less extensive conquest). Obviously, Jewish and Christian biblical fundamentalists support this account in its entirety. However, in addition to the strict fundamentalists, there are many who accept the *essential* reliability of the biblical traditions about the Conquest, though they don't insist that the accounts are accurate in all details. These scholars would agree with John Bright's statement that "the Biblical narrative, at least in all major points, is rooted in history."[2]

Among the prominent supporters of military-conquest theories have been Yehezkel Kaufmann,[3] William Foxwell Albright[4] (and a number of his students, like John Bright,[5] J. L. Kelso,[6] Paul Lapp,[7] and G. E. Wright[8]), Abraham Malamat,[9] and Yigael Yadin.[10] These individuals generally have

---

2. Bright 1972: 130.
3. Kaufmann 1953; 1960: 245-261.
4. Albright 1939; 1960: 108-109.
5. Bright 1972: 127-130. In the latest edition of his *History of Israel,* however, Bright has become a supporter of the internal-revolt hypothesis (Bright 1981: 133-143).
6. Kelso 1968: 32, 47-48.
7. Lapp 1967.
8. Wright 1962a: 69-84.
9. Malamat 1979; 1982.
10. Yadin 1979; 1982.

emphasized the antiquity and reliability of the biblical tradition that Israel gained control of Canaan by force. Paul Lapp's assessment of the biblical version of the Conquest is typical of scholars who accept the Conquest model:

> It is hard to see how this tradition could have been invented in later times, which could be expected to expand traditions related to the founding of the kingdom by David but hardly to have invented a conquest narrative. This Biblical picture may be stressed without pressing any of its details. The literary stratification is diverse, but it is consistent in indicating a substantial conquest in a rather short period of time.[11]

Conquest theorists, especially members of the Albright school of thought, have argued that archaeological evidence justified their acceptance of the essential reliability of the biblical Conquest tradition. The fact that Bethel, Lachish, Tell Beit Mirsim (which Albright claimed was Debir), Hazor, and other Canaanite cities were violently destroyed at the end of the Late Bronze Age was seen as evidence "that during the 13th century a portion at least of the later nation of Israel gained entrance to Palestine by a carefully planned invasion, the purpose of which was not primarily loot but land."[12]

Most of the scholarly supporters of the Conquest model acknowledge that the number of the invading Israelites was probably much smaller than the Bible indicates and that all of the later tribes might not have participated in the invasion. But these scholars believe that the core of later Israel *did* enter Canaan from the outside. They claim that the appearance of small, poor, unfortified Iron Age I villages at new sites or at ones unoccupied for centuries indicates an influx of a relatively large number of seminomadic outsiders at the beginning of the Iron Age.[13]

In the 1930s and 1940s, when Albright and others were constructing the Conquest model, the evidence uncovered by archaeological excavations seemed to support with one or two exceptions the idea of an Israelite conquest of Canaan at the end of the Late Bronze Age. But as more and more archaeological work was undertaken in Israel and Jordan in the decades after World War II, problems for this theory mounted. As we have seen, today it is clear that much of the archaeological evidence from Israel and Jordan is very difficult to reconcile with the biblical narratives of the

---

11. Lapp 1967: 299.
12. Wright 1962a: 84.
13. For example, see, Wright 1962a: 70, 90; Lapp 1967: 295, 299; Bright 1972: 129-130; Yadin 1982: 18-19.

Conquest. The absence of Late Bronze strata of the fifteenth or thirteenth centuries B.C. at Kadesh-Barnea, Arad, Hormah, Heshbon, Dibon, Jericho, Ai, and Gibeon is particularly troublesome. And, since the pottery styles and other aspects of material culture in the Iron I "Israelite" villages is closely related to the previous "Canaanite" culture of the Late Bronze Age, the use of these sites as evidence for the influx of nomads from the desert is highly questionable. Thus, supporters of Conquest theories—once the so-called "archaeological school"—find themselves ironically forced to explain away the many problems that archaeological excavations have created for their view.

One way to deal with problematic evidence from various sites is to question the identification of those sites with particular towns mentioned in the Bible. Thus, as we have seen in Chapter 3, some have argued that et-Tell is not Ai or that Tell Hesban was not the site of Heshbon in Joshua's time. However, this kind of argument cannot eliminate all of the problems, for textual evidence makes the identification of Arad, Dibon, and Gibeon certain, and excavation has shown that they were not occupied in the period the Conquest supposedly occurred. Also, those who believe that the failure of archaeology to agree with the Bible is due largely to incorrectly identified sites must explain why excavations and surveys have turned up no Late Bronze remains in the *entire area* of the Negeb when places like Kadesh-Barnea, Hormah, and Arad, which play an important part in the biblical Conquest narratives, were supposedly located there.

A second approach is to argue that excavations at many sites, including Gibeon, Hebron, and Khirbet Rabud (the probable site of Debir), were limited, that important evidence was probably missed by the excavators. More complete excavation at these sites might reveal the Late Bronze occupation layers or the signs of destruction that were not found in previous "digs." However, the number of sites supposedly conquered by Israel that have failed to produce evidence of that destruction is now so large that it is extremely unlikely that the evidence was accidentally missed at each one. This second approach also fails to account for archaeologists' failure to find any Late Bronze material in the Negeb, even at sites such as Tel Arad, Tel Masos, and Beer-sheba, which *were* extensively excavated.

Such attempts to deal with the archaeological problems on an *ad hoc* basis, site by site, are simply no longer viable. So many sites have now been excavated that it is clear that those providing evidence that supports the biblical story of the Conquest are in a distinct minority. The Late Bronze destructions of Bethel, Lachish, and Hazor cannot be used as "proof" of the Bible's substantial historicity while evidence from most of the other sites is ignored or explained away.

There was widespread destruction in Palestine at the end of the Late Bronze Age, but many of the burned cities were in the plains and valleys, which remained in Canaanite hands down to the time of David and Solomon, not in the hills where Israel seems to have come into being. As Israel Finkelstein has pointed out, those who attempt to remain faithful to both the biblical account of the Conquest and the archaeological evidence must adopt a strange reconstruction in which Israelite tribes destroy a number of key cities in the coastal plain and northern valleys but then fail to settle in those fertile areas. Why would they abandon these desirable regions in order to build small, poor villages in the rocky hill country?[14] This reconstruction is not very persuasive, to say the least.

Obviously, archaeological evidence no longer supports the historical accuracy of the biblical Conquest narratives, and the only way to change that fact is to find an archaeological placement for the Conquest other than the Late Bronze Age. But, as we have seen in Chapter 4, no other archaeological period seems to fit the biblical evidence much better. So, despite its past popularity, the Conquest model seems doomed among scholars.

Settlement By Peaceful Infiltration

A different reconstruction of the Israelite occupation of Canaan was developed in the 1920s and 1930s by German biblical scholar Albrecht Alt.[15] Alt's view of the settlement was supported and further popularized by his student Martin Noth,[16] so it is often known as the Alt-Noth hypothesis. More recently it has been systematically defended by Manfred Weippert.[17]

This theoretical model challenged the traditional idea of an Israelite conquest of Canaan:

> When one looks at the whole range of the Israelite settlements in Palestine it is immediately obvious that the tribes of Israel entered those parts of the country that had only been inhabited sparsely or not at all in the Bronze

---

14. Finkelstein 1988: 302. See also the quote from Martin Noth below on pp. 153–154.
15. Alt 1925; 1936; 1939.
16. Noth 1938; 1960: 68-84.
17. Weippert 1971; 1979.

Age. . . . This fact in itself shows very clearly that the Israelite occupation did not ensue from a warlike encounter between the newcomers and the previous owners of the land. In the parts of the country occupied by the Israelites there were only a few scattered Canaanite settlements, though the tribes may have occupied some of these by military force sooner or later.[18]

Alt and Noth saw the establishment of Israel in terms of a gradual settlement of seminomadic tribes who, with their flocks of sheep and goats, moved peacefully back and forth from the adjoining steppes and desert fringes to the largely unoccupied central hill country of Palestine. Their analysis of the biblical data convinced Alt and Noth that the various Israelite tribes and clans did not all arrive or settle down simultaneously. The "league of twelve tribes" known as Israel in the Bible was created in Palestine; it did not exist in its classic form until the latter part of the period of the "judges." The name *Israel,* though, was older than the tribal confederation that came to use that name. Of the groups that later joined the twelve-tribe league, one or more seem to have called itself Israel at the time the term was mentioned on the Merneptah Stele.[19]

According to Alt and Noth's interpretation of the evidence, warfare between Israel and the Canaanite city-states in the plains and valleys came only in the final stages of the settlement and during the early monarchy, when Israel began to expand its territory. These conflicts became the basis for the development of the later Deuteronomistic tradition in Joshua 1-12, in which a general conquest of the land supposedly took place at the beginning of the settlement. Alt and Noth asserted that many of the Conquest stories developed etiologically—that is, they originally were narratives to explain the existence of institutions, customs, or physical features (like the ruined walls of Ai or a group of five trees near a cave at Makkedah) observed in later times.[20]

One criticism that supporters of the military-conquest model often have directed against Alt, Noth, and their followers is that they failed to utilize the results of archaeology in their attempts to reconstruct the Israelite settlement.[21] This criticism is not valid. Proponents of the peaceful-infiltration theory did not deny the validity of archaeological finds; they only rejected the *interpretation* given to the finds by Albright and his school. Alt and Noth were aware of the archaeological evidence that a number of sites

---

18. Noth 1960: 68.
19. Alt 1925: Section III; Noth 1930; 1960: 68-84.
20. Alt 1936; Noth 1953: 20ff; 1960: 73-74.
21. Bright 1956: 87-89.

in Palestine had been violently destroyed at the end of the Late Bronze Age, but they argued that this evidence was too ambiguous to prove an Israelite conquest. The destructions could have resulted from many causes, including accidentally started fires or natural events like earthquakes. The most likely cause for the destruction of many of the cities was enemy assault, but Egyptian raids into Palestine, marauding Sea Peoples, or forces from other Canaanite city-states could have been the agents of destruction rather than invading Israelite tribes.[22] Such uncertain evidence, they felt, could not negate the conclusions they had reached on the basis of their extensive literary analyses of the biblical text.

In recent years archaeologists such as Yohanan Aharoni,[23] Aharon Kempinski,[24] and Volkmar Fritz[25] have argued that, instead of disproving the peaceful-infiltration hypothesis, the archaeological evidence actually *supports* it. Recent surveys and excavations, they point out, have continued to uncover many small unwalled Iron I "Israelite" villages in the central hills and in Galilee, where the Alt-Noth model predicted they should be concentrated, while none has been found in the coastal plain or northern valleys near the large Canaanite cities. This evidence fits the Alt-Noth hypothesis and demonstrates the basically peaceful nature of the initial stages of the settlement, they contend.

Archaeological discoveries still produce a major problem for the Alt-Noth thesis—the same problem they produce for the Conquest model. Where did the Israelites come from? There is no archaeological evidence of their prior existence in Sinai or in the steppes and desert fringes of Canaan.[26] Another problem with the peaceful-infiltration model is that it unconsciously views the seminomadic or nomadic way of life as a temporary stage of existence between that of primitive hunting, fishing, and gathering and that of sedentary agriculture and civilization.[27] It assumes a "land hunger" on the part of the incoming Israelites that led them to become sedentary as soon as possible. Yet we know that pastoral groups are usually well adapted to their environments and seek to *maintain* their free existence, not to settle down. When the various tribes spread over the hill country of Palestine, why did they build small agricultural villages rather than continue their seminomadic way of life?

22. Noth 1938; 1960: 82. See also Weippert 1971: 128-136 and Fritz 1987: 90-91.
23. Aharoni 1970; 1976; 1978: 158-167.
24. Kempinski 1976.
25. Fritz 1981; 1982.
26. Finkelstein 1988: 304.
27. Chaney 1983: 42-43.

Alt and Noth did not really consider this question, but Manfred Weippert has argued that it was population growth that forced the seminomads to adopt a new, sedentary way of life.[28] However, Weippert's solution is not very likely. In the 1920s and 1930s some 200,000 to 250,000 Bedouin pastoralists lived with their flocks of sheep and goats in the fringe regions of Palestine.[29] In contrast, the sedentary Iron I "Israelite" population has been estimated at only about 55,000 or less.[30] Obviously, the hill country population of Palestine during the Iron I period was nowhere near as large as the seminomadic population that the fringe areas normally could support. So, if the ancient climate of Palestine was much the same as it is now, it is difficult to see excess population as the cause for the Iron I settlement. Even if population pressures had driven the Israelites from the desert fringes, they still could have continued their seminomadic way of life in the hill country. Why didn't they? The Alt-Noth hypothesis does not answer this question.

Furthermore, biblical traditions do not necessarily support the view that the Israelites who left Egypt under Moses and entered Canaan under Joshua had a nomadic or seminomadic background. The patriarchs seem to be depicted as seminomads, but their descendants are portrayed as sedentary inhabitants of Egypt who knew little of the seminomadic life and were very uncomfortable in the desert. Indeed, whenever the going got hard, they were anxious to return to Egypt, and they managed to survive the trek through Sinai only because God aided them with miracles (Exodus 15:22-25; 16:2-15; 17:1-6; Numbers 11:4-6, 22-32; 20:3-11). As Norman Gottwald has pointed out, "The diet of fish and vegetables which they recall was hardly pastoral nomadic fare. In every way the desert is presented as an alien place."[31] Even the prophetic glorification of the wilderness experience does not emphasize a return to *nomadic* life, but rather a reversion to an egalitarian social system and to a pure Yahwistic faith that did not contain elements of Canaanite religion.

Alt and Noth's reliance on etiology as an explanation for the development of many of the biblical Conquest traditions is also somewhat questionable. While undeniably there is an etiological factor in many of the stories in the Book of Joshua, careful examination has shown that this element is usually *secondary*. Details may have been added to various stories

---

28. Weippert 1979: 32-34.
29. See Finkelstein 1988: 308 and the sources cited there.
30. Finkelstein 1988: 330-335.
31. Gottwald 1976: 630.

because of etiological considerations, but it is unlikely that etiology provides an adequate explanation for the existence of most of the basic traditions themselves.[32] Supporters of the Conquest model argue that this strong biblical tradition can be explained only by the assumption that it is rooted in history.

The Internal-Revolt Hypothesis

The third major model for the Israelite settlement in Canaan was first proposed by George Mendenhall in a now-famous article in *The Biblical Archaeologist* in 1962.[33] Mendenhall's thesis has been further developed by Norman Gottwald[34] (though Mendenhall has objected to having his ideas linked with Gottwald's Marxist sociological approach[35]). Among other supporters of variations of this model are C. H. J. de Geus,[36] John Halligan,[37] and Marvin Chaney.[38]

We have already noted that the Iron I "Israelite" culture is derived from that of the Canaanite Late Bronze period. There is no archaeological evidence for the arrival of the large group of outsiders posited by both the Conquest and the peaceful-infiltration models. So, if the Israelites did not enter Canaan from outside, they must have come from within the area of Palestine itself.[39]

Mendenhall's study of the Amarna Letters led him to conclude that the 'apiru who were described as causing so much trouble for some of the Canaanite city-states were not invading nomadic groups as often thought. Rather, they were local population groups (mostly peasants) who had renounced their allegiance to their former city-states and rulers and separated themselves from the feudal society to which they had belonged. Likewise, the term "Hebrew" could be applied to early Israelites because Israel originated from thirteenth and twelfth century B.C. 'apiru who rebelled against the inequities of the Canaanite city-state system.[40]

---

32. Bright 1956: 91-100.
33. Mendenhall 1962. See also Mendenhall 1973 and 1976.
34. Gottwald 1974; 1975; 1976; 1978; 1979; 1983a; 1983b; 1985.
35. Mendenhall 1983.
36. de Geus 1976.
37. Halligan 1983.
38. Chaney 1983.
39. Mendenhall 1962: 107; Gottwald 1975: 92; 1979: 210-211.
40. Mendenhall 1962: 105; 1973: 122-141. See also the further elaboration and defense of Mendenhall's interpretation of the 'apiru in Gottwald 1979: 474-485; Halligan 1983; and Chaney 1983: 72-83.

The revolt hypothesis assumes the existence of a long-standing animosity between peasants, pastoralists, and other members of the Canaanite lower classes who lived in villages near the major cities and the ruling classes who dominated the political and economic life of the city-states. Supposedly, the catalyst that allowed this smoldering conflict to burst into the flame of revolution was provided by a small group of escaped Egyptian slaves who entered Canaan singing the praise of their liberating god, Yahweh. Yahweh not only had triumphed over the power of the Egyptian state and freed His people, but He also demanded that Israelites live together harmoniously in an egalitarian society. The downtrodden of Canaan flocked to join this new movement, which promised equality and social justice in place of the exploitation and mistreatment they had received in the past. "Entire groups having a clan or 'tribal' organization joined the newly-formed community, identified themselves with the oppressed in Egypt, and received deliverance from bondage."[41]

Mendenhall emphasized "the withdrawal, not physically and geographically, but politically and subjectively, of large population groups from any obligation to the existing political regimes."[42] But other advocates of the peasant-revolt thesis find the physical and geographical element in the withdrawal more significant. They point out that it was the rugged hills that provided sanctuary for Canaanites withdrawing from their city-states, and in the hills these groups merged with the small contingent of incoming Yahwists to form the tribes of Israel. That is why many small "Israelite" villages appeared in the hills in the early part of Iron I.[43]

However, Israel Finkelstein has objected that the evidence from the Iron I hill country settlements does *not* support the internal-revolt hypothesis (or "the Sociological School," as he calls it).[44] He claims that advocates of this theory have given insufficient attention to the settlement patterns of both the Late Bronze and Iron Ages. Archaeologists have found no evidence of small, outlying villages around the large Late Bronze city-states as posited by supporters of the revolt hypothesis.[45] Furthermore, the most densely settled area during the Late Bronze era was the southern coast and foothills area adjacent to the Judean Hills. Peasants revolting against the Canaanite cities in this southern region should have fled eastward into

41. The quote is from Mendenhall 1962: 108. See Mendenhall 1962: 107-110; Gottwald 1979: 496, 555-583.

42. Mendenhall 1970: 107.

43. Gottwald 1979: 214; Chaney 1983: 49-50.

44. Finkelstein 1988a: 307-314.

45. Finkelstein 1988a: 311. See also Gonen 1984.

the Judean Hills for refuge. But archaeology indicates that they did not. The Iron I "Israelite" villages were concentrated in the central hill country; very few have been found in the Judean Hills.[46]

It also has been objected that the type of "peasants' revolt" proposed by Mendenhall, Gottwald, and their supporters is a modern construct that has been anachronistically applied to ancient Palestine. No ancient Near Eastern sources describe a social revolution or a large-scale religious conversion like the ones they hypothesize.[47] Moreover, there is little support for the internal-revolt model in the biblical traditions themselves. As J. Maxwell Miller has observed:

> There is not the slightest hint in the biblical traditions regarding the revolution which supposedly brought Israel into existence. Surely one would expect to find some allusion to it in the book of Judges if such a revolution had in fact occurred.[48]

Like the peaceful-infiltration hypothesis, the peasant-revolt theory must explain the Bible's insistence that Israel came into Canaan *from the outside* and *conquered* the Canaanite city-states. While supporters of the revolt model point to elements in biblical tradition, particularly Israelite egalitarianism, as survivals from the era of the revolution that created Israel,[49] their arguments have not convinced most biblical scholars or historians.

Recent Hybrid Models

In the past few years there have been attempts to combine elements of the peaceful-infiltration and internal-revolt models in order to eliminate some of the objections to each of them and better explain the archaeological evidence. These composite theories agree with two contentions of both the Alt-Noth theory and the peasant-revolt hypothesis: that the tribal league known as Israel was created within Palestine from groups with diverse roots, and that the biblical traditions were edited so often during the pre-

---

46. Two hundred and ten Iron I villages have been found in the central hill country of Ephraim and Manasseh; only ten or twelve have been found in Judah. See Finkelstein 1988a: 50-53, 80-91, 121-204, 311.

47. Miller 1977: 279; Soggin 1984: 156-157; Finkelstein 1988a: 314.

48. Miller 1977: 279. See also Lapp 1967: 299.

49. Mendenhall 1962: 108-109, 113-116; 1973: 1-31, 224-226; Gottwald 1979: 63-64, 72-187; Chaney 1983: 67-72.

Roman period that it is now virtually impossible to reconstruct the historical reality of premonarchic Israel from them. However, the two composite models that have attracted some support give slightly different descriptions of the way Israel came into being.

One approach to the problem is to view the emergence of Israel in terms of a "frontier society." Joseph Callaway's excavations at Ai (et-Tell) and Khirbet Raddana revealed that from the beginning of their settlement at these sites the Iron I villagers used terraces and cisterns to make it possible for them to raise grain and garden crops. They had well-developed bronze tools for cutting cisterns and for shaping stone pillars for houses. They also had fixed patterns of house construction, including the tradition of keeping animals in enclosures connected to the houses. Furthermore, the layout of the villages suggested a tradition of sedentary life and agricultural planning. These facts indicated to Callaway that the new settlers had already been farmers before they came to the hill country. They were not seminomads just beginning to settle down.[50]

Like supporters of the revolt hypothesis, Callaway and others have traced the origins of the new settlers to the Canaanite city-states of the coastal plain.[51] However, these scholars see the Iron I villagers as *refugees,* not avowed social revolutionaries. According to Callaway, "the newcomers who established villages in the highlands seem to have fled from conflict in the lowlands and coastal plain areas to escape more warlike newcomers to those regions."[52] On the other hand, Alberto Soggin argues that "groups of city-dwellers will have left the territory of the city-states, probably because they were oppressed by taxation and demands on personal services."[53]

For whatever reasons they fled—attacks by Sea Peoples or oppression by their native rulers—the Canaanite peasants took refuge in a new frontier, the undeveloped hill country of Palestine. Here they developed into the early Israel we know in the Bible, with its emphasis on equality, its distrust of strong centralized government, and its hatred of corvée labor (uncompensated, forced labor on public projects).

It has been pointed out that frontier life tends to produce the kind of egalitarian society that Mendenhall and Gottwald had credited to a peasant revolt:

---

50. Callaway 1985d: 72-75.
51. Callaway 1985d: 75-77. See also Soggin 1984: 158.
52. Callaway 1985d: 75.
53. Soggin 1984: 158.

Having risked their lives to establish themselves in a new territory, frontiersmen are not prepared to hand over their surplus to anyone. Thus frontier conditions often break down the sharp inequalities and exploitative patterns characteristic of agrarian societies.[54]

The frontier-development hypothesis uses such arguments to preserve much of the emphasis of the revolt model while avoiding modern conceptions of an organized revolt that includes widespread military activity against established authorities. Supporters of this view do not have to explain how a peasants' revolt could have been organized or how it could have succeeded against the military power of the Canaanite nobility. Nevertheless, this view still encounters objections. Some archaeologists dispute Callaway's claim (and that of supporters of the peasant-revolt model) that there was a direct connection between Canaanite groups of the Late Bronze Age and the Israelite villagers of Iron I. The pillared ("four-room") houses characteristic of the Iron I villages and the practice of grouping houses to form a defensive belt around many of those villages are features virtually unknown in Late Bronze Age Canaanite cities. So, it is argued, these architectural traditions must have been developed by people who were originally *pastoral* rather than sedentary.[55] Israel Finkelstein notes that "it is particularly significant that the influences of both the tent and the encampment are perceptible in the plans of several early Israelite sites."[56]

However, the pastoralists who settled down to become the Israelites could not have been true nomads or relative newcomers to the land, as Alt and Noth assumed. Their pottery styles, their tools, their use of agricultural terraces to grow grain, and even their cultic practices reflect a Canaanite background, so they must have been in close contact with the Canaanites long before they became sedentary in the twelfth century B.C. In fact, it is claimed, the pastoral Israelites had lived in a symbiotic relationship with the Canaanite city-states throughout much, if not all, of the Late Bronze Age.[57]

Michael B. Rowton has shown that in the ancient Near East most seminomads lived in the vicinity of towns. They were not enemies of the cities; they lived in harmony with them in what Rowton calls a "dimorphic structure." The seminomads grazed their flocks on the stubble left in the

---

54. Lenski and Lenski 1978: 229.
55. Fritz 1987: 97; Finkelstein 1988a: 312-313; 1988b: 42-43.
56. Finkelstein 1988a: 313.
57. Fritz 1987: 97-98; Finkelstein 1988a: 336-338.

fields after harvest, and in return the flocks fertilized the fields for the farmers. The seminomads supplied the cities with products from their flocks and in return acquired grain and luxury goods.[58] As Volkmar Fritz has noted, "This form of nomadism differs radically from that of the bedouin in the desert and entails a partly sedentary life, out of which there develops an economic, and probably a political symbiosis and adoption of cultural goods."[59]

This symbiotic relationship was broken by the destruction of the Canaanite city-states at the end of the Late Bronze period (c. 1200-1150 B.C.), according to the internal nomadic settlement hypothesis. Since they could no longer secure agricultural products from the cities, the pastoralists supposedly had to settle down and begin growing their own crops in addition to tending their herds. Eventually, most of them became fully sedentary farmers; only a few continued to live as seminomads.[60]

The population of Palestine, judged by sedentary-occupation sites, declined drastically after the Middle Bronze Age and then increased again during the Iron Age I. Estimates say that about 140,000 people lived west of the Jordan in the MB II period, while during the Late Bronze Age this number dropped to 60,000 or 70,000.[61] Israel Finkelstein argues that this loss of population was more apparent than real. Large numbers of people, he claims, were forced to become seminomadic (and therefore archaeologically invisible) because of the Egyptian invasions, widespread destruction of towns, and the concomitant stresses within Canaanite society at the end of the Middle Bronze period. The descendants of these farmers-turned-nomads then became sedentary again at the beginning of the Iron Age.[62]

This "symbiosis hypothesis" or "internal nomadic settlement model" is an improvement upon the "peaceful-infiltration theory" from which it primarily derives. However, it still presents certain problems. It has not been established that the four-room or pillared house style common in the Iron I villages developed from tent dwellings or that the village plans reflect the layout of seminomadic encampments.[63] In fact, the practice of grouping houses together so that their walls connect to form a defensive perimeter seems to be a natural response of people familiar with fortified

---

58. Rowton 1974; 1976; 1977. See also Matthews 1978.
59. Fritz 1987: 98.
60. Fritz 1987: 98-99; Finkelstein 1988a: 345-351.
61. Finkelstein 1988a: 341 and the sources cited there. See also Finkelstein 1988b: 41.
62. Finkelstein 1988a: 339-348; 1988b: 40-41.
63. Esse 1988: 10.

towns who do not have the financial and population resources to construct massive defensive walls for themselves.[64] The people who built these villages obviously felt the need for some protection from possible marauders and were intent on defending their homes and their land if necessary. Such people are as likely, if not more likely, to come from a sedentary background as from a seminomadic one.

More importantly, there is the inconsistency of having the stresses within the Canaanite social system and the destructions at the end of the Middle Bronze Age force thousands of farmers to become seminomads—when the destructions at the end of the Late Bronze Age supposedly forced them back into agriculture. Instead of becoming seminomads, why didn't the dispossessed MB II farmers establish small agricultural villages in the hill country, where most of the previously existing towns had been destroyed? After all, this is supposedly what happened in Iron I. Isn't it more likely that such a settlement would have occurred in LB I when the dispossessed groups were still essentially farmers rather than some three hundred years later in Iron I when they long had become accustomed to a seminomadic life?

Finkelstein is aware of this inconsistency, but he argues that "the background of each period was so completely different that absolute comparisons between the two inverse processes cannot be drawn, especially since urban centers continued to flourish in the lowlands of the country during the Late Bronze period."[65] But this does not totally dispose of the problem. It is difficult to imagine that about *half* of the Middle Bronze II population of Palestine could have become pastoralists for some three hundred years without upsetting the delicate balance (or "symbiosis") with the remaining cities.

Furthermore, if ancient seminomads needed to live in symbiosis with towns and cities, how could the tens of thousands of newly created Late Bronze Age seminomads exist in the hill country, where only a handful of towns were to be found? Finkelstein could answer this question by pointing to the Middle Bronze I (or Early Bronze IV) period, when a collapse of

---

64. Nineteenth-century American wagon trains moving through hostile Indian country usually circled wagons at night or when threatened. Most of the people in these wagon trains had been sedentary before moving west and intended to become sedentary again. They were familiar with forts, and created the best defensive "wall" for their encampment that they could. Their practice does not reflect some seminomadic custom. Rather, it suggests that possibly the arrangements of nineteenth- and early-twentieth-century Palestinian bedouin camps were influenced by bedouin acquaintance with cities and fortifications.

65. Finkelstein 1988a: 346, note 40.

urban civilization seems to have led to an extended period of pastoralism in Palestine during which virtually *no* urban centers existed. So it was possible in some instances for seminomads to exist and flourish in the absence of towns and cities. Why, then, must we assume that the destruction of many of the Canaanite cities at the end of the Late Bronze Age would have forced the pastoralists of the hill country to settle down and become agriculturalists?

Finkelstein has presented some archaeological and textual evidence for the existence of seminomadic groups in Palestine during the Late Bronze Age. This evidence includes a few sanctuaries that seem to be unrelated to any settlements, a number of Late Bronze cemeteries that do not seem to have been adjacent to permanent settlements, and the references to Sutu, Shosu, and other seminomadic groups in Egyptian sources.[66] While this evidence does seem to demonstrate that *some* seminomads lived in Palestine and Transjordan in the Late Bronze Age, it does not indicate that these groups were as numerous as the sedentary population of the land. Yet this is what is required by Finkelstein's theory.[67]

The argument that problems at the end of the Middle Bronze Age forced *some* peasants to become seminomads is probably valid. But it is unlikely that we can account in this way for most of the 70,000 to 80,000 people who disappeared between MB II and LB II. So we are left with the questions that Finkelstein himself poses: "Why and to where did over half of the MB II population, i.e., virtually all the inhabitants of the hill country, 'vanish,' " and "from where did the people who settled the hundreds of sites in Iron I 'materialize'?"[68] The answer to that question is not likely to be simply that they became seminomads for a time, and then reverted to a sedentary agricultural existence.

One problem with all of the models we have considered is that they view the Israelite conquest or settlement in relative isolation. They bring in Egyptians or Sea Peoples to explain destructions or periods of cultural decline, but essentially they limit themselves to treatment of Palestinian archaeology and the biblical traditions. This is a great mistake, as Lawrence

66. Finkelstein 1988a: 343-344; 1988b: 41-42.

67. Steven Rosen notes (1988: 53) that the Negeb has preserved traces of nomadic encampments from many different periods, but that archaeologists have found no evidence for Late Bronze Age nomads there. If pastoralists were as plentiful in the Late Bronze Age as Finkelstein claims, and if the climate was similar to that of the present, a number of these nomads should have spent at least some time in the Negeb where traces of their presence would have survived. The absence of such evidence casts serious doubt upon Finkelstein's theory.

68. Finkelstein 1988a: 341.

Stager has recognized. Stager has argued that the appearance of small Iron I agricultural communities in frontier zones was not exclusive to Israel. "A general phenomenon must have equally general causes," he claims. "Comparison with a similar, but widespread phenomenon often undermines purely local explanations."[69]

The emergence of Israel in Canaan should be understood in the context of events taking place throughout the eastern Mediterranean world at the end of the Late Bronze Age. Cities were being destroyed and settlement patterns were changing in Greece, Asia Minor, and Syria as well as in Transjordan and Palestine at the end of the thirteenth century B.C. That these widespread disturbances were all unrelated is extremely unlikely.

---

69. Stager 1985: 83.

6

The End of the Late Bronze Age in the Eastern Mediterranean

The Late Bronze Age saw the zeniths of the Mycenaean civilization in Greece, the Hittite Empire in Asia Minor and northern Syria, and the Egyptian Empire in the Nile Valley, Palestine, and Syria (see Figure 9). Ships carrying trade goods (often designated as "gifts" or "tribute" by the various rulers) crisscrossed the eastern Mediterranean.[1] But toward the end of the thirteenth century, the complex political, economic, and social relationships among and within these civilizations began to unravel. Cities were burned, trade became scarce, and whole populations moved from one place to another.

For a little over a century there was turmoil throughout the area. By the time these troubles ceased and relative calm returned to the region, a new world had dawned, and the empires and civilizations of old were gone or reduced to impotence. In their place there developed new nations and new societies ready to make their mark on the pages of history. Two of the new entities that eventually arose out of the ashes of the Bronze Age destructions were the Classical Greek culture and biblical Israel. When one considers the contributions these two cultures have made to Western

---

1. See Throckmorton 1962 and Bass 1967 and 1987 for information on the cargoes of two Late Bronze Age ships that have been excavated off the south and southwest coasts of Turkey.

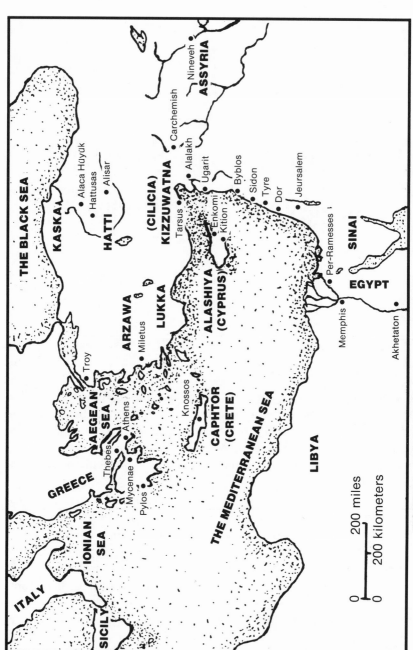

FIGURE 9: THE EASTERN MEDITERRANEAN IN THE LATE BRONZE AGE

Civilization, it becomes clear that the change from the Bronze to the Iron Age in the eastern Mediterranean represents one of the most momentous revolutions in human history.

The Destruction of Mycenaean Civilization

During the thirteenth century B.C., Greek-speaking Mycenaeans, primarily settled in southern Greece, dominated the Aegean world. About a century and a half earlier, mainland groups had invaded Crete, destroyed most of the Minoan palaces, and taken control of the island. The descendants of these invaders seem to have continued their domination of Crete into the thirteenth century B.C. There also were Mycenaean settlements on Rhodes and at Miletus in Asia Minor (perhaps ruled by the king of Ahhiyawa mentioned in Hittite texts).

Mycenaean kings lived in palaces decorated with beautiful frescoes; they presided over extensive bureaucracies, which controlled the local economies as well as many aspects of everyday life; and when they died, they were buried in huge domed tombs near their palaces. Mycenaean craftsmen produced high-quality products that were in demand throughout the eastern Mediterranean. The monumental architecture, flourishing arts and crafts, and widespread trade have given this era the appearance of a "golden age."[2]

But peace did not accompany prosperity in the Aegean region. A few palaces, like the ones at Pylos and Knossos, were defended only by geography or by outlying forts, but most royal dwellings and administrative centers were enclosed within strongly fortified citadels. The rulers of Gla, Athens, Tiryns, and Mycenae found it necessary to enlarge or strengthen their fortification walls during the thirteenth century. After all, it was during that century the palaces at Knossos in Crete and Thebes in Boeotia were both destroyed.[3]

Then came the widespread disasters of the late thirteenth and early twelfth centuries B.C. At the very end of the thirteenth century (c. 1200 B.C.) Pylos was destroyed. At about the same time or soon afterwards,

---

2. For an overview of Mycenaean civilization, see Chadwick 1976; Hooker 1977; and Taylour 1983.

3. The palace at Thebes was destroyed c. 1250 B.C. The destruction of the Mycenaean palace at Knossos traditionally has been dated c. 1400-1380 B.C., the date given by Sir Arthur Evans. A review of the evidence from Knossos now makes it likely, however, that the palace continued to exist under Mycenaean rule into the thirteenth century B.C. Exactly when in the thirteenth century B.C. the palace was destroyed is uncertain. See Hallager 1977.

Thebes was burned again, along with Gla, Iolkos, and Tiryns. Portions of Mycenae were burned at least once and possibly twice during the early twelfth century B.C., but this great citadel survived. Then, around 1150 B.C. Mycenae too was destroyed and abandoned. Population shifts were immense, with refugees settling in Attica, Achaea, the Ionian Islands (especially the island of Kephallenia) off the west coast of Greece, and the far-off island of Cyprus, while areas of Thessaly, Boeotia, and parts of the Peloponnese, which formerly had contained many settlements, became seriously depopulated for about a century. The total population of Greece declined by as much as 75 per cent. The areas that continued to be settled experienced a marked decline in material culture, and the cultural unity of the Mycenaean Age came to an end. The highly centralized Mycenaean palaces, with their elaborate bureaucracies, disappeared, and small, poor agricultural villages took their place.[4]

The situation was much the same in Crete, where there was a great decline in population, and the material culture became very much poorer. People abandoned the previously well-populated coastal areas (especially in South Crete) and built new villages in the hills or in other easily defensible positions.[5]

Like biblical scholars and biblical archaeologists, classical archaeologists have generally been quite parochial in their attempts to explain the changes that occurred at the end of the Bronze Age. Traditionally they have blamed the destruction of Mycenaean civilization on an invasion from the north of semibarbaric Greeks speaking a Dorian dialect, since this seems to have been what the ancient Greeks themselves believed. But archaeologists have been unable to find any artifacts that could be attributed to these newcomers, and linguistic evidence indicates that the Dorian dialect developed in Greece alongside the other Greek dialects, including those that descend from the dialect spoken by the Mycenaeans. The Dorian-invasion theory also has difficulty explaining why many areas, especially those where the Dorians were later settled, were seriously depopulated for some time following the destructions. The Dorians do not seem to have settled in the Peloponnese and Crete until a couple of generations or so *after* the disappearance of the Mycenaean palaces.

Over the past two or three decades a number of other explanations have been advanced to account for the wave of destruction, depopulation, and change in civilization in the Aegean area at the end of the Bronze

---

4. Desborough 1964; 1972; 1975: 658-671; Biers 1980: 63, 94-99.
5. Pendlebury 1939: 303-316; Hutchinson 1962: 320-325; Desborough 1975: 675-677.

Age. Attacks by unknown northerners who did not remain to occupy the areas they destroyed, raids by Sea Peoples, internal conflicts between Mycenaean kings, and economic collapse due to an overly specialized economy have all been blamed by one or more scholars.[6] And some have claimed that a combination of these factors was responsible for the Mycenaean demise.[7]

But all of these theories suffer from the same problem Lawrence Stager saw with models for the Israelite settlement in Palestine: They only provide limited, local explanations for what obviously was a much wider problem. The Mycenaean civilization was not the only one crumbling during the thirteenth and twelfth centuries B.C., and the Aegean area was not the only one experiencing destructions and population shifts. Therefore, any theory that attempts to explain the end of the Mycenaean Age but which cannot also explain what was happening *elsewhere* in the eastern Mediterranean is not likely to be valid.

The End of the Hittite Empire

The Hittites were an Indo-European-speaking people who had settled in central Asia Minor in the third millennium B.C. Starting with only the area around their capital at Hattusas (Boghazköy), the Hittites gradually built an empire that by the thirteenth century B.C. included almost all of Asia Minor and northern Syria. The rulers of this great empire maintained a lively diplomatic correspondence with other great kings—including the rulers of Egypt, Babylon, and Assyria—as well as with allied or vassal kings in western Asia Minor, Ugarit, and Cyprus.[8]

Much of the Hittite expansion southward into Syria had come at the expense of the Egyptian Empire. But in 1258 B.C., during the reign of Ramesses II of Egypt and Hattusilis III of Hatti (which is what the Hittite nation was called), a peace treaty between these two great powers was signed. The alliance between Egypt and Hatti was strengthened a little over a decade later when a daughter of the Hittite king married Ramesses II. Like the Mycenaean kingdoms, in the latter half of the thirteenth century B.C. the Hittite Empire seemed to be at the height of its strength and prosperity.

---

6. See Betancourt 1976 or Stiebing 1981 for a summary of the various theories.

7. See, for example, Biers 1980: 63; M. Wood 1985: 248-249.

8. For an overview of the Hittites and their history, see Goetze 1975; Gurney 1981; or Macqueen 1986.

As they were in the Aegean, in Asia Minor the appearances were deceiving. Rebellions by vassals, particularly in western Anatolia, plagued the Hittite monarchs. Sporadic fighting with the Kaska people of northern Asia Minor continued. The growth of Assyrian power in northern Mesopotamia threatened the eastern holdings of the Hittites. And there were occasional internal conflicts over the succession to the throne.

There also seem to have been crop failures and famine in Asia Minor, for in 1212 B.C., during the reign of Pharaoh Merneptah, the Egyptians sent a large shipment of grain to alleviate hunger in Hittite lands.[9] And, about a generation later, among the last letters received by the king of Ugarit before his city's destruction were three that mentioned famine in Hatti. In one of these letters the last Hittite king, Suppiluliumas II, appealed to his vassal in Ugarit to send two thousand measures of grain to Cilicia immediately because it was a matter of life or death.[10]

However, at this time Ugarit itself seems to have been suffering from drought. Its excavator, Claude F. A. Schaeffer, noted that a fine, powdery, homogeneous yellow-white soil characterized the final Late Bronze stratum at Ugarit. This dry, dusty layer was in marked contrast to the normal dark brown humus layers above and below it.[11] Schaeffer regarded this powdery deposit as clear stratigraphic evidence "of a long period of extreme aridity and heat during the city's last years."[12]

Early in the twelfth century B.C. the Hittite records, as well as those of Ugarit, became silent. Hattusas was violently destroyed along with Troy, Miletus, Tarsus, Alaca Hüyük, Alisar, Carchemish, Alalakh, Ugarit, Qatna, Qadesh, and other cities that had been part of the Hittite Empire.

> The archaeological evidence proves that a catastrophe overtook Anatolia and Syria. Wherever excavations have been made they indicate that the Hittite country was ravaged, its cities burned down. When civilization slowly rises again from the ruins, it is no longer Hittite and clearly bears new characteristics.[13]

Hittite culture did not totally disappear, though. In Syria during the twelfth century B.C. a number of small kingdoms arose whose rulers bore Hittite names and whose religious, literary, artistic, and epigraphic traditions

---

9. Breasted 1906: 244.
10. Astour 1965: 255; Barnett 1975: 369.
11. Nougayrol, *et al.* 1968: 761-762. For an English translation of these pages see Schaeffer 1983.
12. Schaeffer 1983: 75.
13. Goetze 1975: 266.

derived from those of the Hittite Empire. The Assyrians called these kingdoms "Hatti," the old name for the Hittite Empire. But the language of these "Neo-Hittites" was not the Hittite of the former rulers of Hattusas. It was a dialect of Luwian, a related Indo-European language that had been spoken by some groups in the western provinces of the Hittite Empire during the Bronze Age. Obviously, people from western Asia Minor migrated to Syria during the upheaval accompanying the fall of the Hittite Empire, and there they tried to preserve many of the Hittite traditions under which their ancestors had lived.[14]

Around 1160 B.C. an army of Muski (possibly the people the Greeks called the Phrygians) from Anatolia invaded some of the northwestern provinces of Assyria. And about fifty years later the Assyrian king Tiglath-Pileser I defeated a large combined army of Muski and Kaska people in the same area.[15] The Kaska had inhabited an area just south of the Black Sea during the era of the Hittite Empire (see Figure 9), and the Muski seem to have come from east central Asia Minor. Assyrian records thus provide additional evidence of twelfth-century-B.C. migrations from Asia Minor into Syria and northwestern Mesopotamia.

Throughout much of central Asia Minor, the heartland of the Hittites, there is little evidence of new settlements or new peoples for about a century after the collapse of the Hittite Empire. Some think this proves that the newcomers to the area were seminomadic.[16] But, as in Greece, it is likely that the area suffered serious depopulation. The rise of the kingdom of Tabal and the beginning of a new phase of settlement appear to have taken place only after two or more generations had elapsed.

Ramesses III of Egypt claimed in an inscription that Sea Peoples destroyed Hatti and Ugarit, and this explanation for the fall of the Hittite Empire is accepted by many scholars.[17] But there is no evidence that the Sea Peoples penetrated into Anatolia as far eastward as Hattusas, let alone Alaca Hüyük or Alisar. It is also difficult to imagine how wandering tribes without siege equipment could conquer a site as strongly fortified as Hattusas.

One solution to this problem is to describe the invasion as a chain reaction: Northerners from the Balkans crossed into northwestern Asia Minor (their knobbed ware has been found in Troy VIIb) and displaced some of the inhabitants of that region; some of these groups then joined

14. Macqueen 1986: 155.
15. Wiseman 1975: 457; Macqueen 1986: 154-155.
16. Barnett 1975: 418.
17. Bittel 1970: 130-133; Goetze 1975: 266; Bright 1981: 115.

Mycenaean refugees, to form the Sea Peoples who proceeded through southern Asia Minor and Syria to the borders of Egypt; meanwhile, the Kaska people and others revolted against Hittite rule, moved southward and eastward, and destroyed Hattusas and other east central Anatolian cities.[18] This theory has much to commend it, and undoubtedly chain-reaction population movements and internal revolts played important roles in the crisis in the eastern Mediterranean.

But what set off the movements and revolts? The number of invaders from the Balkans does not seem to have been extremely large. Their pottery disappeared quickly in Asia Minor, which probably indicates that its makers were rapidly absorbed by local groups. In normal times, such a small-scale invasion would not have precipitated a cultural collapse, so it is difficult to see the poor, small bands of settlers of Troy VIIb as the initiators of a chain reaction that brought down the mighty Hittite Empire. And, as in Greece, the invasion hypothesis does not explain why some areas seem to have been abandoned for a century or more. The devastation and population movements seem to have been too widespread and too great to be explained simply by invasions or even by chain-reaction invasions accompanied by internal revolts.

The Invasion of the Sea Peoples

Who were the Sea Peoples who some scholars claim destroyed the Hittite Empire and the Mycenaean civilization? The name comes from an Egyptian inscription describing a Libyan invasion of Egypt during the fifth year of Merneptah's reign (c. 1208 B.C.). Joining the Libyans were five groups of outsiders (Shardana, Shekelesh, Akawasha, Lukka, and Tursha), who collectively are called "peoples of the sea."[19]

The Libyans and their allies were defeated, but a generation or so later in the fifth year of Ramesses III (c. 1178 B.C.), the Libyans attacked Egypt again. This time they were supported by tribes known as the Peleset and Tjeker.[20] Then, in Ramesses III's eighth year (c. 1175 B.C.), a great coalition of land and sea raiders moved through Asia Minor and Syria towards Egypt:

---

18. Sandars 1985: 192-202; Macqueen 1986: 51-52, 157-158.
19. Breasted 1906: sections 569ff; Gardiner 1947: 196.
20. Edgerton and Wilson 1936: 30.

The foreign countries made a conspiracy in their islands. All at once the lands were removed and scattered in the fray. No land could stand before their arms, from Hatti, Kode [Cilicia], Carchemish, Arzawa [a Hittite subject state in western Anatolia], and Alashiya [Cyprus] on, being cut off at (one time). A camp (was set up) in one place in Amor [Syria-Palestine]. They desolated its people, and its land was like that which has never come into being. They were coming forward toward Egypt, while the flame was prepared before them. Their confederation was the Peleset, Tjeker, Shekelesh, Denye(n), and Weshesh, lands united. They laid their hands upon the lands as far as the circuit of the earth, their hearts confident and trusting: "Our plans will succeed!"[21]

The invading force was divided into two groups, one moving overland along the coast while the other manned a fleet of ships sailing near the shore. Clearly this was no mere raiding party searching for booty. The Egyptian reliefs at Medinet Habu show that the invading army was accompanied by ox-carts containing women and children. Entire tribes of people were on the move.

Ramesses III defeated the land force in a battle fought somewhere in Lebanon or northern Palestine. However, the Sea Peoples' fleet continued on to Egypt itself. In one of the branches of the Nile the enemy ships seem to have been destroyed by the Egyptian fleet and by Egyptian soldiers firing arrows from the river banks. Egypt was saved, but she had been severely weakened. Soon after the death of Ramesses III, Egyptian control over Palestine and southern Syria ended and Sea Peoples settled at Dor and other coastal sites.

Where did these mysterious Sea Peoples come from? Of the groups mentioned by the Egyptians, only two, the Peleset and the Lukka, can be identified with a high degree of probability, and they seem to have come from the Aegean area. The Peleset almost certainly were the Philistines of the Bible. The ancient Israelites believed that the Philistines had come to Canaan from Caphtor (Deuteronomy 2:23; Jeremiah 47:4; Amos 9:7), a place also mentioned in ancient Akkadian texts as Kaptara and in Egyptian inscriptions as Keftiu (or Kephtiu). The Egyptians described Keftiu as an island "in the midst of the Great Green" (the Mediterranean Sea) and depicted its people wearing Minoan/Mycenaean style garments and bringing objects of Minoan/Mycenaean type as tribute. So Keftiu/Caphtor seems to have been the ancient name for Crete (or possibly for the Minoan/Mycenaean culture area in general, since the Egyptians do not seem to have distinguished

21. J. Wilson 1955: 262. See also Edgerton and Wilson 1936: 53.

between the Minoans of Crete and the Mycenaeans of mainland Greece). This meaning for Caphtor also seems indicated by the fact that other biblical texts refer to some Philistine groups as "Cretans" ("Cherethites," 2 Samuel 8:18 and 20:23; Ezekiel 25:16; Zephaniah 2:5) and to part of the Philistine coast as "the Cretan Negeb" (1 Samuel 30:14).

Archaeology also has traced portions of the Philistine material culture to the Aegean. Much of the pottery that is characteristic of the Iron I strata of Philistine cities in Palestine developed from Mycenaean III C:1 prototypes. And it is important to note that this Philistine pottery of Aegean type was not imported—it was produced in Palestine by potters with Aegean traditions.[22] Other Philistine pottery types are derived from Cypriot, Egyptian, and local Canaanite traditions.[23] But these do not negate an Aegean origin for the Philistines. Many Mycenaeans settled in Cyprus during the thirteenth century B.C., and the island seems to have experienced a major influx of Aegean groups (including some from Crete) during the early twelfth century B.C.[24] So the Philistines could have included groups with an Aegean background who had spent some time in Cyprus before moving on (or before being forced out by new arrivals). The evidence seems to support Trude Dothan's conclusion that the Mycenaean influence was the dominant one in the Philistine pottery tradition, but that "this pottery was not the product of a people coming directly from their country of origin with a homogeneous tradition but rather reflects the cultural influences picked up along the way in the long, slow, meandering migration from their Aegean homeland."[25]

The Lukka were also from the Aegean area, but they almost certainly were not Mycenaeans. Hittite and Ugaritic texts mention a place called Lukka, which seems to have been located somewhere along the western coast of Asia Minor (see Figure 9). The Lukka people (possibly the Lycians later referred to by Greek writers) were Hittite subjects, and they fought as allies of the Hittites at the battle of Qadesh (c. 1275 B.C.).[26]

It is likely that the other Sea Peoples of the Egyptian accounts also came largely from the Aegean region (Greece, Crete, the Aegean islands, and the western coast of Asia Minor). Egyptian artists generally depict the various Sea Peoples wearing kilt-like costumes similar to those of the

22. Aharoni 1978: 183-184; Dothan 1982: 94-160, 198-215.
23. Dothan 1982: 160-198.
24. Karageorghis 1976: 58-89; 1981: 63-70; Sandars 1985: 144-148.
25. Dothan 1982: 217.
26. Barnett 1975: 359-360; Sandars 1985: 37.

Keftiu in Egyptian reliefs or of the Mycenaeans in Mycenaean paintings, and the Sea Peoples' ships, with bird heads on both prow and stern posts, are very much like the one with a bird-headed prow depicted on a Mycenaean stirrup jar.[27] Furthermore, the -*sha* ending on some of the Sea Peoples' tribal names (possibly an Indo-European nominative ending) was common as an ethnic ending in Asia Minor during the Late Bronze Age.[28]

It often has been suggested that the Akawasha (or Ekwesh) be identified as Achaiwoi (Achaeans), a common Homeric name for the Greeks who attacked Troy, and the Denyen as Danaoi (Danaans), a synonym for "Achaeans" in the *Iliad*. The Tursha (or Teresh) are probably mentioned in a Hittite text as Taruisha, a people located in the western part of Asia Minor. They have been equated with the Tyrsenoi (Tyrrhenians), the Greek name for the Etruscans who moved to Italy from Asia Minor, according to Herodotus. The Tjeker may be the Teukroi (Teucrians), who according to Greek tradition moved to Cyprus after the Trojan War. The Shardana (or Sherden) and the Shekelesh may be respectively Sardinians and Sikeloi (Sikels or Sicilians) before they moved to Sardinia and Sicily and gave their names to those islands. It is possible that the Weshesh had some connection with Wilusa (or Wilusia) in northwest Asia Minor.[29] However, none of these identifications of Sea Peoples with groups from Greece or western Asia Minor is as certain as those of the Peleset and Lukka.

It is clear, though, that the Sea Peoples could not have been the supposed mysterious invaders from the north who, according to one theory, destroyed the Mycenaean citadels and then moved on to the Near East. Some of the Sea Peoples were mentioned in Egyptian texts as early as the reign of Amenhotep III in the fourteenth century B.C., and groups of Shardana were hired as mercenaries by the Egyptians during the Eighteenth and Nineteenth Dynasties. It is probable that, in addition to the Lukka, the Tursha and Denyen were Hittite vassals throughout most of the fourteenth and thirteenth centuries B.C.[30] So the Sea Peoples seem to have been on the eastern Mediterranean scene and a part of the Mycenaean and Hittite cultural worlds long before the onset of the disasters at the end of the thirteenth century B.C. They may have been part of chain-reaction invasions and movements, but they almost certainly were not the primary cause of the collapse of the Mycenaean kingdoms or of the Hittite Empire.

---

27. Sandars 1985: illustrations 80-82, 84-87, 112, 119.
28. Barnett 1975: 367.
29. See, for example, Sandars 1985: 106-113, 158, 161-165, 170, 199-201.
30. Albright 1975: 508; Barnett 1975: 359, 368; Sandars 1985: 161-163.

Problems in the Nile Valley

Egypt weathered the thirteenth- and twelfth-century-B.C. tumult better than most other areas of the eastern Mediterranean. The fabric of Egyptian society and civilization remained essentially intact, in contrast to the almost total collapse that took place in Mycenaean and Hittite lands. Egypt was also successful in preventing groups of Libyans and Sea Peoples from occupying the Nile Delta. But not even Egypt could maintain her former strength and grandeur in the face of the widespread calamities. Egyptian control over Palestine and southern Syria came to an end around the middle of the twelfth century B.C., and there are indications of hardship and trouble within the Nile Valley itself during this era.

Near the end of the reign of Ramesses III (c. 1182-1151 B.C.) a very unusual event took place: The craftsmen who cut and decorated the royal tombs in the hills opposite Thebes went on strike.[31] These workers were an elite group of artisans, a kind of Egyptian "middle class," who were paid generous amounts of grain and other food provided by the royal storehouses at Thebes. Each workman's ration was enough to feed about sixteen people. Since the average size of their families was only about eight or nine persons, the necropolis workers had a surplus each month that they could sell or trade to get other goods, including luxuries and furnishings for their own tombs.

Between July and November of Ramesses III's twenty-ninth regnal year (c. 1154 B.C.) the craftsmen's rations arrived late and in reduced quantities. Finally, when they had not received their proper rations for two months, the workers marched off of the job and demanded the grain they were owed. After a strike of eight days they were paid, but they walked out again the next month when once again they were not paid on time. A few weeks later, when he heard about the work stoppage, the vizier ordered that half a month's ration be delivered to the workers immediately. But this payment amounted to only half of what had already been owed for some six weeks, and even this "half-loaf" was not paid in full. Two months later the men left their jobs again, and only after this third strike does it seem that the regular rations began arriving once more.

This incident has often been treated as an isolated case of inefficiency or dereliction of duty on the part of administrators in Thebes.[32] But it

---

31. For a relatively detailed treatment of this strike see J. Wilson 1951: 275-277 or Romer 1984: 116-123.

32. See, for example, Breasted 1909: 496; Faulkner 1975: 246; Romer 1984: 122-123.

was probably one symptom of a grain shortage that would become more acute in succeeding reigns. During the twenty-five years between the end of the reign of Ramesses III (c. 1151 B.C.) and that of Ramesses VII (c. 1127 B.C.), grain prices gradually rose to a level eight (or, for a time, twenty-four) times higher than their earlier rate. They remained at this high level for the rest of the century. Only in the time of Ramesses X (c. 1108-1098) did the prices drop, but even then they remained twice what they had been some sixty years earlier.[33]

We also have evidence that the problems in paying the necropolis workers during the reign of Ramesses III was not a temporary one. In order to collect their grain rations, the craftsmen were forced to strike at least three more times, twice during the reign of Ramesses IX (c. 1126-1108 B.C.) and once in the third year of Ramesses X (c. 1106 B.C.). In the first of these cases the payments were more than three months in arrears at the time that the workers began their protest. When the grain ration got that far behind, it is likely that the strikers' complaints that "we are weak and hungry" were not mere hyperbole.[34]

The grain shortage and rampant inflation encouraged the growth of other evils as well. Among these was dishonesty on the part of various government officials who sought to provide food and wealth for themselves, their families, and friends, with little thought for the rest of Egyptian society. There had probably always been some venal and dishonest officials within the Egyptian bureaucracy, but this problem seems to have become much more widespread during the twelfth century B.C. During a ten-year period (c. 1151-1142 B.C.) in the reigns of Ramesses IV and V, a ship's captain whose job it was to transport a yearly ration of grain from the delta to a temple in Upper Egypt stole 91 per cent of the grain he was supposed to deliver! That this fellow could get away with embezzlement on such a scale for an entire decade indicates that the corruption went much further than the captain and his crew. As John A. Wilson has pointed out, "The ship captain could not have engaged in such wholesale robbery without the knowledge and participation of a host of agents, all the way from the farmers who delivered the grain to his boat in the Delta to the clerks who registered it at the Temple of Khnum at the First Cataract."[35] Somehow, the captain was eventually brought to justice, but it is unlikely that he and his cohorts were the only ones engaging in such embezzlement of royal

---

33. J. Wilson 1951: 274; Butzer 1976: 55-56.
34. J. Wilson 1951: 278.
35. J. Wilson 1951: 280.

and temple revenues.

A second affliction, abetted by high prices and reduced grain yields, was tomb robbery. Even the relatively well-to-do necropolis workers eventually joined in this illegal activity. Because they were not being paid their full rations of food, and because inflation had lessened their ability to buy grain on the open market, they were slowly being reduced to hunger and poverty. During the reign of Ramesses IX (c. 1126-1108) some of these beleaguered craftsmen in the tomb-workers' village at Deir el-Medina began looting the very royal tombs they constructed and decorated. A number of families in the village seem to have been involved and, of course, like the boat captain, they had many accomplices—necropolis police, priests, boatmen, merchants, various officials, and perhaps even the mayor of Western Thebes himself. Eight villagers eventually were caught and made to confess, but no high officials were ever brought to justice. It is compelling that the item most frequently purchased with the loot was food; and another large share went as bribes to granary guards and officials so the thieves could obtain grain in the future.[36]

A final evil spawned by the food shortages was banditry and civil war. Several times during the latter half of the twelfth century B.C. marauding groups of Egyptians and Libyan and Meshwesh mercenaries terrorized the area around Thebes. They looted and killed, at one time destroying an entire town.[37] By the reign of Ramesses XI (c. 1098-1070 B.C.), anarchy had broken out in Thebes. The High Priest of Amun temporarily lost all power, and looters stripped the gold and copper from the walls, doors, and statues of the temples. One eyewitness referred to this period of anarchy as "the year of hyenas, when men starved."[38] Order eventually was restored, but the pharaoh's power continued to wane. By the time Ramesses XI died and the Twentieth Dynasty came to an end, Upper Egypt was already being ruled by an army commander of Libyan descent. The era of Egyptian greatness was over.

The Decline of Assyria and Babylonia

During the late fourteenth and early thirteenth centuries B.C., Assyria had grown into a major power and began to put pressure on the eastern frontiers

---

36. Peet 1930; J. Wilson 1951: 282-288; Romer 1984: 145-162.
37. Černý 1934; 1975: 613, 616-619; J. Wilson 1951: 281; Romer 1984: 168-172.
38. J. Wilson 1951: 280. See also Romer 1984: 168-172.

of the Hittite Empire and expand into eastern Syria. But, toward the end of the reign of Tukulti-Ninurta I (c. 1244-1208 B.C.) Assyria went into rapid decline, as military campaigns ceased and revolts broke out. Assyria was not able to recover from her internal problems and renew her expansion until the second half of the tenth century B.C. Rival Babylon was unable to take advantage of this period of Assyrian weakness, for she too was having problems with internal rebellion as well as with raids by Elamites and seminomadic tribes.[39]

The relatively few written sources that exist for this period of turmoil and weakness in Mesopotamia present a gloomy picture. Seminomadic Aramaeans made frequent incursions. Tiglath-Pileser I of Assyria (c. 1111-1084 B.C.) claimed that he had to cross the Euphrates River twenty-eight times during his reign in pursuit of groups of Aramaeans.[40] And attempted Aramaean movements into Mesopotamia continued to be noted into the tenth century B.C.[41] To these must be added the attempted invasions of the Muski and Kaska mentioned earlier and a number of incursions by Elamites.

There is also written evidence of higher-than-normal temperatures, drought, and famine. The Erra Epic, a poetic composition explaining Babylon's renewed prosperity after this period of crisis, has characters who personify the troubles besetting Babylonia prior to the ninth century B.C.—"scorched (earth)" (Erra), "fiery sun" (Ishum), and "plague" (the Sibitti demons).[42] An Assyrian letter (c. 1090 B.C.) mentions "rains which have been so scanty this year that no harvests were reaped," and an Assyrian chronicle (c. 1082 B.C.) states that "a famine (so severe) occurred (that) [peop]le ate one another's flesh."[43] Drought, famine, and hunger are mentioned at least fourteen times in texts dating from the eleventh and first half of the tenth centuries B.C., and at the very end of the eleventh century the situation was so bad that food and drink offerings for a number of the gods had to be canceled.[44] Considering the importance that ancient Near Eastern peoples placed on maintaining the rites of their gods, especially when divine help was needed, this act could only have been prompted by an extreme emergency.

---

39. For an overview of this period of weakness in Mesopotamia, see Brinkman 1968 and Wiseman 1975.
40. Neumann and Parpola 1987: 178.
41. Neumann and Parpola 1987: 176, 178-181. See also Wiseman 1975.
42. Neumann and Parpola 1987: 179-180.
43. Neumann and Parpola 1987: 178. See also Wiseman 1975: 465.
44. Neumann and Parpola 1987: 176, 178-181.

As one might expect, grain shortages led to higher prices. The normal exchange rate was about thirty seahs (approximately two bushels) of barley for one silver shekel. But in the eleventh and early tenth centuries B.C. the prices for grain tended to be between two and four times higher than the normal rate. The inflationary peak seems to have been reached in the mid-tenth century B.C., when an inscription records that in Babylon a gold shekel would purchase only two seahs of barley.[45] Since one gold shekel was usually worth ten silver shekels, this text indicates that because of the famine grain was selling for one hundred and fifty times its normal price! Obviously, the food shortages in Mesopotamia were even worse than those in Egypt.

Mesopotamia also suffered a significant loss of population in the period just after c. 1200 B.C. Archaeological surveys of southern Mesopotamia indicate that in the old Sumerian heartland just north of the Persian Gulf the population declined by about 25 per cent during this era. But the situation was much worse further to the north. In the Diyala region the loss in population appears to have been about 75 per cent![46]

The Cause of the Turmoil

What could have caused populations to move from parts of Greece and western Asia Minor, produced famine in Hittite lands and in Mesopotamia, been responsible for widespread revolts and conflict, and brought about grain shortages in Egypt? Invasions, loss of trade, overly centralized economies, peasant revolutions against the ruling classes, and dependence on an overspecialized feudal chariot force have all been suggested as causes of collapse in one area or another of the eastern Mediterranean. But none of these explanations is really broad enough to explain all of the evidence, especially the crop failures in the Hittite Empire, Mesopotamia, and Egypt.

More than twenty years ago Rhys Carpenter suggested that the end of the Late Bronze Age in the eastern Mediterranean was due to a climatic change. He argued that a shift in the trade winds and rain pattern could have brought drought and famine to much of southern Greece, Crete, and Asia Minor, while other areas, like the Ionian Islands, Attica, and Achaea, could have received normal or above-normal rainfall amounts. Such a change in the weather over a number of years *could* account for the grain shortages,

---

45. Neumann and Parpola 1987: 181.
46. Brinkman 1984: 172-175.

internal strife, destructions, large-scale movements of people, and depopulation evidenced in the historical sources and archaeological remains.[47]

Carpenter's theory was rejected at the time by most archaeologists and historians because there was little direct evidence to support it. Even today many scholars casually dismiss it from consideration. For example, in a discussion of causes that might have led nomads to become sedentary in Palestine during the Iron I period, Israel Finkelstein lists climatic changes among a number of possible political, social, and economic factors. But he rejects this possibility with the terse remark that "there is, at present, no evidence of any climatic change at the time under discussion."[48]

If most historians and archaeologists have found no evidence for a climatic change at the end of the Late Bronze Age, it is probably because they have not looked very hard. It is natural for social scientists and archaeologists to be more comfortable evaluating *human* factors—invasions, revolutions, economic problems, social unrest—than they are with the kinds of physical evidence studied by climatologists. Over the past two decades, however, an increasing amount of material from a variety of sources has indicated that there probably *was* a climatic change that took place between approximately 1300 and 950 B.C.

The earth's climate is a closed system. What happens in one area is related to what is happening in other areas around the globe.[49] It has been shown, in fact, that in modern times there has been a very close correlation between moisture trends in Europe and those in the Near East. Whenever Europe has been dry, the Near East has also been dry, and whenever Europe has become wetter, so has the Near East.[50] Thus, evidence for a period of major climatic change that affected the eastern Mediterranean can be sought in Europe—and even throughout the northern hemisphere—not just in eastern Mediterranean lands. Such evidence comes from study of a number of climatic indicators (like pollen, tree rings, or lake levels) that reflect past climatic conditions. Then the climatic changes thus indicated are dated by use of radiocarbon dating, tree-ring chronology, other scientific dating methods, or by correlation with archaeological deposits or written material of known date.

Tree rings are excellent indicators of climatic changes. Trees develop wide growth rings in times when the weather is favorable (that is, when

---

47. Carpenter 1966: 59-66.
48. Finkelstein 1988: 345.
49. See Lamb 1982: 11-16.
50. Butzer 1958:136; Bintliff 1982: 143-144; Neumann and Parpola 1987: 162-163.

temperatures are mild during the growing season and moisture is abundant) and narrow ones in periods when the weather is persistently very cold or dry. Since the tree-ring sequence developed from the long-lived bristlecone pine trees of the White Mountains in California covers the past 7,000 years, periods of major climatic change in historical times *can* be precisely dated. A series of narrow tree rings between c. 1300 and 1000 B.C. clearly indicates a change in climate during that time, but whether the change was to colder or drier weather (or both) has not been determined.[51]

Evidence from Europe, Asia, and Africa shows that the climatic change indicated by the bristlecone pine tree rings was not just confined to the White Mountains of California or to the Western Hemisphere. For example:

1. The levels of lakes in Switzerland and Central Europe began declining between about 1400 and 1300 B.C., reaching their lowest point about 1000/ 950 B.C.,[52] which indicates a dry period in Europe during that era. Since the correlation in moisture trends between Europe and the Near East is high, the Near East was also very likely experiencing drier weather during this period.

2. Studies of radiocarbon-dated changes in various European peat-bogs have also indicated periods when the European climate changed from wet to dry. An era of cool, wet climate prevailed from c. 2000 until c. 1400 B.C. A drier period seems to have followed until c. 900 B.C., when once again a change to cooler, wetter conditions prevailed.[53] (The radiocarbon dates used to determine these chronological limits have a standard deviation of about ± 100 years. They are thus in agreement with the dates given above for the period of declining water levels in Swiss lakes.)

3. In the Swiss Alps both pollen evidence and glacier stratigraphy indicate a cool climate between c. 1500 and 1150 B.C. and between c. 800 and 700 B.C., with a warmer phase in between (c. 1150-800 B.C.).[54] (These radiocarbon-derived dates should be used with the caveat mentioned above. It should also be noted that in the Near East cool periods are generally rainy and warm ones are generally dry.)

4. Studies of glaciers in the Himalayas and Karakorum show that in those Asian mountain ranges glaciers advanced between c. 1750 and 1150 B.C. and between c. 750 and 150 B.C. and that the glaciers retreated

51. Lamb 1982: 25-26. Since there is much evidence from other parts of the northern hemisphere that this period was generally *warmer* than usual, the narrow rings probably indicate an extended period of very dry conditions.

52. Brooks 1949: 300; Joos 1982: 50; Neumann and Parpola 1987: 166-167.

53. Barber 1982: 107-110 (note especially p. 110).

54. Bintliff 1982: 148.

between c. 1150 and 750 B.C.[55] This evidence basically agrees with that derived from study of glacial movements in the Swiss Alps and indicates that the warmer climate between c. 1200 ($\pm$ 100) and 800 ($\pm$ 100) was not just confined to Europe.

5. Pollen studies in Kashmir indicate that the monsoon rains declined in volume about 70 per cent from c. 2000 B.C. to about 1500 B.C. They then remained at a low level until the beginning of the Christian era.[56]

6. The decline of the monsoon also seems to have had serious consequences in Africa. Lake Rudolf and Lake Victoria were at high levels shortly before 1300 B.C. However, their levels dropped after that date.[57] Since Lake Victoria is one of the primary sources of the Nile River, its level obviously would have affected the height of the Nile floods in Egypt. The decline of the monsoon, which also feeds the Nile's other sources, would have reduced the waters further.

7. In concert with glaciers in Asia and in Europe, the glacier on Mount Kenya in Africa advanced in the years before c. 1300 B.C. and after c. 540 B.C., but was inactive or retreated in the interval between the beginning of the thirteenth and the end of the seventh centuries B.C.[58]

These and other indications of climatic change in Europe, Asia, and Africa during the time in question are persuasive, but there is also evidence to that effect from the Near East itself. Study of a number of different types of paleoenvironmental data—such as water levels and sedimentation rates in Lake Van, Persian Gulf sediments, and pollen samples from various areas—has enabled P. A. Kay and D. L. Johnson to estimate the Tigris-Euphrates streamflow over the past 6,000 years. The rivers seem to have been generally high between c. 1450 and 1300 B.C. After that their streamflow dropped rapidly, reaching its lowest point c. 1150 B.C. In the years just after c. 950 B.C. the streamflow rapidly rose to high levels once more.[59]

The Nile's annual flood levels were also well below normal for much of the twelfth century B.C. The reduced discharge of the Pelusiac branch of the Nile allowed its mouth to silt up and caused the city of Per-Ramesses to be abandoned during the Twenty-first Dynasty (c. 1070-946 B.C.).[60] And during the reign of Ramesses X (c. 1108-1098 B.C.) Lower Nubia, the area just south of the first cataract, became desiccated due to the Nile's low

---

55. Neumann and Parpola 1987: 167.
56. Bryson and Murray 1977: 107-111; Bintliff 1982: 149; Lamb 1982: 29-30.
57. Neumann and Parpola 1987: 167.
58. Neumann and Parpola 1987: 167.
59. Kay and Johnson 1981; Neumann and Parpola 1987: 164.
60. Butzer 1976: 29.

levels.[61]

Finally, a study of wood charcoal from archaeological sites in the area just north of the Negeb in Israel indicates that at the end of the Late Bronze Age there was a change from Mediterranean to Saharan vegetation. This change in vegetation seems to indicate a shift from a relatively moist climate to a much drier one.[62] While the study made no allowance for the possible importation of wood from other regions, the validity of its conclusions is not likely to be affected, since such imports into this area were probably not very extensive.[63]

All of this evidence indicates a shift to a warmer (and, in the Near East, a drier) climate around the thirteenth and twelfth centuries B.C. When combined with textual references to grain shortages and famine, and with archaeological indications of population decline, it seems absolutely clear that a large climatic change was a major cause of the disturbances at the end of the Late Bronze Age. Some climatologists have even tried to identify the specific weather pattern that would have brought drought to most, but not all, areas of the eastern Mediterranean. They argue that a weather pattern like that of the winter of 1954-1955 fits the archaeological evidence and that such a pattern must have been dominant during the winters for most of the thirteenth and early twelfth centuries B.C.[64] Others think that the frequent recurrence, over a number of years, of a specific pattern of wet and dry areas is unlikely.[65] But it is clear that, while the weather patterns may have varied somewhat from year to year, the general trend in the eastern Mediterranean for at least a century and a half (c. 1300-1150 B.C.) was to drier conditions. This trend seems to have moderated somewhat in most areas during the latter half of the twelfth century B.C. and to have reversed itself in the tenth century B.C., when cooler, moister weather returned.

It was the growing frequency of drought—and the crop failures and hunger it brought with it—that set in motion the internal strife, warfare, plague, piracy, destruction of cities, decline in population, inflation, and population movements that weakened or destroyed the Bronze Age civilizations of the eastern Mediterranean. Obviously, this climatic change must have hit Palestine as well as other parts of the Near East. The widespread

---

61. Romer 1984: 167.
62. Bintliff 1982: 147 describes the contents of an unpublished paper by N. Lipschitz, *et al.* given at the 1979 International Conference of Climate and History at the University of East Anglia.
63. Neumann and Parpola 1987: 165.
64. Bryson, Lamb and Donley 1974; Bryson and Murray 1977: 3-17; Weiss 1982.
65. Neumann and Parpola 1987: 163.

drought might very well have been largely responsible not only for the destruction of most of the Canaanite cities, but also for the creation in Canaan of detached groups of seminomads, refugee peasant farmers, and occasional bands of brigands who, together with a small contingent of escaped slaves from Egypt, would join to form the Israelite tribes.

7

Conclusions

How does the historical context of widespread drought affect or alter the various models of the Israelite settlement proposed earlier? Can any of these models do justice to climatological as well as historical and archaeological evidence? And, if so, how does one explain the existence of the biblical traditions of the Exodus and Conquest from the standpoint of that model?

The Formation of the Israelite Tribes

As we have seen, there is no archaeological indication that a number of outsiders, other than the Philistines and related Sea Peoples, settled in Canaan during the Late Bronze Age or early in the Iron Age. The biblical tradition—which says that large numbers of former Egyptian slaves who had been living in the desert fringes of Sinai invaded Canaan, destroyed most of the Canaanite cities, and occupied the land—is probably not historical. Peaceful-infiltration hypotheses, which derive the Israelite tribes from true desert nomads or from seminomadic groups entering Canaan from outside, also seem to be unsatisfactory. This leaves the internal-revolt hypothesis, the frontier-development model, and the symbiosis theory to choose from, since all of these models derive the Israelite tribes from population groups that were already within Palestine during the Late Bronze period.

Were the people who became Israelites originally farmers or seminomads? And why did they abandon their former way of life, settle in hill country villages, and join together as Israel? The answers provided by our three models contradict each other, and none is really very convincing.

It is unlikely, for example, that widespread peasant revolts would have erupted almost spontaneously at the end of the Late Bronze Age in Canaan. It *is* possible that a number of individual farmers fled to the hills to escape warfare or taxation, but in the normal course of things the numbers of such refugees would have been small—too small to account for the numbers of early Iron I villages established in the hill country. It is also possible that some seminomads might have become sedentary when the cities that had supplied their agricultural needs were destroyed. That tens of thousands of seminomads made this choice at the beginning of the Iron Age, however, is highly improbable.

Knowing that a vast climatic change to drier conditions pervaded the eastern Mediterranean at the end of the Bronze Age makes the task of explaining the breakup of Canaanite society and the formation of the new Israelite confederation much easier. After all, drought and famine have long been known to destroy the normal bonds that hold societies, and even families, together. Disease (which at first tends to cause death primarily among the very young and very old) is one of the early products of a drought that extends over a number of years.[1] When people no longer can feed their families and themselves adequately many choose to flee the drought and disease-stricken area, while others remain and fight over the scarce food supplies. In recent times towns have even been sacked and pillaged by their own people during times of drought.[2]

We no longer need to rely solely on invasions of Egyptians, Sea Peoples, or Israelites to explain the destruction of Canaanite cities at the end of the thirteenth and early in the twelfth centuries B.C. Some towns may have been destroyed by Egyptians or Sea Peoples, but others undoubtedly were sacked as a result of internecine fighting among local rulers struggling to control a larger portion of the diminishing food supplies. And, since grain and other commodities were collected from the farmers in the countryside and stored in the cities before being redistributed, some cities might have been destroyed by their own citizens who had been made desperate by

---

1. See Bryson and Murray 1977: 97. It is interesting to note that in the thirteenth- and twelfth-century-B.C. cemetery at Tell es-Sa'idiyeh in the Jordan Valley a number of graves contained two or three bodies buried together. These seem to have been family members (including children) who died about the same time. Thirty-two per cent of the skeletons uncovered belonged to children, most of them infants. See Pritchard 1980.

2. Carpenter 1966: 69.

hunger and fear. Dry conditions over the better part of a century also "fits" the archaeological evidence that the Canaanite cities were destroyed over the span of a generation or two rather than all at once.

We also no longer have to wonder why large numbers of people became detached from their former Canaanite city-states. There may have been some long-standing resentment on the part of many peasants toward the ruling classes, as supporters of the revolt model claim, but it probably was hunger, and not ideology or class consciousness, that drove the peasants to revolt against the system. It is also likely that the destructions of numerous cities made it difficult for some seminomads to maintain their former way of life, as the symbiosis hypothesis asserts, but urban decline alone did not force them to become sedentary. Almost certainly drought, famine, and internal strife were what finally drove large numbers of both peasants and seminomads to sever their established communal ties and seek refuge in the hills.

All in all, the evidence for climatic change noted in Chapter 6 meshes quite well with the archaeological evidence from Palestine. The Middle Bronze II era, a flourishing period characterized by numerous cities and a large population, coincided with a period of relatively cool weather and adequate rainfall. Egyptian invasions during the early part of the New Kingdom destroyed many of the Palestinian MB II cities and brought about a transition to the Late Bronze Age around 1500 B.C. The destruction and unrest generated by the Egyptian military campaigns probably caused a significant decline in the size of the Palestinian population. By the latter part of the Late Bronze Age there seem to have been only about half as many people in Palestine as there had been during the Middle Bronze II period.[3]

Some of the missing people may have become seminomads (whose presence is difficult for archaeologists to detect), but most of the loss in population was probably real. It has been claimed that continued Egyptian military campaigns and exploitation of Canaanite resources in addition to conflicts between Canaanite city-states account for the failure of the population to increase to its former levels after the initial wave of destruction was over.[4] However, the Egyptians do not seem to have conducted many campaigns in the Palestinian hill country or in the Transjordanian highlands, yet settlement in those areas declined drastically as well during the Late Bronze period.[5] One possible factor

---

3. Finkelstein 1988: 339-341.
4. R. Gonen as cited in Finkelstein 1988: 341.
5. Finkelstein 1988: 340.

in the failure of the Late Bronze population to return to former levels was the climate: cool, moist weather was drawing to a close during the fifteenth-fourteenth centuries B.C.

Most of the paleoclimatic data I have described indicate that warm, dry conditions were already well established in the eastern Mediterranean by c. 1300 B.C., and the change to that weather pattern probably did not occur overnight. There would have been a period of years, probably a century or more, during which the change from a generally moist pattern to a generally dry one took place. This gradual climatic change almost certainly would have been felt first in marginal areas like the Negeb (which was not occupied at all during the Late Bronze Age). Portions of the Palestinian hill country and the Transjordanian plateau also would have gradually become less attractive for settlement. Few Canaanites would have been alarmed by the declining rainfall during the fourteenth century B.C., but the areas suitable for settlement would have been reduced nonetheless, and the crop yield of areas already inhabited might have declined as well. Along with Egyptian raids and demands for tribute, this gradual weather change probably made a return to the high population figures of the MB II period impossible.

This argument is reinforced by evidence that climate altered population numbers earlier in history. The widespread urbanization of the Early Bronze Age seems to have taken place during a cool, moist climatic phase in the Near East, which lasted from about 3500 to 2100 B.C. (plus or minus two hundred years, since these dates come from radiocarbon analysis).[6] During the EB era, for example, settlements expanded into areas which are now deserts. But virtually all of the Early Bronze towns and villages were destroyed around 2300-2200 B.C., and in most of the Negeb occupation was not resumed until the Iron Age II. It so happens, as Barbara Bell has shown, that the level of the Nile floods also seriously declined between 2300 and 2100 B.C., causing famine and turmoil in Egypt.[7]

There thus seems to have been another relatively dry period in the Near East during the Egyptian First Intermediate Period and the Palestinian Middle Bronze I (or early Bronze IV) Period. During this era, urban civilization virtually disappeared in Palestine and Transjordan. The size of the population dropped drastically, leaving the land to groups of pastoral seminomads. The revival of urbanism occurred only after 2000 B.C., when relatively moist weather seems to have returned, weather that was less moist, however, than what had prevailed just before and after c. 3000 B.C.. This clear correspondence

---

6. Bintliff 1982: 147-148; Lamb 1982: 29.
7. Bell 1971; 1975.

TABLE 10

Climate, History, and Archaeology in Palestine and the Near East, c. 3500-950 B.C.

DATE	CLIMATE IN THE REGION	HISTORY AND ARCHAEOLOGY
3500	Beginning of a cool, moist period	
3250		
	High Nile floods	Beginning of the Egyptian Old Kingdom
3000		Extensive urbanization in Palestine, Transjordan, Syria, and Asia Minor
2750		Occupation in the Negeb and Sinai
	Gradual decrease in moisture	
2500		
	End of moist era	Destruction of EB cities in Syria-Palestine, Transjordan, and Asia Minor
2250		
	Very low Nile floods, dry weather in Near East and Europe	Pastoral, non-urban period in Palestine; First Intermediate Period in Egypt; nomads invade Mesopotamia
2000	Transition from dry to moist weather	Renewed urban settlements in Palestine (MB II A)
	High Nile floods	Egyptian Middle Kingdom
1750		Extensive urbanization in Palestine
		Egyptian New Kingdom; Egyptian conquest of Palestine
1500	Transition from moist era to drier period	Decline in settlement in Palestinian hill country
1250	Onset of very dry era	
		Destruction of Palestinian LB II sites
	Low Nile; low Tigris and Euphrates	End of the Hittite Empire; grain shortages in Egypt; famine in Mesopotamia
	End of drought and trend toward moister era	Iron I settlements in the hill country of Palestine and in Transjordan
1000	Start of moist period	Renewed settlement in the Negeb; urbanized Iron II Period

between climatic conditions and occupation patterns in Palestine and Transjordan over more than twenty-five hundred years (c. 3500-950 B.C.) was almost certainly not due to chance (see Table 10).

Surely, the Late Bronze Age decline of settlement in the Palestinian and Transjordanian hill country was related to the gradual onset of dry weather. Settlements in the coastal plain and Jordan Valley generally had springs or seasonally flowing streams in addition to rainfall to provide water for agriculture. But in most parts of the hill country, agriculture depended on rainfall alone. In a period of decreasing rainfall, life would have been harder there than in areas that received even less rainfall but whose springs and streams were fed by drainage from the hills.

By the latter part of the thirteenth century B.C., the effects of the increasingly dry climate began to be felt throughout the eastern Mediterranean area. The Hittites appealed to pharaoh Merneptah to send grain to relieve their famine, and about the same time Libyans and their Sea People allies invaded the Nile Delta, "fighting to fill their bodies daily" and "to seek the necessities of their mouths."[8] When the drought was at its height, between c. 1200 and 1150 B.C., a wave of destruction swept over most of the Mycenaean centers in Greece as well as over numerous cities in the Hittite Empire, Cyprus, Syria, and Palestine. Tribes from the Aegean area caused havoc before settling in parts of Cyprus, Lebanon, and Palestine, and groups from Asia Minor migrated into northern Syria. This drought and turmoil must also have transformed many Canaanite peasants and seminomads into stateless brigands or fleeing refugees.

The dry weather seems to have abated somewhat around 1150 B.C., allowing most of the various groups of marauders and refugees to settle down. In some areas, though, like parts of Mesopotamia, periods of famine and social unrest continued sporadically for about a century after the worst part of the drought had ended. In Palestine and Transjordan groups of stateless peasant farmers and seminomads seem to have found refuge in the hill country, as increasing rainfall made subsistence-level farming possible in those areas again. The hill country would have been especially attractive then: There were few settlers already there who might contest the settlement of refugees, and the rough hill country was less likely to be invaded by the Philistines or the remaining Canaanite nobles who were contending for the coastal areas. It is not surprising that many of the villages built by these stateless refugees, who had just suffered through severe drought and famine, included numerous storage pits for grain and plaster-lined cisterns to collect and store water.

---

8. Breasted 1905: 580; 1906: 467.

To determine precise absolute or relative dates for the appearance of the various Iron I settlements in the Palestinian hill country is difficult. Nonetheless, it is unlikely that more than a handful of sites were settled earlier than 1150 B.C. They seem to have been concentrated first in the central hill country (the Hill Country of Ephraim) and in Galilee, and only later to have spread into the Judean Hills and the Negeb. Since the Negeb normally gets less rain than the central or Galilean hill country, it makes sense that when rainfall began to increase during the latter half of the twelfth and early part of the eleventh centuries B.C., it would take longer for it to become attractive for habitation. It is more difficult to explain the small number of early Iron I settlements in the Judean Hills, however. It is possible that the rainfall pattern in the Iron I period was somewhat different from the current one—or there may have been other factors involved, like vegetation, soil, or difficulty of terrain. The main expansion into (or population growth within) the Negeb, the Hill Country of Judah, and much of the Edomite territory in southern Transjordan would come in the Iron II period, which according to the climatological evidence was a time of renewed cool, moist weather in the Near East.

Of course, only the earliest Iron I villages in the hill country were built and occupied by refugees who had fled from the effects of drought in other parts of the country. The settlements constructed in the latter part of Iron I probably were the result of normal population growth as climatic conditions slowly improved.

Some of the people who settled in the Palestinian hill country and the Transjordanian plateau may have already been organized into tribes, but probably most had no tribal allegiances before they settled down. As their need for protection and internal governance began to be felt, various groups of hill-country refugees joined together to create a number of tribal organizations through a process Norman Gottwald has called "retribalization."[9]

Tribal organization does not imply seminomadic status, as was assumed often in the past. Many sedentary peoples, including the ancient Greeks and Romans, were organized into tribes. And we must assume, as do supporters of the internal-revolt and the hybrid models, that a number of tribes were created in Palestine and Transjordan during the twelfth century B.C. These tribes then formed several alliances or confederations among themselves that, as a result of conflict with other groups, developed into the "national" entities of Israel, Ammon, Moab, and Edom.

Some might consider this scenario a bit far-fetched, but we know that

---

9. Gottwald 1979: 323-334.

something similar was going on in Greece at around this time. The Mycenaean kingdoms, with their highly centralized economies and large bureaucracies, were destroyed during the era of drought and famine. In their place there gradually arose small farming villages usually grouped around urban centers ruled by petty kings and nobles. In time these urban centers became the city-states of Classical Greece. After c. 700 B.C., when textual sources become more plentiful, we learn that the population of each *polis* ("city-state") was usually divided into tribes, phratries ("brotherhoods," a collection of clans), and *genê* ("families" or "clans"), whose members supposedly shared a common ancestry. However, there is no evidence of such tribes or phratries in Mycenaean times and they play a very minor role in the Homeric poems. These new groups must have been created during the early stages of the Greek Dark Ages and were just starting to become important by the time of Homer (c. 800-750 B.C.).[10]

In the past various scholars have tried to trace the origins and premonarchic histories of individual Israelite tribes from data recorded in the Bible.[11] Such attempts, we know now, are futile. Biblical lists of the tribes of Israel differ from one another, suggesting that in premonarchic times the make-up of the individual tribes, and of Israel itself, was fairly fluid. Furthermore, the archaeological and climatological evidence forces us to question whether much, if any, of the material in Genesis-Judges is based on genuine early traditions rooted in history. As George Ramsey has noted, "there continues the teasing thought that at least some of our reports of tribal settlements are but fictional stories designed to do something quite other than convey precise information about the past."[12]

The only reliable references we have to premonarchic Israel are Merneptah's "victory hymn" and the Song of Deborah. Merneptah's poem indicates that there *was* an entity called *Israel* in the central hill country of Palestine at the end of the thirteenth century B.C. And, since the hieroglyphic determinative used for Israel is the one for "people" rather than the one for "land" or "place," it is likely that "Israel" designated a nonsedentary or only partially sedentary group. We have no way of determining whether this "Israel" was a single "tribe" or a confederation of two or more "tribes" in Merneptah's time.

In the Song of Deborah (Judges 5:2-31), an ancient poem which most

---

10. See, for example, Forrest 1966: 45-55; Fine 1983: 43-61.
11. For example, see Noth 1960: 73-80; de Vaux 1978: 523-678; Ramsey 1981: 81-90; Miller and Hayes 1986: 94-107.
12. Ramsey 1981: 98.

biblical scholars date to the twelfth or early eleventh century B.C., only a short time after the events it narrates, Israel seems to consist of a confederation of ten tribes. Fighting with Barak and Deborah against unnamed "kings of Canaan" were warriors from the tribes of Ephraim, Benjamin, Machir (later a division of Manasseh), Zebulun, Issachar, and Naphtali, while the tribes of Reuben, Gilead (the later Gad?), Dan, and Asher are rebuked for their nonparticipation. The most important omission in the poem is any reference to Judah. It is likely that Judah was an independent coalition of tribes in southern Palestine that originally was separate from Israel. It does not seem to have become part of the Israelite confederation until the end of the period of the "judges," and possibly not even until the time of David.[13]

The details of how a number of tribes were formed from disparate groups of refugees trying to make a new start in the hills and of how these tribes became the coalition known as Israel probably will never be known. Like the development of the Greek *polis* system, the formation of Israel (and of Ammon, Moab, and Edom) is lost in a "Dark Age." But it seems clear, as a constantly growing number of scholars agree, that Israel was created within Canaan from groups of people whose background was primarily Canaanite. The genealogies relating the Israelite tribes to one another by tracing their origins to the children of Jacob (Israel), and the traditions that insist that these tribes conquered Canaan after entering from the outside, do not appear to be accurate. Something other than "historical kernels" must account for the presence of these traditions in the Bible.

Was the Exodus Historical?

And what about the Exodus accounts? Are *they* historical? John Bright has asserted: "There can really be little doubt that ancestors of Israel had been slaves in Egypt and had escaped in some marvelous way. Almost no one today would question it."[14] Undoubtedly he is correct. Most biblical scholars, archaeologists, and historians—even ones like myself and supporters of the revolt hypothesis or hybrid models, who are generally skeptical about the accuracy of biblical traditions concerning early Israel—usually agree that an exodus took place, though on a much smaller scale than the Bible indicates.[15]

Many are still convinced by the argument that it is unlikely that any

---

13. Cohen 1976: 499; Miller and Hayes 1986: 105-106.
14. Bright 1981: 120.
15. Gottwald 1979: 35-38; Soggin 1984: 109-111; Finkelstein 1988: 348.

nation would *make up* a tradition that its founders had suffered shameful servitude in a foreign land. More persuasive, however, are elements in the story that have the "ring of truth" to them: the reference in Exodus 1:11 to building Per-Ramesses, a city abandoned about the time the Israelite monarchy began; the name "Moses," which comes from an Egyptian word meaning "begotten" or "child of," and for which the biblical narrative provides an inaccurate Hebrew folk etymology (Exodus 2:10); and the indications within the story that the group leaving Egypt was small—only two midwives were needed to handle the births of Hebrew children (Exodus 1:15), and the Israelites needed divine help to defeat a seminomadic tribe of Sinai whose numbers could not have been large (Exodus 17:8-13)—in contradiction to the later editor's estimate that 600,000 men plus children (and women?) left Egypt (Exodus 12:37-38). Such elements in the narrative do not *prove* the historicity of the entire account, but they do suggest an "historical kernel" and that at least much of the outline of the story might be accurate. So, while a twelve-tribe coalition of Israelites may not have entered Canaan from the outside, at least *some* individuals who became part of Israel probably did so. The existence of this outside group within Israel seems to be the simplest and most persuasive way to explain the early and persistent tradition of an Israelite exodus from Egypt.

The presence of an influential non-Canaanite element within Israel also seems to be indicated by Israel's worship of Yahweh, a god who was foreign to Palestine. Claims that Yahweh was worshipped in Early Bronze Age Ebla in Syria or among the Amorites of the Middle Bronze Age have not been substantiated.[16] In fact, there is no convincing evidence for the worship of Yahweh anywhere prior to the emergence of Israel in the Iron Age. The Bible associates the pre-Mosaic cult of Yahweh with Sinai and with the Midianites, and possibly this tradition is correct. We have no evidence for it, though, other than the Bible itself. On the other hand, we do have a fair amount of extrabiblical evidence about Canaanite religion, and this material allows us to be almost certain that Yahweh was not a member of the Canaanite pantheon.[17] So, if most of the individuals who became part of Israel were originally Canaanites, as we have argued, Yahweh worship must have been introduced into Israel from the outside.

Some scholars have argued that the traditions of the Exodus were originally separate from those related to a theophany at Mount Sinai or Horeb.[18] If

---

16. Cross 1973: 60-67; de Vaux 1978: 341-343; Bermant and Weitzman 1979: 178-182 (contra Pettinato 1976: 48; 1981: 276-277).

17. Albright 1968: 115-150.

18. Von Rad 1938; 1962: 124, 187-188; Noth 1960: 133-134.

such a view is correct, it is possible that Yahweh worship was introduced into Israel by a group other than the one that brought the tradition of the Exodus. It is much more likely, however, that only one group of outsiders was involved. The Exodus group and the Yahweh worshippers were probably one and the same,[19] and they must have been very influential in the formative stages of the Israelite tribes.

Possible Origins of the Conquest Tradition

We can only speculate on how the newly formed Israelite confederation of tribes came to worship Yahweh or how later Israel produced the now-familiar traditions about the Exodus, Conquest, and settlement in Canaan. There is a considerable body of evidence favoring the view that Yahweh was originally worshipped as a war god—a divine warrior who would defend His people and defeat their enemies.[20] This is the role He plays in both the Song of Deborah and the Song of the Sea, which seem to be the two earliest compositions in the Bible. As we have seen, the Song of Deborah is probably premonarchic and the Song of the Sea probably dates from the era of the United Monarchy. It might have been Yahweh's original role as a warrior/ protector that led to His becoming accepted by Israel during the formative period, when the new settlers and new tribes in the hill country were facing increasing pressures from outside groups.

The degree to which Yahweh was worshipped throughout Israel in premonarchic times, however, remains unknown. Possibly a covenant with Yahweh was agreed upon when the Israelite confederation of tribes was created, but it is now virtually impossible to get behind the later conceptions of the covenant and of early Israelite history to determine what really happened. We can be fairly sure, however, that many, if not most, of the new Israelites continued to worship Ba'al and other Canaanite deities along with (or, in some cases, instead of) Yahweh, since the Bible does describe such "backsliding" in the period of the "judges" and throughout the era of the monarchy. The later Yahwistic prophets and biblical authors believed that Israel had committed itself to worship Yahweh *alone* and that those who participated in Canaanite cults were being unfaithful to the Mosaic covenant. But, for most later Israelites, the acceptance of aspects of Canaanite religion was probably just a continuation of ancestral practices that existed when Israel was formed out of groups

---

19. Ramsey 1981: 51-52.
20. Cross 1966; 1973: 91-111; P. Miller 1973; Gottwald 1979: 682-683.

of stateless Canaanites.[21]

One way to promote the worship of Yahweh and to foster a new Israelite identity among people of Canaanite background was to connect Yahweh with the local cults of Canaanite deities such as El and Ba'al, a practice that seems to have become official policy during the monarchy's early period. Canaanite shrines at Shechem, Bethel, and other sites seem to have been adopted by Yahwists, and the deities (like El Berith, El Bethel, and El Shaddai) worshipped at these shrines were claimed to be earlier manifestations of Yahweh.[22] There is even evidence that, down to the time of Josiah's reforms in the seventh century B.C., Yahweh, like Ba'al, was thought to have had the fertility goddess Asherah as His consort.[23]

This religious syncretism was strongly opposed by ardent Yahwists like the prophets, who also opposed royal attempts to present Yahweh as a national deity who would always defend His people and His "son," the king. It is from the Yahwistic roots of the prophets that Deuteronomy and the Deuteronomistic History would spring. And it is this literature that opposes all things Canaanite and that claims that the Israelites took possession of Canaan through a military campaign in which they destroyed most Canaanite cities and exterminated their inhabitants.

Pre-Deuteronomistic Conquest traditions probably developed as a result of late-twelfth- or eleventh-century B.C. conflicts between Canaanite city-states and the new Israelite tribal confederation—as Alt, Noth, and other supporters of the peaceful-infiltration hypothesis have claimed. But the early traditions in the Song of Deborah and the Song of the Sea simply describe Yahweh's victories over specific enemies (Sisera and pharaoh's army, respectively) and state that non-Israelite groups—the Philistines, Edomites, Moabites, and "all the inhabitants of Canaan"—have been seized with fear and dread of Yahweh. This is normal nationalistic religious propaganda of the type we find in the literature of other Near Eastern peoples. There is no indication in these poems that the Israelites were expected to destroy all Canaanites and take possession of the entire land, as the Deuteronomistic tradition would claim.

The form that the Deuteronomistic Conquest tradition took seems to have been due to political as well as religious considerations. Marvin Chaney has made this point quite well:

---

21. For a discussion of the "Yahweh-alone" party as a minority movement in Israel and Judah prior to the time of Josiah, see Lang 1983.

22. See, for example, Cross 1973: 44-60; de Vaux 1978: 274-287.

23. Meshel 1979; Freedman 1987.

If the "first edition" of the "Deuteronomistic History" is viewed as a programmatic piece written to support the Josianic reform, its framer's propensities are readily understandable. For that archaizing reform of the late 7th century B.C. sought to weld Judah and the remnants of the northern Kingdom into a united, centralized, pure, and militantly independent nation, realizing its manifest destiny under both Mosaic and Davidic covenants. This program could hardly have been better legitimated than by an interpretation of pre-Davidic history which emphasized the unfailing success of Israel's national and territorial aspirations if and when political cohesion and military discipline were maintained and all vestiges and bearers of "foreign culture" eradicated. Faced with northern suspicions of the centralized leadership of a Davidite, the "Deuteronomistic Historian" urged that the paradigm for such national leadership and its success predated the Davidic monarchy in the person of a northerner—Joshua, the Ephraimite.[24]

We should not be surprised to find no mention of drought, famine, or Canaanite refugees in the biblical narratives about Israel's settlement in Canaan. If such traditions did once exist, they were almost certainly suppressed by David or Solomon (or both), monarchs who were seeking to create a sense of national identity and unity within a very diverse population. These rulers had to stress the differences between Israel and the Edomites, Moabites, Ammonites, and those Canaanites still occupying cities in the valleys and coastal plain. To this end they promoted the traditions of that portion of the Israelite population that had come out of Egypt, and they encouraged the development of traditions that connected the Israelite tribes to one another through a family relationship.

So well did the early rulers' policies succeed that even during the Divided Monarchy the sense of unity between the southern and northern kingdoms remained relatively strong. And later the Deuteronomistic reformers could inveigh against the Canaanites and attack the remaining elements of Israel's Canaanite heritage as signs of apostasy without creating a significant backlash. By the seventh century B.C. Israelites clearly had forgotten their Canaanite background, so they could accept the idea that their ancestors had come into the land from the outside and driven out the native population.

It is only in recent times, through the development of biblical criticism and archaeological research, that we have come to recognize that the Conquest narratives are not historical. And with the discovery that there was a change in climate between the thirteenth and tenth centuries B.C., we are finally beginning to understand the historical context in which the Israelite settlement

---

24. Chaney 1983: 47.

did take place. It occurred as part of a widespread crisis that saw old empires and civilizations toppled and new nations and new social and economic systems created. Edom, Moab, and Ammon would become small kingdoms. The Phoenician city-states, freed from Egyptian and Hittite dominance, would become trade centers whose ships would traverse the entire Mediterranean and even venture into the Atlantic. Aramaean kingdoms, especially the one centered on Damascus, would become centers for the overland caravan trade. A number of small kingdoms would emerge in Asia Minor, while in Greece the *polis* or city-state system would begin to rise. And in Palestine a small group of escaped Egyptian slaves would join contingents of Canaanite refugees in the hills and together create a confederation of tribes known as Israel.

We do not yet know how all of these developments occurred. Much scholarly work remains to be done. One can hope, however, that the research of biblical scholars, archaeologists, historians, sociologists, anthropologists, climatologists, and other specialists will continue to converge, and to more brightly illuminate this most significant era in Western history.

Bibliography

Ackroyd, P. R.
  1967   "Samaria." In *Archaeology and Old Testament Study*. Edited
          by D. Winton Thomas. Oxford: Oxford University Press.

Aharoni, Yohanan
  1975a   "Arad." In *Encyclopedia of Archaeological Excavations in
          the Holy Land*. Vol. I. Edited by M. Avi-Yonah. Englewood
          Cliffs, N.J.: Prentice-Hall, 74-88.
  1975b   "Beersheba, Tel." In *Encyclopedia of Archaeological
          Excavations in the Holy Land*. Vol. I. Edited by M. Avi-
          Yonah. Englewood Cliffs, N.J.: Prentice-Hall, 160-168.
  1976a   "Nothing Early and Nothing Late: Re-writing Israel's
          Conquest." *Biblical Archeologist* 39/2 (May): 55-76.
  1976b   "Arad." In *The Interpreter's Dictionary of the Bible*. Supple-
          mentary Volume. Nashville: Abingdon Press, 38-39.
  1978   *The Archaeology of the Land of Israel*. Translated by Anson
          F. Rainey (1982). Philadelphia: The Westminster Press.
  1979   *The Land of the Bible: A Historical Geography*. 2nd ed. Trans-
          lated and edited by Anson F. Rainey. London: Burns and
          Oates.

Aharoni, Yohanan and Michael Avi-Yonah
  1968   *The Macmillan Bible Atlas*. New York: Macmillan.

Ahituv, S.
  1972   "Did Ramesses II Conquer Dibon?" *Israel Exploration Journal*
          22: 141-142.

Ahlström, G. W. and D. Edelman
1985   "Merneptah's Israel." *Journal of Near Eastern Studies* 44/1 (January): 59-61.

Albright, William Foxwell
1934   "The Kyle Memorial Excavation at Bethel." *Bulletin of the American Schools of Oriental Research* 56: 2-15.
1939   "The Israelite Conquest of Canaan in the Light of Archaeology." *Bulletin of the American Schools of Oriental Research* 74: 11-23.
1945   "The Chronology of the Divided Monarchy of Israel." *Bulletin of the American Schools of Oriental Research* 100: 16-22.
1955   "Palestinian Inscriptions." In *Ancient Near Eastern Texts Relating to the Old Testament.* 2nd ed. Edited by J. B. Pritchard. Princeton, N.J.: Princeton University Press, 320-322.
1957   *From the Stone Age to Christianity.* 2nd ed. Baltimore: Johns Hopkins Press.
1960   *The Archaeology of Palestine.* 3rd revised edition. Baltimore: Penguin Books.
1965   "Some Remarks on the Archaeological Chronology of Palestine Before About 1500 B.C." In *Chronologies in Old World Archaeology.* Edited by R. W. Ehrich. Chicago: University of Chicago Press, 47-57.
1967   "Debir." In *Archaeology and Old Testament Study.* Edited by D. Winton Thomas. London: Oxford University Press, 207-220.
1968   *Yahweh and the Gods of Canaan.* Garden City, N.Y.: Doubleday.
1975a   "The Amarna Letters From Palestine." In *The Cambridge Ancient History.* 3rd edition. Vol. II, Part 2, Chapter XX. Edited by I. E. S. Edwards, *et al.* Cambridge: Cambridge University Press, 98-116.
1975b   "Beit Mirsim, Tell." In *Encyclopedia of Archaeological Excavations in the Holy Land.* Vol. I. Edited by M. Avi-Yonah. Englewood Cliffs, N.J.: Prentice-Hall, 171-178.

Alt, Albrecht
1925   *Die Landnahme der Israeliten in Palästina* (Reformationsprogram der Universität Leipzig 1925). Translation, "The

Settlement of the Israelites in Palestine." In A. Alt, *Essays on Old Testament History and Religion.* Translated by R. A. Wilson. Oxford: Basil Blackwell (1966), 135-169.

1936   "Josua." In *Werden und Wesen des Alten Testaments* (Beihefte zur *Zeitschrift für die Alttestamentliche Wissenschaft* 66). Edited by P. Volz, F. Stummer, and J. Hempel. Berlin: Töpelmann, 13-29. Reprinted in *Kleine Schriften zur Geschichte des Volkes Israels.* Munich: C. H. Beck'sche Verlagsbuchhandlung, 1953. Vol. I. 176-192.

1939   "Erwägungen über die Landnahme der Israeliten in Palästina." *Palästinajahrbuch des Deutschen evangelischen Instituts für Altertumswissenschaft des Heiligen Landes zu Jerusalem* 35: 8-63. Reprinted in *Kleine Schriften zur Geschichte des Volkes Israels.* Munich: C. H. Beck'sche Verlagsbuchhandlung, 1953, Vol. I. 126-175.

Alvarez, W., L. Alvarez, F. Asaro, and H. Michel
1980   "Extraterrestrial Cause for the Cretaceous-Tertiary Extinction." *Science* 208: 1095-1108.

Alvarez, W., E. Kauffman, F. Surlyk, L. Alvarez, F. Asaro, and H. Michel
1984   "Impact Theory of Mass Extinctions and the Invertebrate Fossil Record." *Science* 223: 1135-1141.

Amiran, Ruth
1970   *Ancient Pottery of the Holy Land.* New Brunswick, N.J.: Rutgers University Press.

Amiran, Ruth and J. E. Worrell
1976   "Hesi, Tell." In *Encyclopedia of Archaeological Excavations in the Holy Land.* Vol. II. Edited by M. Avi-Yonah. Englewood Cliffs, N.J.: Prentice-Hall, 514-520.

Anati, Emmanuel
1985   "Has Mt. Sinai Been Found?" *Biblical Archaeology Review* 11/4 (July/August): 42-57.

1987   *The Mountain of God.* New York: Rizzoli Publications.

Andersen, K. T.
   1969   "Die Chronologie der Könige von Israel und Juda." *Studia Theologica* 23: 67-112.

Anderson, Bernhard W.
   1986   *Understanding the Old Testament.* 4th edition. Englewood Cliffs, N.J.: Prentice-Hall.

Anderson, G. W.
   1966   *The History and Religion of Israel.* London: Oxford University Press.

Archaeology Staff
   1988   "Newsbriefs: Exodus Redux." *Archaeology* 41/2 (March/April): 20.

Astour, Michael
   1965   "New Evidence on the Last Days of Ugarit." *American Journal of Archaeology* 69: 253-258.

Avigad, N.
   1978   "Samaria." In *Encyclopedia of Archaeological Excavations in the Holy Land.* Vol. IV. Edited by M. Avi-Yonah. Englewood Cliffs, N.J.: Prentice-Hall, 1032-1050.

Avi-Yonah, M.
   1977   "Medeba (Madeba)." In *Encyclopedia of Archaeological Excavations in the Holy Land.* Vol. II. Edited by M. Avi-Yonah. Englewood Cliffs, N.J.: Prentice-Hall, 819-823.

Bailey, M. E., S. V. M. Clube, and W. M. Napier
   1986   "The Origin of Comets." *Vistas in Astronomy* 29: 53-110.

Baillie, M. G. L. and M. A. R. Munro
   1988   "Irish Tree Rings, Santorini and Volcanic Dust Veils." *Nature* 332 (March 24): 344-346.

Barber, K. E.
   1982   "Peat-bog Stratigraphy as a Proxy Climate Record." In

Climatic Change in Later Prehistory. Edited by A. F. Harding. Edinburgh: Edinburgh University Press, 103-113.

Barnett, R. D.
1975   "The Sea Peoples" and "Phrygia and the Peoples of Anatolia in the Iron Age." In *Cambridge Ancient History.* 3rd edition. Vol. II, Part 2. Edited by I. E. S. Edwards, *et al.* Cambridge: Cambridge University Press, 359-378 and 417-442.

Bartlett, John R.
1978   "The Conquest of Sihon's Kingdom: A Literary Re-examination." *Journal of Biblical Literature* 97/3 (September): 347-351.

Bass, George F.
1967   *Cape Gelidonya: A Bronze Age Shipwreck.* Philadelphia: American Philosophical Society.
1987   "Oldest Known Shipwreck Reveals Splendors of the Bronze Age." *National Geographic Magazine* 172/6 (December): 692-732.

Batto, Bernard F.
1983   "The Reed Sea: *Requiescat in Pace.*" *Journal of Biblical Literature* 102/1 (March): 27-35.
1984   "Red Sea or Reed Sea?: How the Mistake Was Made and What *Yam Sup* Really Means." *Biblical Archaeology Review* 10/4 (July/August): 57-63.

Begrich, J.
1929   *Die Chronologie der Könige von Israel und Juda.* Tübingen: J. C. B. Mohr.

Bell, Barbara
1971   "The Dark Ages in Ancient History: I. The First Dark Age in Egypt." *American Journal of Archaeology* 75: 1-26.
1975   "Climate and the History of Egypt: The Middle Kingdom." *American Journal of Archaeology* 79: 223-269.

Bennett, Crystal
  1964   "Umm el-Biyara-Petra." *Revue Biblique* 71: 250-253.
  1966   "Fouilles d'Umm el-Biyara." *Revue Biblique* 73: 372-403.
  1969   "Tawilan (Jordanie)." *Revue Biblique* 76: 386-390.
  1970   "Tawilan (Jordanie)." *Revue Biblique* 77: 371-374.
  1972   "A Brief Note on Excavations at Tawilan, Jordan, 1968-70." *Levant* 4: v-vii and pl. II.
  1973   "Excavations at Buseirah, Southern Jordan, 1971: A Preliminary Report." *Levant* 5: 1-11 and pls. I-VIII.
  1974   "Excavations at Buseirah, Southern Jordan, 1972: Preliminary Report." *Levant* 6: 1-24.
  1975   "Excavations at Buseirah, Southern Jordan, 1973: Third Preliminary Report." *Levant* 7: 1-19.
  1977   "Excavations at Buseirah, Southern Jordan, 1974: Fourth Preliminary Report." *Levant* 9: 1-10.

Bennett, John G.
  1963   "Geophysics and Human History." *Systematics, the Journal of the Institute for the Comparative Study of History, Philosophy and the Sciences* 1/2 (September): 127-156.

Bermant, Chaim and Michael Weitzman
  1979   *Ebla: A Revelation in Archaeology.* New York: Times Books.

Betancourt, Philip P.
  1976   "The End of the Greek Bronze Age." *Antiquity* 50: 40-47.
  1987   "Dating the Aegean Late Bronze Age With Radiocarbon." *Archaeometry* 29/1 (February): 45-49.

Betancourt, Philip P. and H. N. Michael
  1987   "Dating the Aegean Late Bronze Age With Radiocarbon: Addendum." *Archaeometry* 29/2 (August): 212-213.

Betancourt, Philip P. and Gail A. Weinstein
  1976   "Carbon 14 and the Beginning of the Late Bronze Age in the Aegean." *American Journal of Archaeology* 80/4 (Fall): 329-348.

Bienkowski, Piotr
1986   *Jericho in the Late Bronze Age.* Warminster, England: Aris and Phillips, Ltd.

Bierbrier, M. L.
1975   *The Late New Kingdom in Egypt (c. 1300-664 B.C.): A Genealogical and Chronological Investigation.* Warminster, England: Aris and Phillips Ltd.

Biers, William R.
1980   *The Archaeology ot Greece: An Introduction.* Ithaca, N.Y.: Cornell University Press.

Bietak, Manfred
1981   *Avaris and Piramesse: Archaeological Exploration in the Eastern Nile Delta.* London: Oxford University Press.
1984   "Problems of Middle Bronze Age Chronology: New Evidence from Egypt." *American Journal of Archaeology* 88: 471-485.
1988   "Contra Bimson, Bietak Says Late Bronze Age Cannot Begin as Late as 1400 B.C." *Biblical Archaeology Review* 15/4 (July/August): 54-55.

Bimson, John J.
1978   "Can There Be a Revised Chronology Without a Revised Stratigraphy?" In *Ages in Chaos?* (Proceedings of the Residential Weekend Conference, Glasgow, 7-9 April, 1978). *S.I.S. Review* 6/1-3 (1982): 16-26.
1981   *Redating the Exodus and Conquest.* 2nd ed. Sheffield, England: The Almond Press.
1985   "Queries and Comments—Is Et-Tell the Site of 'Ai?" *Biblical Archaeology Review* 11/5 (September/October): 78-79.
1988   "A Reply to Baruch Halpern's 'Radical Exodus Dating Fatally Flawed,' in *BAR,* November/December 1987." *Biblical Archaeology Review* 15/4 (July/August): 52-55.

Bimson, John J. and David Livingston
1987   "Redating the Exodus." *Biblical Archaeology Review* 13/5 (September/October): 40-53, 66-68.

Bintliff, J. L.
1982   "Climatic Change, Archaeology and Quaternary Science in the Eastern Mediterranean Region." In *Climatic Change in Later Prehistory*. Edited by A. F. Harding. Edinburgh: Edinburgh University Press, 143-161.

Biran, Avraham
1969   "Tel Dan." *Israel Exploration Journal* 19: 121-123.
1975   "Dan, Tel." In *Encyclopedia of Archaeological Excavations in the Holy Land*. Vol. I. Edited by M. Avi-Yonah. Englewood Cliffs, N.J.: Prentice-Hall, 313-321.
1980   "Tel Dan: Five Years Later." *Biblical Archeologist* 43: 168-182.
1984   "The Triple Arched Gate of Laish at Tel Dan." *Israel Exploration Journal* 34: 1-19.
1985   "Tel Dan, 1984." *Israel Exploration Journal* 35: 186-189.
1987   "*BAR* Interview: Avraham Biran—Twenty Years of Digging at Tel Dan." *Biblical Archaeology Review* 13/4 (July/August): 12-25.

Bittel, Kurt
1970   *Hattusha, the Capital of the Hittites*. New York: Oxford University Press.

Blenkinsopp, Joseph
1985   "The Documentary Hypothesis in Trouble." *Bible Review* 1/4 (Winter): 22-32.

Blong, R. J.
1980   "The Possible Effects of Santorini Tephra Fall on Minoan Crete." In *Thera and the Aegean World*. Vol. 2. Edited by C. Doumas, London: Thera and the Aegean World, 217-226.

Boardman, John
1964   *The Greeks Overseas*. Baltimore: Penguin Books.

Boling, Robert G.
1975   *Judges (The Anchor Bible,* 6A). Garden City, N.Y.: Doubleday.

Boling, Robert G. and G. Ernest Wright
1982   *Joshua (The Anchor Bible,* 6). Garden City, N.Y.: Doubleday.

Breasted, James Henry
1906   *Ancient Records of Egypt.* Vol. 3. Chicago: University of Chicago Press.
1909   *A History of Egypt.* 2nd ed., New York: Charles Scribner's Sons.

Bright, John
1942   "Has Archaeology Found Evidence of the Flood?" *Biblical Archaeologist* 5/4 (December): 55-62.
1956   *Early Israel in Recent History Writing.* London: SCM Press.
1972   *A History of Israel.* 2nd ed. Philadelphia: The Westminster Press.
1981   *A History of Israel.* 3rd ed. Philadelphia: The Westminster Press.

Brinkman, J. A.
1968   *A Political History of Post-Kassite Babylonia, 1158-722 B.C.* Rome: Pontifical Biblical Institute.
1984   "Settlement Surveys and Documentary Evidence: Regional Variation and Secular Trends in Mesopotamian Demography." *Journal of Near Eastern Studies* 43/3 (July): 169-180.

Brooks, C. E. P.
1949   *Climate Through the Ages.* 2nd edition. London: E. Benn.

Bryson, Reid A., H. H. Lamb, and D. L. Donley
1974   "Drought and the Decline of Mycenae." *Antiquity* 48: 46-50.

Bryson, Reid A. and Thomas J. Murray
1977   *Climates of Hunger: Mankind and the World's Changing Weather.* Madison, Wis.: University of Wisconsin.

Bryson, Reid A. and Christine Padoch
1981   "On the Climates of History." In *Climate and History.* Edited by R. I. Rotberg and T. K. Rabb. Princeton, N.J.: Princeton University Press, 3-17.

Budyko, M. I.
    1982   *The Earth's Climate: Past and Future.* New York: Academic
            Press.

Butzer, Karl W.
    1958   *Quaternary Stratigraphy and Climate in the Near East.* Bonn:
            F. Dümmlers Verlag.
    1976   *Early Hydraulic Civilization in Egypt.* Chicago: University
            of Chicago Press.

Cadogan, Gerald
    1987   "Unsteady Date of a Big Bang." *Nature* 328 (August 6-12):
            473.

Callaway, Joseph A.
    1968   "New Evidence on the Conquest of 'Ai." *Journal of Biblical
            Literature* 87: 312-320.
    1975   "Ai." In *Encyclopedia of Archaeological Excavations in the
            Holy Land.* Vol. I. Edited by M. Avi-Yonah. Englewood Cliffs,
            N.J.: Prentice-Hall, 36-52.
    1976   "Ai." In *The Interpreter's Dictionary of the Bible.* Supple-
            mentary Volume. Nashville: Abingdon Press, 14-16.
    1985a   "Was My Excavation of Ai Worthwhile?" *Biblical Archaeology
            Review* 11/2 (March/April): 68-69.
    1985b   "Queries and Comments—Joseph Callaway Replies." *Biblical
            Archaeology Review* 11/4 (July/August): 23-24.
    1985c   "A New Perspective on the Hill Country Settlement of Canaan
            in Iron Age I." In *Palestine in the Bronze and Iron Ages:
            Papers in Honour of Olga Tufnell.* Edited by J. N. Tubb.
            London: Institute of Archaeology, 31-49.
    1985d   "Response." In *Biblical Archaeology Today: Proceedings of
            the International Congress on Biblical Archaeology, Jeru-
            salem, April 1984.* Jerusalem: Israel Exploration Society, 72-
            77.

Carpenter, Rhys
    1968   *Discontinuity in Greek Civilization.* New York: W. W. Norton
            and Company.

Casperson, Lee W.
    1986   "The Lunar Dates of Thutmose III." *Journal of Near Eastern
            Studies* 45/2 (April): 139-150.
    1988   "The Lunar Date of Ramesses II." *Journal of Near Eastern
            Studies* 47/3 (July): 181-184.

Černý, Jaroslav
    1934   "Fluctuations in Grain Prices during the Twentieth Egyptian
            Dynasty." *Archiv Orientali* 6: 173ff.
    1975   "Egypt: From the Death of Ramesses III to the End of the
            Twenty-first Dynasty." In *Cambridge Ancient History.* 3rd
            edition. Vol. II, Part 2. Edited by I. E. S. Edwards, *et al.*
            Cambridge: Cambridge University Press, 606-657.

Chadwick, Jeffrey and Ben Lomond
    1985   "Queries and Comments—Ai and the Bible." *Biblical
            Archaeology Review* 11/4 (July/August): 20-22.

Chadwick, John
    1976   *The Mycenaean World.* Cambridge: Cambridge University
            Press.

Champion, Sara
    1980   *Dictionary of Terms and Techniques in Archaeology.* New
            York: Facts on File.

Chaney, Marvin L.
    1983   "Ancient Palestinian Peasant Movements and the Formation
            of Premonarchic Israel." In *Palestine in Transition: The
            Emergence of Ancient Israel.* Edited by D. N. Freedman and
            D. F. Graf. Sheffield, England: The Almond Press, 39-90.

Clube, S. V. M.
    1985   "Giant Comets and Their Role in History." Unpublished paper
            presented at the Fourteenth International Conference on the
            Unity of the Sciences, Houston, Texas, November 30.

Clube, S. V. M. and W. M. Napier
    1982   *The Cosmic Serpent.* London: Faber and Faber.

1986   "Giant Comets and the Galaxy: Implications of the Terrestrial Record." In *The Galaxy and the Solar System*. Edited by M. S. Matthews, R. Smoluckowski, and J. Bahcall. Tucson, Ariz.: University of Arizona Press.

Coats, George W.
1976   "Tradition Criticism, O.T." In *The Interpreter's Dictionary of the Bible*. Supplementary Volume. Nashville: Abingdon Press, 912-914.

Cohen, M. A.
1976   "Judah, Formation of." In *The Interpreter's Dictionary of the Bible*. Supplementary Volume. Nashville: Abingdon Press, 498-499.

Cohen, Rudolph
1981   "Did I Excavate Kadesh-Barnea?" *Biblical Archaeology Review* 7/3 (May/June): 21-33.

Cohen, Simon
1962   "Azmon." In *The Interpreter's Dictionary of the Bible*. Vol. 1. Nashville: Abingdon Press, 327.

Corney, Richard W.
1962   "Libnah." In *The Interpreter's Dictionary of the Bible*. Vol. 3. Nashville: Abingdon Press, 123.

Courville, Donovan A.
1971   *The Exodus Problem and Its Ramifications*. 2 vols. Loma Linda, Calif.: Challenge Books.
1985   "The Problem of Adjusting the Date Limits of the Archaeological Ages to Meet Velikovsky's Revision." In *Proceedings of the Second Seminar of Catastrophism and Ancient History*. Edited by M. A. Luckerman. Los Angeles: Catastrophism and Ancient History Press, 7-13.
1986   "On the Survival of Velikovsky's Thesis in *Ages in Chaos*." In *Proceedings of the Third Seminar of Catastrophism and Ancient History*. Edited by M. A. Luckerman. Los Angeles: Catastrophism and Ancient History Press, 65-75.

Cross, Frank Moore
    1966   "The Divine Warrior in Israel's Early Cult." In *Biblical Motifs: Origins and Transformations*. Edited by A. Altmann. Cambridge, Mass.: Harvard University Press, 11-30.
    1973   *Canaanite Myth and Hebrew Epic*. Cambridge, Mass.: Harvard University Press.

Crowfoot, J. W. and Kathleen Kenyon
    1957   *Samaria-Sebaste III: The Objects from Samaria*. London: Palestine Exploration Fund.

Crowfoot, J. W., K. Kenyon and E. L. Sukenik
    1942   *Samaria Sebaste II: The Buildings at Samaria*. London: Palestine Exploration Fund.

Culver, R. B. and P. A. Ianna
    1984   *The Gemini Syndrome*. Rev. ed. Buffalo, N.Y.: Prometheus Books.

Dahood, Mitchell
    1966   *Psalms I, 1-50 (The Anchor Bible*, 16). Garden City, N.Y.: Doubleday.
    1968   *Psalms II, 51-100 (The Anchor Bible*, 17). Garden City, N.Y.: Doubleday.
    1970   *Psalms III, 101-150 (The Anchor Bible*, 17A). Garden City, N.Y.: Doubleday.

Damrosch, David
    1987   *The Narrative Covenant: Transformations of Genre in the Growth of Biblical Literature*. San Francisco: Harper and Row.

de Geus, C. H. J.
    1976   *The Tribes of Israel*. Studia semitica Neerlandica 18. Assen: Van Gorcum.

Desborough, V. R. d'A.
    1964   *The Last Mycenaeans and Their Successors*. Oxford: Clarendon Press.

1975   "The End of the Mycenaean Civilization and the Dark Age: (a) The Archaeological Background." In *Cambridge Ancient History*. 3rd edition. Vol. II, Part 2. Edited by I. E. S. Edwards, *et al.* Cambridge: Cambridge University Press, 658-677.

de Vaux, Roland
1970   "On Right and Wrong Uses of Archaeology." In *Near Eastern Archaeology in the Twentieth Century*. Edited by J. A. Sanders. Garden City, N.Y.: Doubleday, 64-80.
1971   "Palestine in the Early Bronze Age." In *Cambridge Ancient History*. 3rd edition. Vol. I, Part 2. Edited by I. E. S. Edwards, *et al.* Cambridge: Cambridge University Press, 208-237.
1978   *The Early History of Israel*. Translated by David Smith. Philadelphia: The Westminster Press.

Dever, William G.
1976   "Gezer." In *Encyclopedia of Archaeolgical Excavations in the Holy Land*. Vol. II. Edited by M. Avi-Yonah. Englewood Cliffs, N.J.: Prentice-Hall, 428-443.
1980   "New Vistas on the EB IV ("MB I") Horizon in Syria-Palestine." *Bulletin of the American Schools of Oriental Research* 237: 35-64.
1985a   "Relations Between Syria-Palestine and Egypt in the 'Hyksos' Period." In *Palestine in the Bronze and Iron Ages: Papers in Honour of Olga Tufnell*. Edited by J. N. Tubb. London: Institute of Archaeology, 69-87.
1985b   "From the End of the Early Bronze Age to the Beginning of the Middle Bronze." In *Biblical Archaeology Today: Proceedings of the International Congress on Biblical Archaeology, Jerusalem, April 1984*. Jerusalem: Israel Exploration Society, 113-135.

De Vries, Simon J.
1962   "Chronology of the OT." In *The Interpreter's Dictionary of the Bible*. Vol. I. Nashville: Abingdon Press, 580-599.
1976   "Chronology, OT." In *The Interpreter's Dictionary of the Bible*. Supplementary Volume. Nashville: Abingdon Press, 161-166.

Dornemann, Rudolph H.
1983   *The Archaeology of the Transjordan in the Bronze and Iron Ages.* Milwaukee: Milwaukee Public Museum.

Dothan, Moshe
1977   "Kadesh-Barnea." In *Encyclopedia of Archaeological Excavations in the Holy Land.* Vol. III. Edited by M. Avi-Yonah. Englewood Cliffs, N.J.: Prentice-Hall, 697-699.

Dothan, Trude
1982   *The Philistines and Their Material Culture.* New Haven, Conn.: Yale University Press.

Doumas, Christos
1983   *Thera: Pompeii of the Ancient Aegean.* London: Thames and Hudson.

Drower, Margaret S.
1973   "Syria c. 1500-1400 B.C." In *Cambridge Ancient History.* 3rd edition. Vol. II, Part 1. Edited by I .E. S. Edwards, *et al.* Cambridge: Cambridge University Press, 417-525.

Edgerton, W. F. and John A. Wilson
1936   *Historical Records of Ramesses III.* Chicago: University of Chicago Press.

Eissfeldt, O.
1975   "Palestine in the Time of the Nineteenth Dynasty: (a) The Exodus and Wanderings." In *Cambridge Ancient History.* 3rd edition. Vol. II, Part 2. Edited by I. E. S. Edwards, *et al.* Cambridge: Cambridge University Press, 307-330.

Ellenberger, C. Leroy
1982   "Could a Volcanic Eruption of Thera be Visible in the Nile Delta?" ("Queries and Comments"). *Biblical Archaeology Review* 8/1 (January/February): 14.

Esse, Douglas L.
1988   "Review of Israel Finkelstein, *The Archaeology of the Israelite*

Settlement." Biblical Archaeology Review 14/5 (September/
October): 6-12.

Faulkner, R. O.
1975   "Egypt: From the Inception of the Nineteenth Dynasty to
the Death of Ramesses III." In *Cambridge Ancient History*.
3rd edition. Vol. II, Part 2. Edited by I. E. S. Edwards, *et
al*. Cambridge: Cambridge Universiy Press, 217-251.

Fine, John V. A.
1983   *The Ancient Greeks: A Critical History*. Cambridge, Mass.:
Harvard University Press.

Finegan, Jack
1963   *Let My People Go: A Journey Through Exodus*. New York:
Harper and Row.
1964   *Handbook of Biblical Chronology: Principles of Time
Reckoning in the Ancient World and Problems of Chronology
in the Bible*. Princeton, N.J.: Princeton University Press.

Finkelstein, Israel
1986   "Shiloh Yields Some, But Not All, of Its Secrets." *Biblical
Archaeology Review* 12/1 (January/February): 22-41.
1988a   *The Archaeology of the Israelite Settlement*. Jerusalem: Israel
Exploration Society.
1988b   "Searching for Israelite Origins." *Biblical Archaeology Review*
14/5 (September/October): 34-45.

Foerster, G.
1975   "Dor." In *Encyclopedia of Archaeological Excavations in the
Holy Land*. Vol. I. Edited by M. Avi-Yonah. Englewood Cliffs,
N.J.: Prentice-Hall, 334-337.

Forrest, W. G.
1966   *The Emergence of Greek Democracy, 800-400 B.C.* New York:
McGraw-Hill.

Franken, H. J.
1975   "Palestine in the Time of the Nineteenth Dynasty: (b) Archaeo-

logical Evidence." In *Cambridge Ancient History*. 3rd edition. Vol. II, Part 2. Edited by I. E. S. Edwards, *et al.* Cambridge: Cambridge University Press, 331-337.

1976   "The Problem of Identification in Biblical Archaeology." *Palestine Exploration Quarterly* 108: 3-11.

Freedman, David Noel

1976   "Deuteronomic History." In *The Interpreter's Dictionary of the Bible*. Supplementary Volume. Nashville: Abingdon Press, 226-228.

1976   "Source Criticism, O.T." In *The Interpreter's Dictionary of the Bible*. Supplementary Volume. Nashville: Abingdon Press, 838-839.

1987   "Yahweh of Samaria and His Asherah." *Biblical Archaeologist* 50/4 (December): 241-249.

Fretheim, Terence

1976   "Elohist." In *The Interpreter's Dictionary of the Bible*. Supplementary Volume. Nashville: Abingdon, 259-263.

Fritz, Volkmar

1981   "The Israelite 'Conquest' in Light of Recent Excavations at Khirbet el-Meshash." *Bulletin of the American Schools of Oriental Research* 241: 61-73.

1982   "The Conquest in the Light of Archaeology." In *Proceedings of the Eighth World Congress of Jewish Studies*. Jerusalem: 15/21.

1987   "Conquest or Settlement? The Early Iron Age in Palestine." *Biblical Archaeologist* 50/2 (June): 84-100.

Galanopoulos, A. G. and E. Bacon

1969   *Atlantis: The Truth Behind the Legend*. Indianapolis and New York: Bobbs-Merrill Company.

Gardiner, Alan

1918   "The Delta Residence of the Ramessides." *Journal of Egyptian Archaeology* 5: 127-138, 179-200, 242-271.

1924   "The Geography of the Exodus: An Answer to Professor Naville and Others." *Journal of Egyptian Archaeology* 10: 87-96.

1946   "Davies's Copy of the Great Speos Artemidos Inscription."
        Journal of Egyptian Archaeology 32: 43-56.
1947   *Ancient Egyptian Onomastica, I.* Oxford: Oxford University
        Press.
1961   *Egypt of the Pharaohs.* Oxford: Oxford University Press.

Garstang, John
1931   *The Foundations of Bible History: Joshua, Judges.* New York:
        Richard R. Smith, Inc.

Garstang, John and J. B. E. Garstang
1940   *The Story of Jericho.* London: Hodder and Stoughton.

Geraty, Lawrence T.
1983   "Heshbon: The First Casualty in the Israelite Quest for the
        Kingdom of God." In *The Quest for the Kingdom of God:
        Studies in Honor of George E. Mendenhall.* Edited by H. B.
        Huffmon, F. A. Spina, and A. R. W. Green. Winona Lake,
        Ind.: Eisenbrauns, 239-248.

Glock, Albert E.
1978   "Taanach." In *Encyclopedia of Archaeological Excavations
        in the Holy Land.* Vol. IV. Edited by M. Avi-Yonah. Engle-
        wood Cliffs, N.J.: Prentice-Hall, 1138-1147.

Glueck, Nelson
1934   *Explorations in Eastern Palestine, I* (Annual of the American
        Schools of Oriental Research, Vol. 14). New Haven, Conn.:
        American Schools of Oriental Research.
1935   *Explorations in Eastern Palestine, II* (Annual of the American
        Schools of Oriental Research, Vol. 15). New Haven, Conn.:
        American Schools of Oriental Research.
1939   *Explorations in Eastern Palestine, III* (Annual of the American
        Schools of Oriental Research, Vols. 18-19). New Haven, Conn.:
        American Schools of Oriental Research.
1951   *Explorations in Eastern Palestine, IV* (Annual of the American
        Schools of Oriental Research, Vols. 25-28). New Haven, Conn.:
        American Schools of Oriental Research.
1967   "Transjordan." In *Archaeology and Old Testament Study.*

Edited by D. Winton Thomas. London: Oxford University Press, 429-452.
1970   *The Other Side of the Jordan.* Revised edition. Cambridge, Mass.: American Schools of Oriental Research.

Goedicke, Hans
1982   "Goedicke Defends His Exodus Thesis" ("Queries and Comments"). *Biblical Archaeology Review* 8/2 (March/April): 12.
1987   "Exodus: The Ancient Egyptian Evidence." A paper delivered at the "Who Was the Pharaoh of the Exodus?" symposium, Memphis, Tennessee, April 23-25.

Goetze, A.
1975   "The Hittites and Syria (1300-1200 B.C.)." In *Cambridge Ancient History.* 3rd edition. Vol. II, Part 2. Edited by I. E. S. Edwards, *et al.* Cambridge: Cambridge Universiy Press, 252-273.

Gold, V. R.
1962   "Punon." In *The Interpreter's Dictionary of the Bible.* Vol. 3. Nashville: Abingdon Press, 968.

Goldsmith, Donald, ed.
1977   *Scientists Confront Velikovsky.* New York: W. W. Norton and Company.

Gonen, Rivka
1984   "Urban Canaan in the Late Bronze Age." *Bulletin of the American Schools of Oriental Research* 253: 61-73.
1987   "Israelite Occupation of Canaan." A paper presented at the "Who Was the Pharaoh of the Exodus?" symposium, Memphis, Tennessee, April 23-25.

Gophna, R.
1975   "Beersheba." In *Encyclopedia of Archaeological Excavations in the Holy Land.* Vol. I. Edited by M. Avi-Yonah. Englewood Cliffs, N.J.: Prentice-Hall, 152-159.

Gottwald, Norman K.
    1974   "Were the Early Israelites Pastoral Nomads?" In *Rhetorical Criticism: Essays in Honor of James Muilenburg.* Edited by J. J. Jackson and M. Kessler. Pittsburgh: Pickwick Press, 223-255.
    1975   "Domain Assumptions and Societal Models in the Study of Pre-Monarchic Israel." *Supplements to Vetus Testamentum* 28: 89-100.
    1976   "Nomadism." In *The Interpreter's Dictionary of the Bible.* Supplementary Volume. Nashville: Abingdon Press, 629-631.
    1978   "Were the Early Israelites Pastoral Nomads?" *Biblical Archaeology Review* 4/2 (June): 2-7.
    1979   *The Tribes of Yahweh: A Sociology of the Religion of Liberated Israel, 1250-1050 B.C.E.* Maryknoll, N.Y.: Orbis Books.
    1983a   "Two Models for the Origins of Ancient Israel: Social Revolution or Frontier Development." In *The Quest for the Kingdom of God: Studies in Honor of George E. Mendenhall.* Edited by H. B. Huffmon, F. A. Spina, and A. R. W. Green. Winona Lake, Ind.: Eisenbrauns, 5-24.
    1983b   "Early Israel and the Canaanite Socio-Economic System." In *Palestine in Transition: The Emergence of Ancient Israel.* Edited by D. N. Freedman and D. F. Graf. Sheffield, England: The Almond Press, 25-37.
    1985   "The Israelite Settlement as a Social Revolutionary Movement." In *Biblical Archaeology Today: Proceedings of the International Congress on Biblical Archaeology, Jerusalem, April 1984.* Jerusalem: Israel Exploration Society, 34-46.

Grant, Michael
    1976   *Cities of Vesuvius: Pompeii and Herculaneum.* New York: Penguin Books.

Gray, John
    1970   *I and II Kings: A Commentary.* 2nd ed. Philadelphia: The Westminster Press.

Greenberg, Moshe
    1955   *The Ḫab/piru.* New Haven, Conn.: American Oriental Society.

Gurney, Oliver R.
1981   *The Hittites.* 2nd revised edition. New York: Penguin Books.

Hallager, Erik
1977   *The Mycenaean Palace at Knossos: Evidence for the Final Destruction in the III B Period.* Stockholm: Medelhavsmuseet.

Halligan, John M.
1983   "The Role of the Peasant in the Amarna Period." In *Palestine in Transition: The Emergence of Ancient Israel.* Edited by D. N. Freedman and D. F. Graf. Sheffield, England: The Almond Press, 15-24.

Halpern, Baruch
1983   *The Emergence of Israel in Canaan.* Chico, Calif.: Scholars Press.
1987   "Radical Exodus Redating Fatally Flawed." *Biblical Archaeology Review* 13/6 (November/December): 56-61.

Hamilton, R. W.
1962   "Lachish." In *The Interpreter's Dictionary of the Bible.* Vol. 3. Nashville: Abingdon, 53-57.

Hammer, C. V., H. B. Clausen, W. L., Friedrich and H. Tauber
1987   "The Minoan Eruption of Santorini in Greece Dated to 1645 B.C.?" *Nature* 328 (August 6-12): 517-519.

Hammond, P. C.
1965   "Hebron." *Revue Biblique* 72: 267-270.
1966   "Hebron." *Revue Biblique* 73: 566-569.
1968   "Hebron." *Revue Biblique* 75: 253-2258

Haran, Menahem
1976   "Exodus, The." In *The Interpreter's Dictionary of the Bible.* Supplementary Volume. Nashville: Abingdon, 304-310.

Harding, G. L.
1958   "Recent Discoveries in Jordan." *Palestine Exploration Quarterly* 90: 7-18.

Harrison, R. K.
    1969   *Introduction to the Old Testament.* Grand Rapids, Mich.:
            Wm. B. Eerdmans.

Hart, S.
    1986   "Edom Survey Project, 1985." *Palestine Exploration Quarterly*
            118: 77-78.

Hart, S. and R. K. Falkner
    1985   "Preliminary Report on a Survey in Edom, 1984." *Annual*
            of the Department of Antiquities of Jordan 29: 255-277.

Hayes, William C.
    1970   "Chronology: I. Egypt—to the End of the Twentieth Dynasty."
            In *Cambridge Ancient History.* 3rd edition. Edited by I. E. S.
            Edwards, *et al.* Cambridge: Cambridge University Press, 173-
            193.
    1973a   "Egypt: From the Death of Ammenemes III to Seqenenre
            II." In *Cambridge Ancient History.* 3rd edition. Vol. II, Part
            1. Edited by I. E. S. Edwards, *et al.* Cambridge: Cambridge
            Universiy Press, 42-76.
    1973b   "Egypt: Internal Affairs From Tuthmosis I to the Death of
            Amenophis III." In *Cambridge Ancient History.* 3rd edition.
            Vol. II, Part 1. Edited by I. E. S. Edwards, *et al.* Cambridge:
            Cambridge University Press, 313-416.

Hempel, Johannes
    1962   "Psalms, Book of." In *The Interpreter's Dictionary of the Bible.*
            Vol. III, Nashville: Abingdon Press, 942-958.

Hennessy, J. B.
    1967   *The Foreign Relations of Palestine During the Early Bronze*
            Age. London: Bernard Quaritch.

Herrmann, Siegfried
    1975   *A History of Israel in Old Testament Times.* Translated by
            John Bowden. Philadelphia: Fortress Press.
    1985   "Basic Factors of Israelite Settlement in Canaan." In *Biblical*
            Archaeology Today: Proceedings of the International Congress

on Biblical Archaeology, Jerusalem, April 1984. Jerusalem: Israel Exploration Society, 47-53.

Herzog, Ze'ev
1980   "Beer-Sheba of the Patriarchs." *Biblical Archaeology Review* 6/6 (November/December): 12-28.
1984   *Beer-Sheba II: The Early Iron Age Settlements*. Tel Aviv: The Institute of Archaeology and Ramot Publishing Company.

Holladay, John S.
1982   *Cities of the Delta, Part III: Tell el-Maskhuta: Preliminary Report on the Wadi Tumilat Project, 1978-79*. Malibu, Calif.: Undena Publications.

Hooker, J. T.
1977   *Mycenaean Greece*. London: Routledge and Kegan Paul.

Horn, Siegfried H.
1976a   "Heshbon." In *Encyclopedia of Archaeological Excavations in the Holy Land*. Vol. II. Edited by M. Avi-Yonah. Englewood Cliffs, N.J.: Prentice-Hall, 510-514.
1976b   "Heshbon." In *The Interpreter's Dictionary of the Bible*. Supplementary Volume. Nashville: Abingdon Press, 410-411.
1977   "What We Don't Know About Moses and the Exodus." *Biblical Archaeology Review* 3/2 (June): 22-31.
1986   "Why the Moabite Stone Was Blown to Pieces." *Biblical Archaeology Review* 12/3 (May/June): 50-61.

Hutchinson, R. W.
1962   *Prehistoric Crete*. Baltimore: Penguin Books.

Jack, J. W.
1925   *The Date of the Exodus in the Light of External Evidence*. Edinburgh: T. & T. Clark.

James, F. W.
1975   "Beth-Shean" (parts 1-3). In *Encyclopedia of Archaeological Excavations in the Holy Land*. Vol. I. Edited by M. Avi-Yonah, Englewood Cliffs, N.J.: Prentice-Hall, 207-212.

Joos, Marcel
    1982   "Swiss Midland-lakes and Climatic Changes." In *Climatic Change in Later Prehistory*. Edited by A. F. Harding. Edinburgh: Edinburgh University Press, 44-51.

Joukowsky, Martha
    1980   *A Complete Manual of Field Archaeology*. Englewood Cliffs, N.J.: Prentice-Hall.

Kafafi, Z.
    1985   "Egyptian Topographical Lists on the Late Bronze Age in Jordan (East Bank)." *Biblische Notizen* 29: 17-21.

Kantor, Helene J.
    1965   "The Relative Chronology of Egypt and Its Foreign Correlations Before the Late Bronze Age." In *Chronologies in Old World Archaeology*. Edited by R. W. Ehrich. Chicago: University of Chicago Press, 1-46.

Karageorghis, Vassos
    1976   *View from the Bronze Age: Mycenaean and Phoenician Discoveries at Kition*. New York: E. P. Dutton.
    1981   *Ancient Cyprus: 7,000 Years of Art and Archaeology*. Baton Rouge, La.: Louisiana State University Press.

Kaufmann, Yehezkel
    1953   *The Biblical Account of the Conquest of Palestine*. Jerusalem: The Magnes Press.
    1960   *The Religion of Israel From Its Beginnings to the Babylonian Exile*. Translated and abridged by Moshe Greenberg. Chicago: University of Chicago Press.

Kay, P. A. and D. L. Johnson
    1981   "Estimation of Tigris-Euphrates Streamflow from Regional Paleoenvironmental Proxy Data." *Climatic Change* 3: 251-263.

Kelso, James L.
    1968   *The Excavation of Bethel (1934-1960)* (Annual of the American

Schools of Oriental Research, Vol. 39). Cambridge, Mass.:
American Schools of Oriental Research.

1975   "Bethel." In *Encyclopedia of Archaeological Excavations in
the Holy Land*. Vol. I. Edited by M. Avi-Yonah. Englewood
Cliffs, N.J.: Prentice-Hall, 207-212.

Kemp, Mark
1988   "Power Surge." *Discover* 9/4 (April): 40-41.

Kempinski, Aharon
1976   "Israelite Conquest or Settlement? New Light from Tell
Masos." *Biblical Archaeology Review*. 2/3 (September): 25-
30.
1977   "Masos, Tel." In *Encyclopedia of Archaeological Excavations
in the Holy Land*. Vol. III. Edited by M. Avi-Yonah.
Englewood Cliffs, N.J.: Prentice-Hall, 816-819.

Kenyon, Kathleen M.
1957   *Digging Up Jericho*. New York: Frederick A. Praeger.
1967   "Jericho." In *Archaeology and Old Testament Study*. Edited
by D. Winton Thomas. London: Oxford University Press,
264-275.
1971   "Syria and Palestine c. 2160-1780 B.C.: The Archaeological
Sites." In *Cambridge Ancient History*. 3rd edition. Vol. I,
Part 2. Edited by I. E. S. Edwards, *et al.* Cambridge: Cambridge University Press, 567-594.
1973a   "Palestine in the Middle Bronze Age." In *Cambridge Ancient
History*. 3rd edition. Vol. II, Part 1. Edited by I. E. S. Edwards, *et al.* Cambridge: Cambridge Universiy Press, 77-116.
1973b   "Palestine in the Time of the Eighteenth Dynasty." In *Cambridge Ancient History*. 3rd edition. Vol. II, Part 1. Edited
by I. E. S. Edwards, *et al.* Cambridge: Cambridge Universiy
Press, 526-556.
1978   *The Bible and Recent Archaeology*. Atlanta: The John Knox
Press.
1981   *Excavations at Jericho, Vol. 3: The Architecture and
Stratigraphy of the Tell*. Edited by T. A. Holland. London:
British School of Archaeology in Jerusalem.

Kikawada, Isaac M. and Arthur Quinn
1985   *Before Abraham Was.* Nashville: Abingdon Press.

Kitchen, Kenneth A.
1964   "Some New Light on the Asiatic Wars of Rameses II." *Journal of Egyptian Archaeology* 50: 47-70.

Knudtzon, J. A.
1915   *Die El-Amarna Tafeln.* 2 vols. Leipzig: Hinrichs.

Kochavi, Moshe
1972   *Judea, Samaria and the Golan, Archaeological Survey 1967-68.* Jerusalem: Carta. (In Hebrew.)
1974   "Khirbet Rabud = Debir." *Tel-Aviv* I: 2-33.
1976   "Debir (City)." In *The Interpreter's Dictionary of the Bible.* Supplementary Volume. Nashville: Abingdon, 222.
1977   "Malhata, Tel." In *Encyclopedia of Archaeological Excavations in the Holy Land.* Vol. III. Edited by M. Avi-Yonah. Englewood Cliffs, N.J.: Prentice-Hall, 771-775.
1978   "Rabud, Khirbet." In *Encyclopedia of Archaeological Excavations in the Holy Land.* Vol. IV. Edited by M. Avi-Yonah. Englewood Cliffs, N.J.: Prentice-Hall, 995.
1985   "The Israelite Settlement in Canaan in the Light of Archaeological Surveys." In *Biblical Archaeology Today: Proceedings of the International Congress on Biblical Archaeology, Jerusalem, April 1984.* Jerusalem: Israel Exploration Society, 54-60.

Kraft, Charles F.
1962   "Judges, Book of." In *The Interpreter's Dictionary of the Bible.* Vol. 2. Nashville: Abingdon Press, 1013-1023.

Krahmalkov, Charles R.
1981   "A Critique of Professor Goedicke's Exodus Theories." Biblical Archaeology Review 6/5 (September/October): 51-54.

Kramer, Samuel Noah
1963   *The Sumerians.* Chicago: University of Chicago Press.

La Marche, V. C. and K. K. Hirschboeck
    1984   "Frost Rings in Trees as Records of Major Volcanic Erup-
            tions." *Nature* 307 (January 12-18): 121-126.

Lamb, H. H.
    1982   "Reconstruction of the Course of Postglacial Climate Over
            the World." In *Climatic Change in Later Prehistory*. Edited
            by A. F. Harding. Edinburgh: Edinburgh University Press,
            11-32.

Lang, Bernhard
    1983   *Monotheism and the Prophetic Minority*. Sheffield, England:
            The Almond Press.

Lapp, Paul
    1967   "The Conquest of Palestine in the Light of Archaeology."
            Concordia Theological Monthly 38: 283-300.

Laughlin, John C. H.
    1981   "The Remarkable Discoveries at Tel Dan." *Biblical Archae-
            ology Review* 7/5 (September/October): 20-37.

Leichty, Earl
    1975   *The Omen Series Shumma Izbu*. Locust Valley, N.Y.: J. J.
            Augustine Publisher.

Lenski, G. and J. Lenski
    1978   *Human Societies: An Introduction to Macrosociology*. 3rd
            edition. New York: McGraw-Hill.

Livingston, David
    1970   "The Location of Biblical Bethel and Ai Reconsidered."
            Westminster Theological Journal 33: 20-44.
    1971   "Traditional Site of Bethel Questioned." *Westminster
            Theological Journal* 34: 39-50.
    1987   "The Identity of Bethel and Ai." A paper delivered at the
            "Who Was the Pharaoh of the Exodus?" symposium, Mem-
            phis, Tennessee, April 23-25.

Lo, Henrietta W.
1987   "Velikovsky's Interpretation of the Evidence Offered by China in His *Worlds in Collision." The Skeptical Inquirer* 11: 282-291.

Lohfink, Norbert
1976   "Deuteronomy." In *The Interpreter's Dictionary of the Bible.* Supplementary Volume. Nashville: Abingdon Press, 229-232.

Luce, John V.
1969   *Lost Atlantis: New Light on an Old Legend* (British title: *The End of Atlantis*). New York: McGraw-Hill.
1976   "Thera and the Destruction of Minoan Crete: A New Interpretation of the Evidence." *American Journal of Archaeology* 80: 9-16.

Luckerman, Marvin Arnold
1980   "A Different View on the Chronology of Hazor." *Catastrophism and Ancient History* 2/2 (June): 95-115.

MacDonald, Burton
1983   "The Late Bronze and Iron Age Sites of the Wadi el Hasa Survey, 1979." In *Midian, Moab and Edom: The History and Archaeology of Late Bronze and Iron Age Jordan and North-West Arabia.* Edited by J. F. A. Sawyer and D. J. A. Clines. Sheffield, England: The Almond Press, 18-28.

MacKie, Euan
1978   "Radiocarbon Dating and Egyptian Chronology." *Ages in Chaos?* (Proceedings of the Residential Weekend Conference, Glasgow, 7-9 April, 1978). *S.I.S. Review* 6/1-3 (1982): 56-63.

Macqueen, J. G.
1986   *The Hittites and Their Contemporaries in Asia Minor.* Revised edition. New York and London: Thames and Hudson.

Malamat, Abraham
1979   "Israelite Conduct of War in the Conquest of Canaan." In

Symposia Celebrating the Seventy-Fifth Anniversary of the Founding of the American Schools of Oriental Research (1900-1975). Edited by Frank Moore Cross. Cambridge, Mass.: American Schools of Oriental Research, 35-55.

1982   "How Inferior Israelite Forces Conquered Fortified Canaanite Cities." *Biblical Archaeology Review* 8/2 (March/April): 25-35.

Marinatos, S.
1939   "The Volcanic Destruction of Minoan Crete." *Antiquity* 13: 425-439.
1972   "Thera: Key to the Riddle of Minos." *National Geographic Magazine* 141/1 (January): 40-52.

Matthews, V. H.
1978   *Pastoral Nomadism in the Mari Kingdom (ca. 1850-1760 B.C.).* Cambridge: Cambridge University Press.

Mattingly, G. L.
1983   "The Exodus-Conquest and the Archaeology of Transjordan: New Light on An Old Problem." *Grace Theological Journal* 4: 245-262.
1987   "Another Look At Transjordan." A paper presented at the "Who Was the Pharaoh of the Exodus?" symposium, Memphis, Tennessee, April 23-25.

Mavor, James W.
1969   *Voyage to Atlantis.* New York: G. P. Putnam's Sons.

May, Herbert G., ed.
1962   *Oxford Bible Atlas.* London: Oxford University Press.

Mayes, A. D. H.
1983   *The Story of Israel Between Settlement and Exile: A Redactional Study of the Deuteronomistic History.* London: SCM Press.

Mays, James L.
1969   *Amos: A Commentary.* Philadelphia: The Westminster Press.

Mazar, Amihai
    1985   "The Israelite Settlement in Canaan in the Light of Archaeo-
            logical Excavations." In *Biblical Archaeology Today: Proceed-
            ings of the International Congress on Biblical Archaeology,
            Jerusalem, April 1984.* Jerusalem: Israel Exploration Society.

Mazar, Benjamin
    1965   "The Sanctuary of Arad and the Family of Hobab the Kenite."
            Journal of Near Eastern Studies 24: 297-303.

McCoy, F. W.
    1980   "The Upper Thera (Minoan) Ash in Deep-Sea Sediments:
            Distribution and Comparison With Other Ash Layers." In
            Thera and the Aegean World. Vol. 2. Edited by C. Doumas.
            London: Thera and the Aegean World, 57-58.

McGovern, Patrick E.
    1986   *The Late Bronze and Early Iron Ages of Central Transjordan:
            The Baq'ah Valley Project, 1977-1981.* Philadelphia: University
            Museum.

McKenzie, John L.
    1966   *The World of the Judges.* Englewood Cliffs, N.J.: Prentice-
            Hall.
    1983   "The Sack of Israel." In *The Quest For the Kingdom of God:
            Studies in Honor of George E. Mendenhall.* Edited by H. B.
            Huffmon, F. A. Spina, and A. R. W. Green. Winona Lake,
            Ind.: Eisenbrauns, 25-34.

Meek, Theophile J.
    1960   *Hebrew Origins.* 3rd revised edition (Torchbook edition). New
            York: Harper and Brothers.

Mendenhall, George E.
    1962   "The Hebrew Conquest of Palestine." *Biblical Archaeologist*
            25: 66-87. Reprinted with slight revisions in *The Biblical
            Archaeologist Reader.* Vol. 3. Edited by E. F. Campbell and
            D. N. Freedman. Garden City, N.Y.: Doubleday, 100-120.
            Page references cited here are to the reprinted version.

1973   *The Tenth Generation: The Origins of the Biblical Tradition.*
Baltimore: Johns Hopkins University Press.

1976   " 'Change and Decay in All Around I See': Conquest, Covenant and the Tenth Generation." *Biblical Archaeologist* 39:
152-157.

1983   "Ancient Israel's Hyphenated History." In *Palestine in
Transition. The Emergence of Ancient Israel.* Edited by D. N.
Freedman and D. F. Graf. Sheffield, England: The Almond
Press, 91-103.

Meshel, Ze'ev
1979   "Did Yahweh Have a Consort?" *Biblical Archaeology Review*
5/2 (March/April): 24-35.

Mihelic, Joseph L. and G. Ernest Wright
1962   "Plagues in Exodus." In *The Interpreter's Dictionary of the
Bible.* Vol. III. Nashville: Abingdon Press, 822-824.

Milgrom, J.
1976a   "Leviticus." In *The Interpreter's Dictionary of the Bible.*
Supplementary Volume. Nashville: Abingdon Press, 541-545.

Miller, J. Maxwell
1976a   "Joshua, Book of." In *The Interpreter's Dictionary of the Bible.*
Supplementary Volume. Nashville: Abingdon Press, 493-496.

1976b   *The Old Testament and the Historian.* Philadelphia: Fortress
Press.

1977a   "The Israelite Occupation of Canaan." In *Israelite and Judean
History.* Edited by John H. Hayes and J. Maxwell Miller.
Philadelphia: The Westminster Press, 213-284.

1977b   "Archaeology and the Israelite Conquest of Canaan: Some
Methodological Observations." *Palestine Exploration Quarterly* 109: 87-93.

Miller, J. Maxwell and John H. Hayes
1986   *A History of Ancient Israel and Judah.* Philadelphia: The
Westminster Press.

Miller, Patrick D., Jr.
1973   *The Divine Warrior in Early Israel* (Harvard Semitic Monographs, 5). Cambridge, Mass.: Harvard University Press.

Mittmann, S.
1970   *Beiträge zur Siedlungs— und Territorialgeschichte des nördlichen Ostjordanlandes (Abhandlungen des Deutschen Palästina-Vereins).* Wiesbaden: Otto Harrassowitz.

Morrison, David
1977   "Planetary Astronomy and Velikovsky's Catastrophism." In *Scientists Confront Velikovsky.* Edited by D. Goldsmith. New York: W. W. Norton, 145-176.

Mulholland, J. D.
1977   "Movements of Celestial Bodies—Velikovsky's Fatal Flaw." In *Scientists Confront Velikovsky.* Edited by D. Goldsmith. New York: W. W. Norton, 105-115.

Naville, E.
1903   *The Store-City of Pithom and the Route of the Exodus.* 4th ed. London: Egypt Exploration Fund.
1924   "The Geography of the Exodus." *Journal of Egyptian Archaeology* 10: 18-39.

Needham, Joseph
1959   *Science and Civilization in China, Vol. 3: Mathematics and the Sciences of the Heavens and the Earth.* Cambridge: Cambridge University Press.

Neugebauer, Otto
1957   *The Exact Sciences in Antiquity.* 2nd ed. Providence, R.I.: Brown University Press.

Neumann, J. and Simo Parpola
1987   "Climatic Change and the Eleventh-Tenth-Century Eclipse of Assyria and Babylonia." *Journal of Near Eastern Studies* 46/3 (July): 161-182.

Noth, Martin
1930   *Das System der zwölf Stamme Israels.* Stuttgart: W. Kohl-hammer.
1935   "Bethel und 'Ai." *Palästinajahrbuch* 31: 7-29.
1938   "Grundsätzliches zur geschichtlichen Deutung archäologischer Befunde auf dem Boden Palästinas." *Palästinajahrbuch* 37: 7-22.
1943   *Überlieferungs geschichtliche Studien I.* Tübingen: Max Niemeyer Verlag. The 2nd ed., 1957, was translated into English under the title *The Deuteronomistic History.* Sheffield, England: JSOT Press, 1981.
1948   *A History of Pentateuchal Traditions.* Translated and introduced by B. W. Anderson. Englewood Cliffs, N.J.: Prentice-Hall, 1972. Originally published as *Überlieferungsgeschichte des Pentateuch* in 1948.
1953   *Das Buch Josua.* 2nd ed. Tübingen: J. C. B. Mohr.
1960   *The History of Israel.* Translated by P. R. Ackroyd from the 2nd ed. of *Geschichte Israels.* New York: Harper and Brothers.
1962   *Exodus, A Commentary.* Translated by J. Bowden. Philadelphia: The Westminster Press.
1965   *Leviticus, A Commentary.* Translated by J. E. Anderson. Philadelphia: The Westminster Press.

Nougayrol, J., *et al.*
1968   *Ugaritica.* Vol. 5. Paris: Imprimerie Nationale.

Olavarri, Emilio
1965   "Sondages a 'Aro'er sur l'Arnon." *Revue Biblique* 72: 77-94.
1969   "Fouilles a 'Aro'er sur l'Arnon." *Revue Biblique* 76: 250-259.
1975   "Aroer." In *Encyclopedia of Archaeological Excavations in the Holy Land.* Vol. I. Edited by M. Avi-Yonah. Englewood Cliffs, N.J.: Prentice-Hall, 98-100.

Oppenheim, A. Leo
1964   *Ancient Mesopotamia.* Chicago: University of Chicago Press.

Oren, Eliezer D.
1981   "How Not to Create a History of the Exodus—A Critique

of Professor Goedicke's Theories." *Biblical Archaeology Review* 6/6 (November/December): 46-53.

1982   "Oren Replies to the Goedicke Letter" ("Queries and Comments"). *Biblical Archaeology Review* 8/2 (March/April): 12.

Ovadiah, A.
1976   "Gaza." In *Encyclopedia of Archaeological Excavations in the Holy Land.* Vol. II. Edited by M. Avi-Yonah. Englewood Cliffs, N.J.: Prentice-Hall, 408-417.

Owen, T.
1982   "Planetary Atmospheres and the Search for Life." *Physics Teacher* 20 (February): 90-96.

Parr, Peter
1968   "The Origin of the Rampart Fortifications of Middle Bronze Age Palestine and Syria." *Zeitschrift des Deutschen Palästina-Vereins* 84: 18-45.

Peet, T. Eric
1923   *Egypt and the Old Testament.* Liverpool: The University Press of Liverpool.
1930   *The Great Tomb Robberies of the Twentieth Egyptian Dynasty.* 2 vols. Oxford: Oxford University Press.

Pendlebury, J. D. S.
1939   *The Archaeology of Crete.* Norton Library edition. New York: W. W. Norton and Company.

Petrie, W. M. Flinders
1906   *Hyksos and Israelite Cities.* London: Egyptian Research Account.
1911   *Egypt and Israel.* London: Society for Promoting Christian Knowledge.

Pettengill, G. H., D. B. Campbell, and H. Masursky
1980   "The Surface of Venus." *Scientific American* 243/2 (August): 45-67.

Pettinato, Giovanni
　　1976　　"The Royal Archives of Tell-Mardikh-Ebla." *Biblical Archaeologist* 39/2 (May): 44-52.
　　1981　　*The Archives of Ebla.* Garden City, N.Y.: Doubleday.

Pfeiffer, Robert H.
　　1948　　*Introduction to the Old Testament.* Rev. ed. New York: Harper and Row.

Pichler, H.
　　1980　　"Discussion." In *Thera and the Aegean World.* Vol. 2. Edited by C. Doumas. London: Thera and the Aegean World, 324-325.

Pichler, H. and W. L. Friedrich
　　1980　　"Mechanism of the Minoan Eruption of Santorini." In *Thera and the Aegean World.* Vol. 2. Edited by C. Doumas. London: Thera and the Aegean World, 15-30.

Platon, Nicholas
　　1971　　*Zakros: The Discovery of a Lost Palace of Ancient Crete.* New York: Charles Scribner's Sons.

Posener, G.
　　1971　　"Syria and Palestine c. 2160-1780 B.C.: Relations With Egypt." In *Cambridge Ancient History.* 3rd edition. Vol. I, Part 2. Edited by I. E. S. Edwards, *et al.* Cambridge: Cambridge University Press, 532-558.

Pritchard, James B.
　　1959　　*Hebrew Inscriptions and Stamps from Gibeon.* Philadelphia: The University Museum.
　　1962　　*Gibeon, Where the Sun Stood Still.* Princeton, N.J.: Princeton University Press.
　　1964　　*Winery, Defenses, and Soundings at Gibeon.* Philadelphia: The University Museum.
　　1965　　"Culture and History." In *The Bible in Modern Scholarship.* Edited by J. P. Hyatt. Nashville: Abingdon Press, 313-324.

1969   *The Ancient Near East in Pictures Relating to the Old Testament.* Princeton, N.J.: Princeton University Press.

1976   "Gibeon." In *Encyclopedia of Archaeological Excavations in the Holy Land.* Vol. II. Edited by M. Avi-Yonah. Englewood Cliffs, N.J.: Prentice-Hall, 446-450.

1980   *The Cemetery at Tell es-Sa'idiyeh, Jordan.* Philadelphia: The University Museum.

Rainey, Anson F.

1970   "Bethel is Still Beitin." *Westminster Theological Journal* 33: 175-188.

1976a   "Eglon (City), 1. Tell 'Aitun?" In *The Interpreter's Dictionary of the Bible.* Supplementary Volume. Nashville: Abingdon, 252.

1976b   "Libnah (City)." In *The Interpreter's Dictionary of the Bible.* Supplementary Volume. Nashville: Abingdon, 546.

1980   "Review of John Bimson, *Redating the Exodus and Conquest.*" *Israel Exploration Journal* 30: 249-251.

Ramsey, George W.

1981   *The Quest for the Historical Israel.* Atlanta: John Knox Press.

Redford, Donald B.

1963   "Exodus I.11." *Vetus Testamentum* 13: 401-418.

1967   *History and Chronology of the Eighteenth Dynasty of Egypt: Seven Studies.* Toronto: University of Toronto Press.

1982   "Contact Between Egypt and Jordan in the New Kingdom: Some Comments on Sources." In *Studies in the History and Archaeology of Jordan, I.* Edited by A. Hadidi. Amman: Department of Antiquities, 115-119.

1984   *Akhenaton: The Heretic King.* Princeton, N.J.: Princeton University Press.

Reed, William L. and Fred V. Winnett

1964   *The Excavations at Dibôn (Dhibân) in Moab* (Annual of the American Schools of Oriental Research, Vols. 36-37), New Haven, Conn.: American Schools of Oriental Research.

Reiner, E. and D. Pingree
1975   *Babylonian Planetary Omens, Part 1: Enuma Anu Enlil.*
Malibu, Calif.: Undena Publications.

Reisner, G.A., C. S. Fisher and D. G. Lyon
1924   *Harvard Excavations at Samaria.* 2 vols. Cambridge, Mass.:
Harvard University Press.

Rendsburg, Gary A.
1986   *The Redaction of Genesis.* Winona Lake, Ind.: Eisenbrauns.

Rendtorff, Rolf
1977   *Das Überlieferungsgeschichtliche Problem des Pentateuch*
(Beihefte zur *Zeitschrift für die alttestamentliche Wissenschaft*
147). Berlin: de Gruyter.

Renfrew, Colin
1979   *Before Civilization: The Radiocarbon Revolution and*
Prehistoric Europe. Cambridge: Cambridge University Press.

Richard, Suzanne
1987   "The Early Bronze Age: The Rise and Collapse of Urbanism."
Biblical Archaeologist 50/1 (March): 22-43.

Romer, John
1984   *Ancient Lives: Daily Life in Egypt of the Pharaohs.* New
York: Holt, Rinehart and Winston.

Rose, D. Glenn
1976   "Eglon (City), 2. Tell el-Hesi?" In *The Interpreter's Dictionary*
of the Bible. Supplementary Volume. Nashville: Abingdon, 252-
253.

Rosen, Steven A.
1988   "Finding Evidence of Ancient Nomads." *Biblical Archaeology*
Review 14/5 (September/October): 46-53.

Rowley, H. H.
1950a   *From Joseph to Joshua: Biblical Traditions in the Light of*

Archaeology. London: Oxford University Press.
1950b   *The Growth of the Old Testament.* Harper Torchbooks edition (1963). New York: Harper and Row.

Rowton, Michael B.
1974   "Enclosed Nomadism." *Journal of the Economy and Social History of the Orient* 17:1-30.
1976   "Dimorphic Structure and the Problem of the 'Apiru-'Ibrim." *Journal of Near Eastern Studies* 35/1 (January): 13-20.
1977   "Dimorphic Structure and the Parasocial Element." *Journal of Near Eastern Studies* 36 (April): 181-198.

Rudman, Burton S.
1981   "Goedicke's Exodus Theories Anticipated by *BAR* Reader and Others" ("Queries and Comments"). *Biblical Archaeology Review* 7/6 (November/December): 14-16.

Sagan, Carl
1977   "An Analysis of *Worlds in Collision.*" In *Scientists Confront Velikovsky.* Edited by D. Goldsmith. New York: W. W. Norton, 41-104.

Sandars, Nancy K.
1985   *The Sea Peoples: Warriors of the Ancient Mediterranean.* Revised edition. New York and London: Thames and Hudson.

Sarna, Nahum M.
1986   *Exploring Exodus: The Heritage of Ancient Israel.* New York: Schocken Books.

Sauer, James A.
1985   "Ammon, Moab and Edom." In *Biblical Archaeology Today: Proceedings of the International Conference on Biblical Archaeology, Jerusalem, April 1984.* Jerusalem: Israel Exploration Society, 206-214.
1986   "Transjordan in the Bronze and Iron Ages: A Critique of Glueck's Synthesis." *Bulletin of the American Schools of Oriental Research* 263: 1-26.

Schaeffer, Claude F. A.
1983   "The Last Days of Ugarit." An exerpt from *Ugaritica* 5 (1968). Translated by Michael D. Coogan. *Biblical Archaeology Review* 9/5 (September/October): 74-75.

Schmid, Hans H.
1976   *Der sogenannte Jahwist: Beobachtungen und Fragen zur Pentateuchforschung.* Zurich: Theologischer Verlag.

Schmidt, W. H.
1965   "Die deuteronomistische Redaktion des Amosbuches." *Zeitschrift für die alttestamentliche Wissenschaft* 77: 168-192.

Shanks, Hershel
1981   "The Exodus and the Crossing of the Red Sea, According to Hans Goedicke." *Biblical Archaeology Review* 6/5 (September/October): 42-50.
1987   "Dever's 'Sermon on the Mound.' " *Biblical Archaeology Review* 13/2 (March/April): 54-57.

Sharer, Robert J. and Wendy Ashmore
1987   *Archaeology: Discovering Our Past.* Mountain View, Calif.: Mayfield Publishing Company.

Shaw, Ian M. E.
1985   "Egyptian Chronology and the Irish Oak Calibration." *Journal of Near Eastern Studies* 44/4 (October): 295-317.

Shea, William H.
1986   "Some New Factors Bearing Upon the Date of the Exodus." In *Proceedings of the Third Seminar of Catastrophism and Ancient History.* Edited by M. A. Luckerman. Los Angeles: Catastrophism and Ancient History Press, 29-35.

Silberman, Neil Asher
1982   *Digging for God and Country: Exploration, Archaeology, and the Secret Struggle for the Holy Land, 1799-1917.* New York: Alfred A. Knopf.

Snaith, Norman H.
  1965   "סוּף יָם": The Sea of Reeds: The Red Sea." *Vetus Testamentum* 15: 395-398.

Soggin, J. Alberto
  1972   *Joshua: A Commentary.* Translated by R. A. Wilson. Philadelphia: The Westminster Press.
  1981   *Judges: A Commentary.* Translated by John Bowden. Philadelphia: The Westminster Press.
  1984   *A History of Ancient Israel: From the Beginnings to the Bar Kochba Revolt, A.D. 135.* Translated by John Bowden. Philadelphia: The Westminster Press.

Speiser, Ephraim A.
  1964   *Genesis (The Anchor Bible 1).* Garden City, N.Y.: Doubleday.

Stager, Lawrence E.
  1985   "Response." In *Biblical Archaeology Today: Proceedings of the International Congress on Biblical Archaeology, Jerusalem, April 1984.* Jerusalem: Israel Exploration Society, 83-86.

Stanley, Daniel J. and Harrison Sheng
  1986   "Volcanic Shards From Santorini (Upper Minoan Ash) in the Nile Delta, Egypt." *Nature* 320 (April 24): 733-735.

Stern, Ephraim
  1978   "Es-Safi, Tell." In *Encyclopedia of Archaeological Excavations in the Holy Land.* Vol. IV. Edited by M. Avi-Yonah. Englewood Cliffs, N.J.: Prentice-Hall, 1024-1027.

Stiebing, William H.
  1971   "Hyksos Burials in Palestine: A Review of the Evidence." *Journal of Near Eastern Studies* 30/2 (April): 110-117.
  1973   "A Criticism of the Revised Chronology." *Pensée* 3/3 (Fall): 10-12.
  1974   "Rejoinder to Velikovsky." *Pensée* 4/5 (Winter): 24-26.
  1980   "The End of the Mycenaean Age." *Biblical Archeologist* 43/1 (Winter): 7-21.

1984   *Ancient Astronauts, Cosmic Collisions and Other Popular Theories About Man's Past.* Buffalo, N.Y.: Prometheus Books.

1985   "Should the Exodus and the Israelite Settlement be Redated?." *Biblical Archaeology Review* 11/4 (July/August): 58-69.

1987   "The Israelite Exodus and the Volcanic Eruption of Thera." *Catastrophism and Ancient History* 9/2 (July): 69-79.

1988a   "New Archaeological Dates for the Israelite Conquest, Part I: Proposals for an EB III Conquest," *Catastrophism and Ancient History* 10/1 (January): 5-16.

1988b   "New Archaeological Dates for the Israelite Conquest, Part II: An MB II C Conquest." *Catastrophism and Ancient History* 10/2 (in press).

Storck, Herbert A.
1986   "Interaction: Another Look at Velikovsky's Ages in Chaos." *Catastrophism and Ancient History* 8/1 (January): 80-84.

Tadmor, H.
1984   "Appendix 2, Chronology of the First Temple Period: A Presentation and Evaluation of the Sources." In J. Alberto Soggin. *A History of Ancient Israel: From the Beginnings to the Bar Kochba Revolt, A.D. 135.* Philadelphia: The Westminster Press, 368-383.

Taylour, William
1983   *The Mycenaeans.* Revised edition. New York: Thames and Hudson.

Thiele, Edwin R.
1965   *The Mysterious Numbers of the Hebrew Kings: A Reconstruction of the Chronology of the Kingdoms of Israel and Judah.* Revised edition. Grand Rapids, Mich.: Wm. B. Eerdmans.

1977   *A Chronology of the Hebrew Kings.* Grand Rapids, Mich.: Zondervan.

Thompson, Thomas L. and Dorothy Irvin
1977   "The Joseph and Moses Narratives." In *Israelite and Judean*

History. Edited by John H. Hayes and J. Maxwell Miller. Philadelphia: The Westminster Press, 149-212.

Throckmorton, Peter
1962   "Oldest Known Shipwreck Yields Bronze Age Cargo." *National Geographic Magazine* 121/5 (May): 696-711.

Tucker, Gene M.
1971   *Form Criticism of the Old Testament*. Philadelphia: Fortress Press.
1976   "Form Criticism, O.T." In *The Interpreter's Dictionary of the Bible*. Supplementary Volume. Nashville: Abingdon Press, 342-345.

Tufnell, Olga
1967   "Lachish." In *Archaeology and Old Testament Study*. Edited by D. Winton Thomas. London: Oxford University Press, 296-308.

Tushingham, A. D.
1953   "Excavations at Old Testament Jericho." *Biblical Archaeologist* 16: 46-67.
1954   "Excavations at Old Testament Jericho." *Biblical Archaeologist* 17: 98-104.
1972   *The Excavations at Dibon (Dhiban) in Moab: The Third Campaign, 1952-53* (Annual of the American Schools of Oriental Research, Vol. 40). Cambridge, Mass.: American Schools of Oriental Research.
1975   "Dibon." In *Encyclopedia of Archaeological Excavations in the Holy Land*. Vol. I. Edited by M. Avi-Yonah. Englewood Cliffs, N.J.: Prentice-Hall, 330-333.

Uphill, E. P.
1968   "Pithom and Raamses: Their Location and Significance, Part 1." *Journal of Near Eastern Studies* 27: 291-316.
1969   "Pithom and Raamses: Their Location and Significance, Part 2." *Journal of Near Eastern Studies* 28: 15-39.

Ussishkin, David
1977   "Lachish." In *Encyclopedia of Archaeological Excavations in the Holy Land*. Vol. III. Edited by M. Avi-Yonah. Englewood Cliffs, N.J.: Prentice-Hall, 735-753.
1979   "Answers at Lachish." *Biblical Archaeology Review* 5/6 (November/December): 16-39.
1987   "Lachish—Key to the Israelite Conquest of Canaan?" *Biblical Archaeology Review* 13/1 (January/February): 18-39.

Van der Waerden, Bartel L.
1974   *Science Awakening, Vol. 2: The Birth of Astronomy*. Leiden: Noordhoff International Publishing.

Vaninger, Stan F.
1983   "Abraham to Hezekiah: An Archaeological Revision, Part I." *Catastrophism and Ancient History* 5/2 (July): 69-85.
1983   "Abraham to Hezekiah: An Archaeological Revision, Part II." *Catastrophism and Ancient History* 6/1 (January): 5-18.

Van Seters, John
1966   *The Hyksos: A New Investigation*. New Haven, Conn.: Yale University Press.
1972   "The Conquest of Sihon's Kingdom: A Literary Examination." *Journal of Biblical Literature* 91/2 (June): 182-197.
1975   *Abraham in History and Tradition*. New Haven, Conn.: Yale University Press.
1980   "Once Again—the Conquest of Sihon's Kingdom." *Journal of Biblical Literature* 99/1 (March): 117-119.
1982   "More Holes in Goedicke's Exodus Theories" ("Queries and Comments"). *Biblical Archaeology Review* 8/1 (January/February): 12.
1983   *In Search of History: Historiography in the Ancient World and the Origins of Biblical History*. New Haven, Conn.: Yale University Press.

Velikovsky, Immanuel
1950   *Worlds in Collision*. Garden City, N.Y.: Doubleday.
1952   *Ages in Chaos*. Garden City, N.Y.: Doubleday.
1973a   "The Pitfalls of Radiocarbon Dating." *Pensée* 3/2 (Spring-

Summer): 12-14, 50.

1973b   "A Reply to Stiebing." *Pensée* 4/1 (Winter): 38-42.

1974   "A Concluding Retort." *Pensée* 4/5 (Winter): 26, 49.

Vincent, L. H.

1937   "Les Fouilles d'Et-Tell." *Revue Biblique* 46: 231-266.

Vitaliano, Dorothy B.

1973   *Legends of the Earth.* Bloomington, Ind.: Indiana University Press.

1978   "Atlantis from the Geologic Point of View." In *Atlantis: Fact or Fiction?* Edited by E. Ramage. Bloomington, Ind.: Indiana University Press, 137-160.

Von Rad, Gerhard

1938   *Das formgeschichtliche Problem des Hexateuchs.* Translated by E. W. Trueman Dicken as "The Form-Critical Problem of the Hexateuch." In G. Von Rad. *The Problem of the Hexateuch and Other Essays.* Edinburgh: Oliver and Boyd.

1962   *Old Testament Theology.* Vol. I. Translated by D. M. G. Stalker. New York: Harper and Row.

Waltke, Bruce K.

1972   "Palestinian Artifactual Evidence Supporting the Early Date for the Exodus." *Bibliotheca Sacra* 129: 33-47.

Ward, William A.

1973   "A Possible New Link Between Egypt and Jordan During the Reign of Amenhotep III." *Annual of the Department of Antiquities of Jordan and Amman* 18: 45-46.

Warren, P. M.

1987   "Absolute Dating of the Aegean Late Bronze Age." *Archaeometry* 29/2 (August): 205-211.

Weippert, Manfred

1971   *The Settlement of the Israelite Tribes in Palestine.* Translated by J. D. Martin. Studies in Biblical Theology, 21. London: SCM Press.

1979   "The Israelite 'Conquest' and the Evidence from Transjordan." In *Symposia Celebrating the Seventy-Fifth Anniversary of the Founding of the American Schools of Oriental Research (1900-1975).* Edited by Frank Moore Cross. Cambridge, Mass.: American Schools of Oriental Research, 15-34.

Weiser, Artur
    1929   *Die Profetie des Amos* (Beiheft zur *Zeitschrift für die alttestamentliche Wissenschaft* 53). Berlin: de Gruyter.
    1962   *The Psalms: A Commentary.* Translated by Herbert Hartwell. Philadelphia: The Westminster Press.

Weiss, B.
    1982   "The Decline of Late Bronze Age Civilizations as a Possible Response to Climatic Change." *Climatic Change* 4: 172-198.

Weisskopf, Victor
    1986   "Search for Simplicity: Maxwell, Rayleigh, and Mt. Everest." *American Journal of Physics* 54/1 (January): 13-14.

Wellhausen, Julius
    1885   *Prolegomena to the History of Israel.* Edinburgh: A. and C. Black. Originally published as *Prolegomena zur Geschichte Israels.* Berlin: Georg Reimer, 1883.

Wente, Edward F.
    1980   "Genealogy of the Royal Family." In *An X-Ray Atlas of the Royal Mummies.* Edited by James E. Harris and Edward F. Wente. Chicago: University of Chicago Press, 122-162.

Wente, Edward F. and Charles C. Van Siclen, III
    1976   "A Chronology of the New Kingdom." *Chicago Studies in Ancient Oriental Civilization* 39: 217-61.

Wilson, Ian
    1985   *Exodus: The True Story Behind the Biblical Account.* San Francisco: Harper and Row.

Wilson, John A.
1951   *The Burden of Egypt.* Chicago: University of Chicago Press.
1955   "Egyptian Historical Texts," "Egyptian Hymns and Prayers," and "Egyptian Oracles and Prophecies." In *Ancient Near Eastern Texts Relating to the Old Testament.* 2nd ed. Edited by James B. Pritchard. Princeton, N.J.: Princeton University Press, 227-264, 325-381, 441-449.

Winnett, F. V.
1949   *The Mosaic Tradition.* Toronto: University of Toronto Press.
1965   "Re-examining the Foundations." *Journal of Biblical Literature* 84: 1-19.

Wiseman, D. J.
1975   "Assyria and Babylonia c. 1200-1000 B.C." In *Cambridge Ancient History.* 3rd edition. Vol. II, Part 2. Edited by I. E. S. Edwards, *et al.* Cambridge: Cambridge University Press, 443-481.

Woldering, Irmgard
1963   *The Art of Egypt.* New York: Greystone Press.

Wood, Bryant G.
1987   "The Archaeology and History of Jericho in the Late Bronze Age." A paper presented at the "Who Was the Pharaoh of the Exodus?" symposium, Memphis, Tennessee, April 23-25.

Wood, Leon J.
1970   "The Date of the Exodus." In *New Perspectives on the Old Testament.* Edited by J. Barton Payne. Waco, Tex.: Word Books.
1986   *A Survey of Israel's History.* Revised and enlarged by David O'Brien. Grand Rapids, Mich.: Zondervan.

Wood, Michael
1985   *In Search of the Trojan War.* New York: Facts on File.

Wright, G. Ernest
    1962a   *Biblical Archaeology.* 2nd ed., Philadelphia: The Westminster
             Press.
    1962b   "Exodus, Book of." In *The Interpreter's Dictionary of the
             Bible.* Vol. 2. Nashville: Abingdon Press, 188-197.
    1975   "Beth-Shemesh." In *Encyclopedia of Archaeological
             Excavations in the Holy Land.* Vol. I. Edited by M. Avi-
             Yonah. Englewood Cliffs, N.J.: Prentice-Hall, 248-253.

Wright, H. E., Jr.
    1968   "Climatic Change in Mycenaean Greece." *Antiquity* 42: 123-
             127.

Yadin, Yigael
    1975   *Hazor: The Rediscovery of a Great Citadel of the Bible.* New
             York: Random House.
    1976   "Hazor." In *Encyclopedia of Archaeological Excavations in
             the Holy Land.* Vol. II. Edited by M. Avi-Yonah. Englewood
             Cliffs, N.J.: Prentice-Hall, 474-495.
    1979   "The Transition from a Semi-Nomadic to a Sedentary Society
             in the Twelfth Century B.C.E." In *Symposia Celebrating the
             Seventy-Fifth Anniversary of the Founding of the American
             Schools of Oriental Research (1900-1975).* Edited by Frank
             Moore Cross. Cambridge, Mass.: American Schools of Oriental
             Research, 57-68.
    1982   "Is the Biblical Account of the Israelite Conquest of Canaan
             Historically Reliable?" *Biblical Archaeology Review* 8/2
             (March/April): 16-23.
    1985   "Biblical Archaeology Today: The Archaeological Aspect."
             In *Biblical Archaeology Today: Proceedings of the Interna-
             tional Congress on Biblical Archaeology, Jerusalem, April
             1984.* Jerusalem: Israel Exploration Society, 21-27.

Yeivin, Samuel
    1971   *The Israelite Conquest of Canaan.* Istanbul: Nederlands
             Historisch-Archaeologisch Instituut in Het Nabije Oosten.

Zevit, Ziony
    1985a   "The Problem of Ai." *Biblical Archaeology Review* 11/2

(March/April): 58-69.

1985b   "Queries and Comments—Ziony Zevit Replies." *Biblical Archaeology Review* 11/4 (July/August): 22-23.

1985c   "Queries and Comments—Ziony Zevit Replies." *Biblical Archaeology Review* 11/5 (September/October): 79-80.

Index